IMAGES
of America

REXBURG

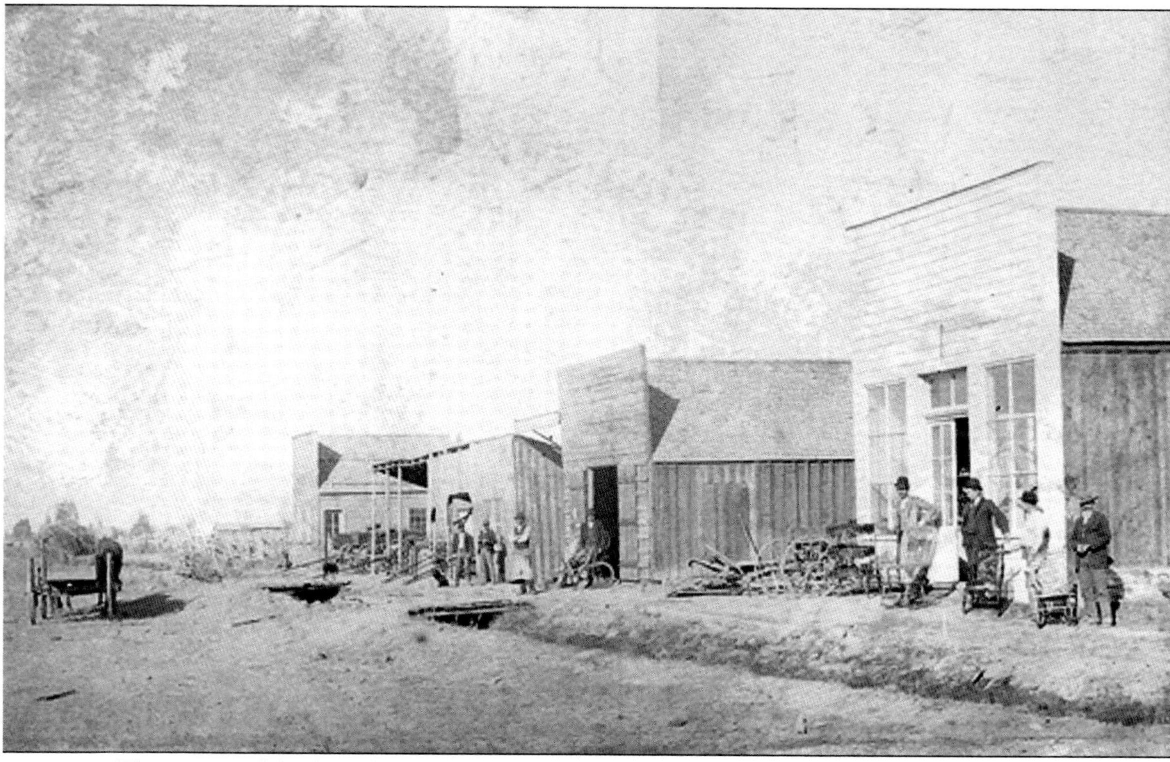

This is one of the first photographs taken of Rexburg, Idaho, at the corner of North Center and Main Streets in 1886. The only business identified is Bramwell's Blacksmith Shop. (Courtesy of Upper Snake River Valley Historical Society.)

On the Cover: The photograph was taken in 1915 on the south side of West Main Street. From left to right are the Idaho Hotel, Hegsted and Jenson's General Merchandise, Electric Theater, Len Root Harness Shop, and Henry Jacob Bigler's Commercial Hotel and Merchandise Store. (Authors' collection.)

IMAGES
of America

REXBURG

Lowell J. and Mardi J. Parkinson

ARCADIA
PUBLISHING

ISBN 978-1-4671-3220-6

Published by Arcadia Publishing
Charleston, South Carolina

Printed in the United States of America

Library of Congress Control Number: 2014933150

For all general information, please contact Arcadia Publishing:
Telephone 843-853-2070
Fax 843-853-0044
E-mail sales@arcadiapublishing.com
For customer service and orders:
Toll-Free 1-888-313-2665

Visit us on the Internet at www.arcadiapublishing.com

This book is dedicated to our parents: the late John D. and Verla Jensen Parkinson and Morris D. and Josephine Alzola Madsen.

Contents

ACKNOWLEDGMENTS

Lowell Parkinson, a sixth-generation resident of Rexburg, who at the tender age of 10 was mesmerized with the early pioneer stories and photographs of the Rexburg area, should be acknowledged for his precociousness in recording histories and his collection of over 2,000 period images of the area. Earl Garner came to Rexburg crossing the North Fork of the Snake River in 1883, and his accounts of life in Rexburg told to this young boy became the inspiration for collecting these histories and photographs.

Mardi Parkinson, a third-generation resident of Rexburg, was responsible for encouragement, timeless hours of research, organization, and typing the script in this book.

Special indebtedness goes to Terrell and Margaret Porter Arnold, whose personal knowledge and archival pictures are a treasure to the community of Rexburg. Margaret's father, Arthur Porter, kept personal journals, was the owner of the *Journal* newspaper and a mayor of Rexburg, and was cognizant of the events of the city.

Acknowledgements go to Cleo Johnson's endless research of the origin of the historic buildings of Rexburg; Louis Clements, who is the cornerstone of the Upper Snake River Valley Historical Society and has written many books on Rexburg; and Jill Spencer, curator at the flood museum. Special appreciation goes to Dean Rasmussen for the use of his photograph archives and Diana Fuller for her research and pictures of the first settlers of Rexburg. Lowell appreciated the history he received from his mother, Verla Parkinson, and for her memories of Rexburg. Thanks to Lloyd Miller for sharing pictures from the William Lloyd Adams archives. We would also like to acknowledge Lola Webster, Gary Archibald, Dwight Davidson, Judge Harold Forbush, Dorothy Kennedy, and the *Rexburg Standard Journal*. Special thanks goes to photographer Allan Morton.

Great appreciation is extended to the late Dr. Samuel Merrill Beal, former professor at Ricks Academy and Idaho State University and an Idaho state historian, for having the foresight to interview a few of the original 11 men who came to Rexburg in 1883 and acquire pictures of Beaver Dick from the Leigh family archives.

Unless otherwise noted, all images are courtesy of the authors.

Introduction

Historians' perceptions on history vary as they take the facts and present and interpret them in their own words. Two local historians who were major in contributing the historical facts of Rexburg were Dr. Samuel Merrill Beal and Louis Clements. This book may be similar to their accounts, but history is history. These men laid the blueprints of history that are used by present-day historians.

In 1810, Maj. Andrew Henry, who was associated with the Missouri Fur Company, built a cottonwood log fort along the Snake River, seven miles north of the current site of Rexburg. He stayed one year and then moved on. Capt. Wilson Price Hunt and a party of 62 trappers representing the Hudson Bay Fur Company arrived at the fort on October 8, 1811. Later that year, Captain Hunt and a party explored and found the natural hot springs used by the Indians 25 miles from the fort at the base of the Big Hole Mountain Range. He was the first white man to visit the hot springs. Robert Stuart, a fur trapper, also stopped at the hot springs in 1812.

In 1844, Jesuit priest Fr. Pierre De Smet traveled through the area to Henry's Lake, where he held the first Catholic communion with a band of Couer d'Alene Indians.

Prior to the 1860s, Mormon president and territorial governor of Utah Brigham Young procured the service of frontiersman and mountain man Jim Bridger to explore the southeast and east area of Idaho for colonization. Jim Bridger returned to Salt Lake and reported in the positive.

Richard "Beaver Dick" Leigh was one of the more interesting first recorded white men to settle in the Rexburg area. He came to the area around 1870 and fell in love with the mountains and rivers while eking out a living by trapping.

Mormon president John Taylor chose wagon master and frontiersman Thomas E. Ricks to explore an area east of the three buttes along the Snake River. Ten men led by Ricks journeyed to the area that would later be transformed into the city of Rexburg. The company arrived on March 10, 1883. The location they choose was situated at 4,865 feet above sea level at the foot of two mesas that would later be called the Rexburg bench and the upper bench. From the upper mesa, it connected to the foot of the Big Hole Mountain Range.

In 1883, the town was called Ricksburg in honor of Thomas E. Ricks. Ricks asked for the name to be changed to Rexburg, using the German spelling of his last name. In 1889, at the height of the polygamy persecution of the Mormons in Idaho and Utah, H.N. "Kentucky" Smith was associated with anti-Mormon political issues. Under his political influence, the post office in Rexburg was renamed Kaintuck, even though the town retained its name Rexburg. Because of this conflict, the name *Rexburg* did not appear on any territorial maps of Idaho until after 1887, when the Edmund Tucker Act was passed by Congress, abolishing polygamy in the United States.

The Church of Jesus Christ of Latter-day Saints (known as the Mormon or LDS Church) was adamant about the education of its children. The Mormon Church established an academy in 1888, and after several name changes, in 1903, it became known as the Ricks Academy, honoring Thomas E. Ricks. In 1923, the academy's name was changed to Ricks College, and in 2001, it was made into a four-year university as Brigham Young University–Idaho (BYU–Idaho). On February 18, 1913, Bill No. 173 was signed by Gov. John M. Haines of Idaho, creating Madison as the 33rd county and Rexburg as the county seat.

Agriculture was the economic foundation of the community. Wheat, barley, oats, sugar beets, cattle, and sheep were the major contributing commodities in the late 19th and early 20th centuries. In 1961, Harvey Summers and his three sons drilled the first irrigation well on the lower Rexburg bench. This event changed the agriculture industry in Madison County from dryland farming to deep well irrigation farming, which brought about the cultivation of potatoes.

On June 5, 1976, the Teton Dam, located in the northeast corner of Madison County, burst, sending 280,000 acre-feet of water rushing down into the valley, destroying more than a third of the city of Rexburg. Sadly, a majority of Rexburg's historic buildings were destroyed, and the pictorial histories of Rexburg and Madison County were washed away by the floodwaters. It was the biggest life-changing event in Rexburg since its conception. When the surviving residents of the flood talk about history, they reference "before" the flood and "after" the flood.

One

Early Explorers

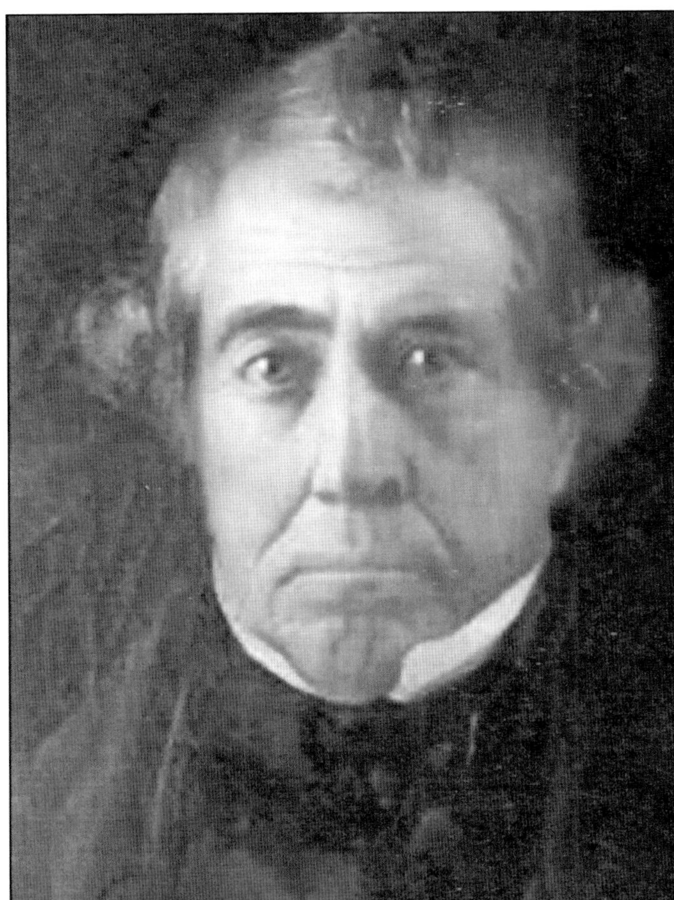

Maj. Andrew Henry (1775–1832) was a fur trader associated with the Missouri Fur Company. In 1810, he built a cottonwood log fort called Fort Henry, located along Henry's Fork of the Snake River, seven miles north of the current courthouse in Rexburg. The site was excavated in 1933 by Dr. Samuel Beal and students from the college who found a rock engraved with "Fort Henry 1810."

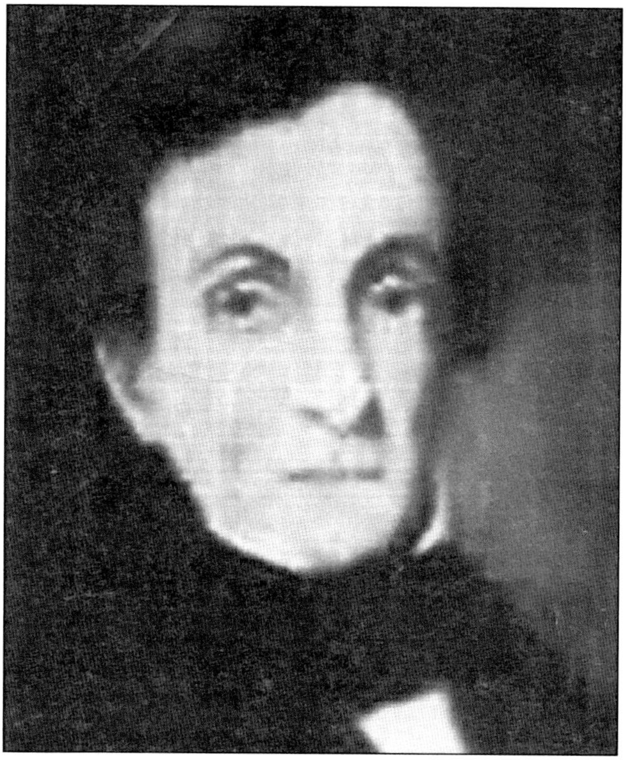

Wilson Price Hunt (1783–1842) was employed by John Jacob Astor. In the fall of 1811, Hunt's expedition visited Fort Henry, and while at the fort, he learned of a hot springs at the base of the Big Hole Mountains. Consequently, he became the first white man to visit the hot springs.

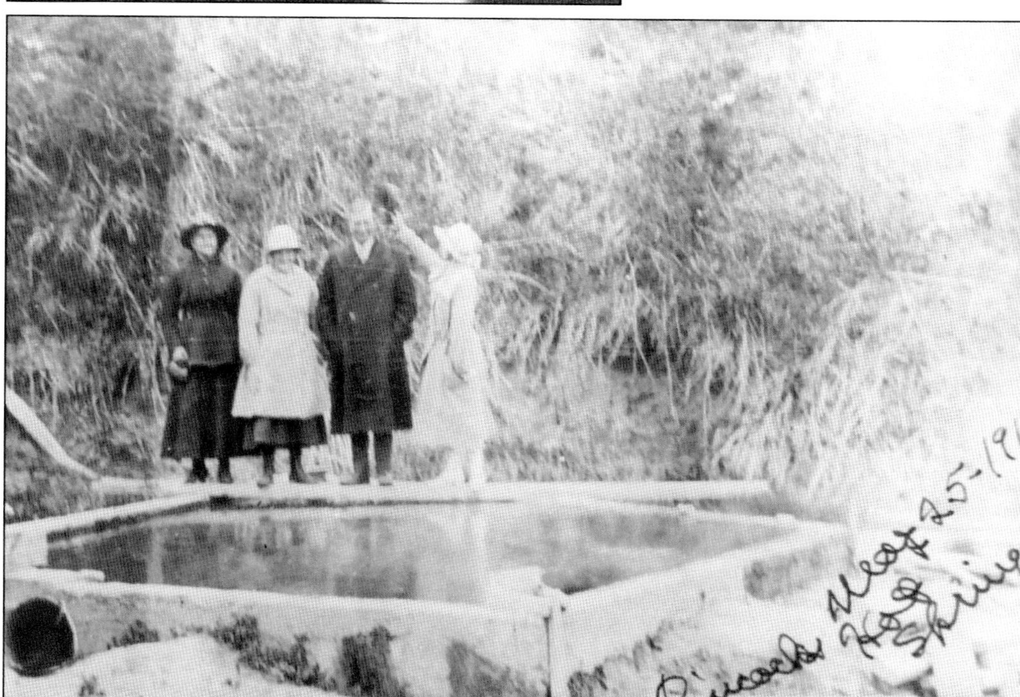

In this May 25, 1918, photograph, standing at the source of the hot springs visited by Wilson Price Hunt are, from left to right, Anna Carlson, Alice and Morgan Harris, and Carla Carlson. This picture was taken by Isabel Wilson. (Courtesy of Roland Brown.)

Robert Stuart (1785–1848) was a partner with John Jacob Astor, and on an 1811 journey from Oregon to the East Coast, the Stuart party floated down the Snake River. They were afraid the Blackfeet Indians were close by, so they abandoned their raft at present-day Table Rock and followed Canyon Creek to the hot springs used by the local Indians.

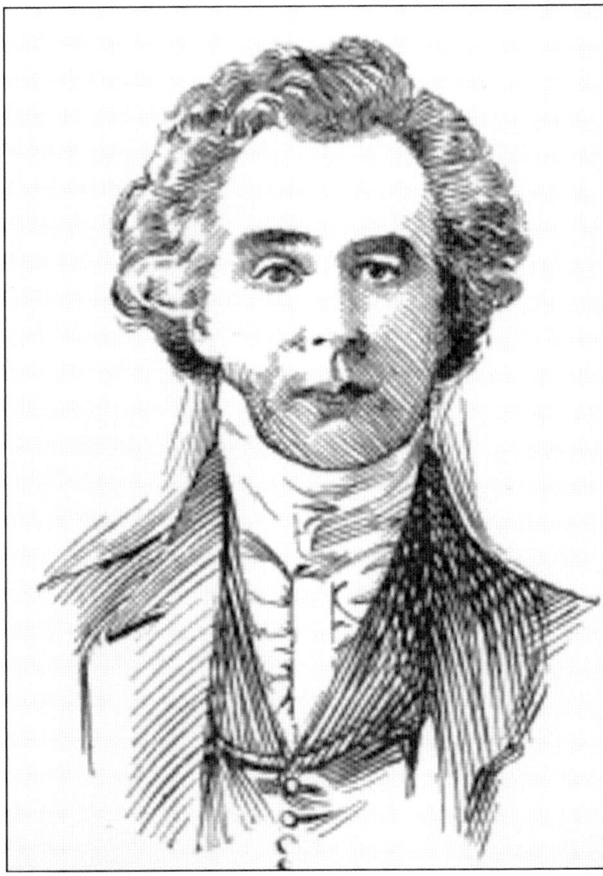

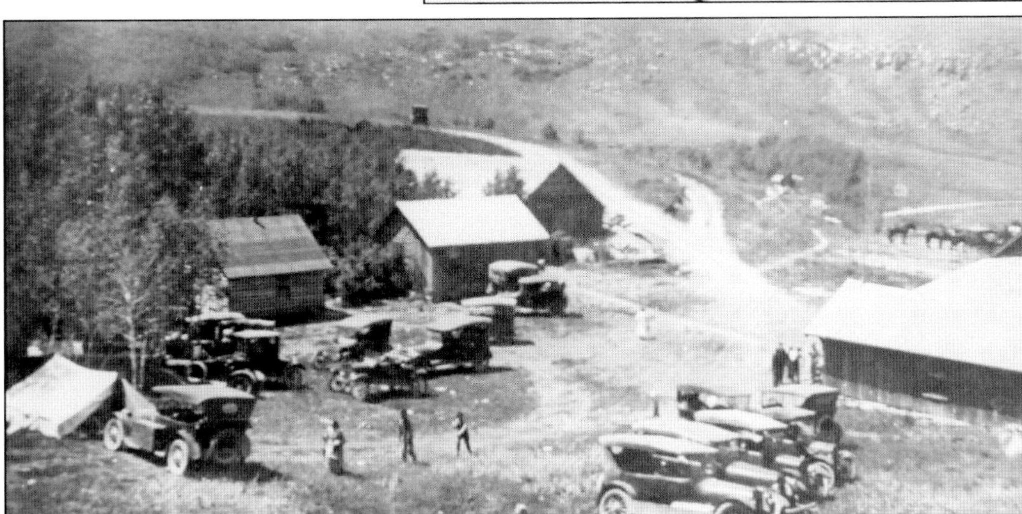

John and James Pincock bought farmland from a Mr. Butler in Green Canyon in 1898 and dug three hot pools. A building erected in 1912 became known as Pincock Hot Springs. In 1944, the Pincocks sold the hot springs to Robert Thueson. He constructed a new building and pool in 1948, renamed Green Canyon Hot Springs. Darrell Neibaur traded his farm for the swimming pool in 1952.

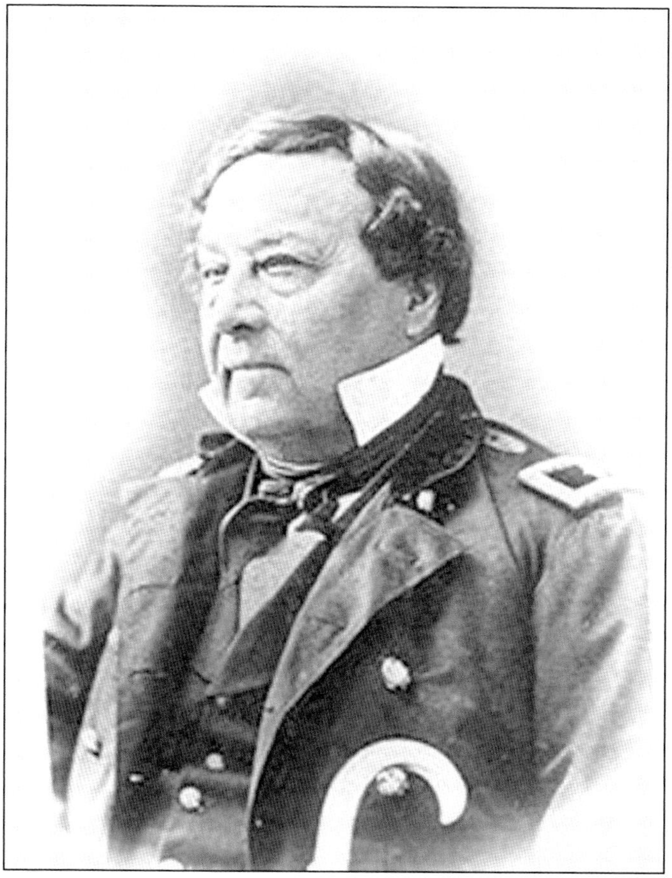

Capt. Benjamin De Bonneville (1796–1878) was a French-born officer in the US Army and an explorer of the American West. He was appointed to lead one of the expeditions to the Oregon country. In the spring of 1833, he explored along the Snake River and Henry's Fork near the site of Fort Henry.

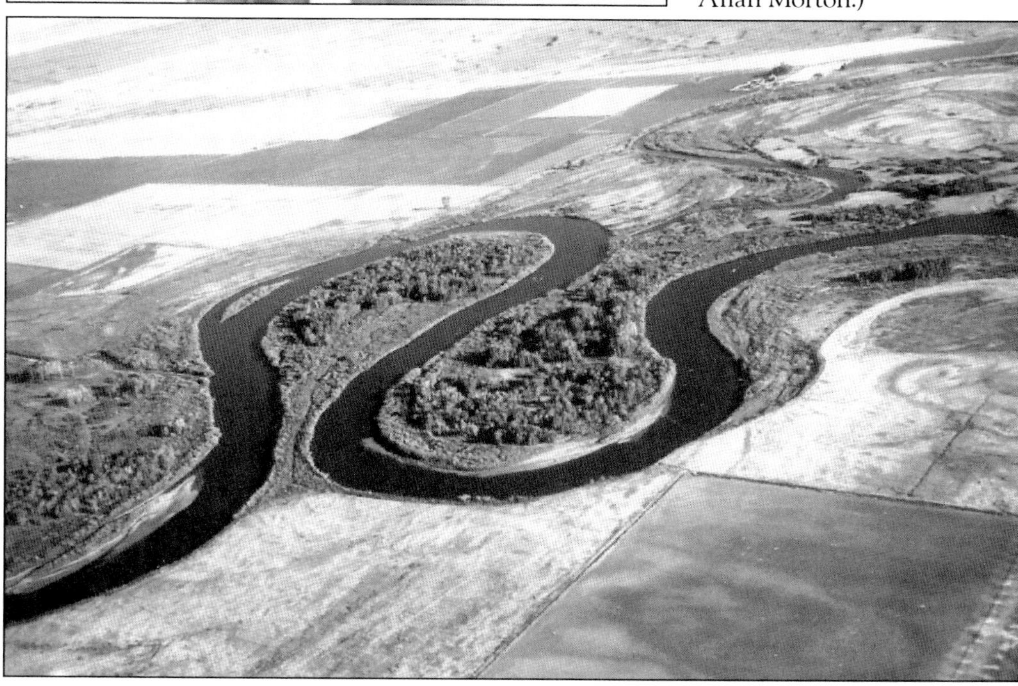

This photograph shows the convergence of the Snake and Teton Rivers west of Rexburg. The river served as the highway for fur traders and is the largest North American river to empty into the Pacific Ocean as it traverses across the state of Idaho. Fifteen major dams crisscross this river, and it is the lifeblood for agriculture in the Snake River basin. (Courtesy of Allan Morton.)

Fr. Pierre-Jean De Smet (1801–1873) was a Jesuit priest. In 1844, he passed through an area south of Rexburg on his way from Pierre's Hole in the Teton basin to Henry's Lake, where he performed the first Catholic communion in the Idaho territory for a band of Flathead and Nez Percé Indian tribes.

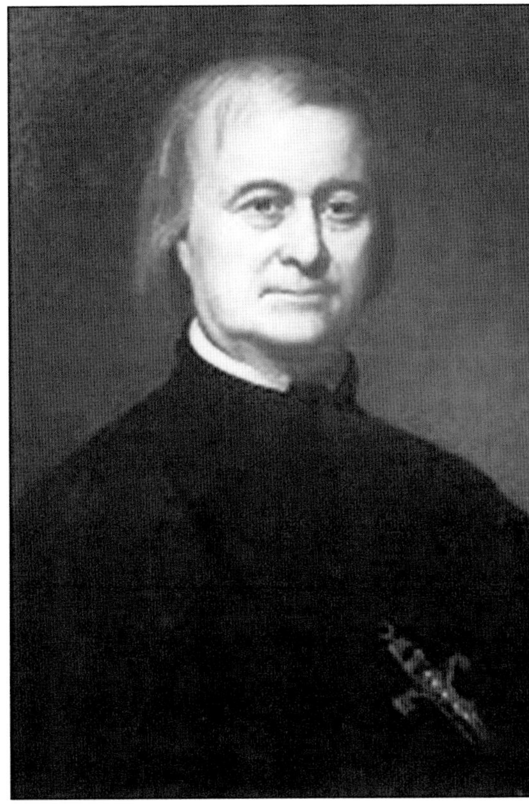

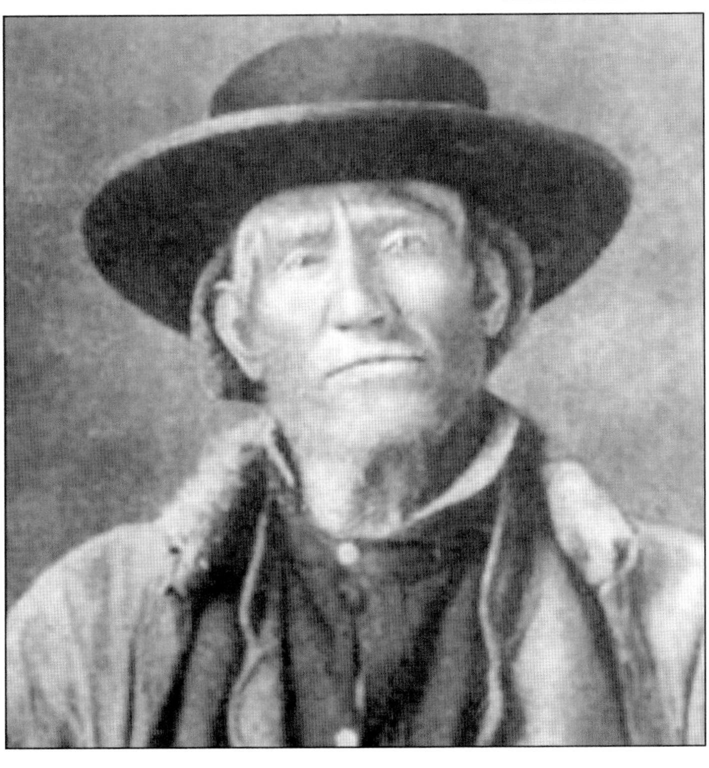

Jim Bridger (1804–1881) explored the Western United States between 1820 and 1850. He was commissioned by Brigham Young to explore the southeast and eastern areas of the Idaho territory for the possibility of colonization and farming. He was one of many mountain men who visited Fort Henry in its declining days.

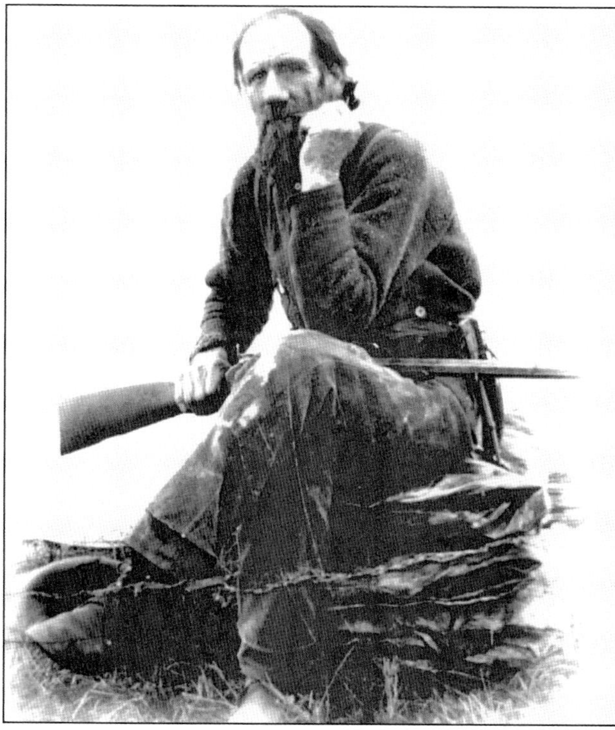

The more fascinating of the first white settlers of the area was Richard "Beaver Dick" Leigh. He settled on the bank of the Snake River, west of Rexburg. He learned the art of trapping with the Hudson Bay Fur Company and went west, where he met Mormon president Brigham Young, who gave him the nickname of "Beaver Dick" because of his two protruding front teeth. (Courtesy of Dr. Samuel Beal.)

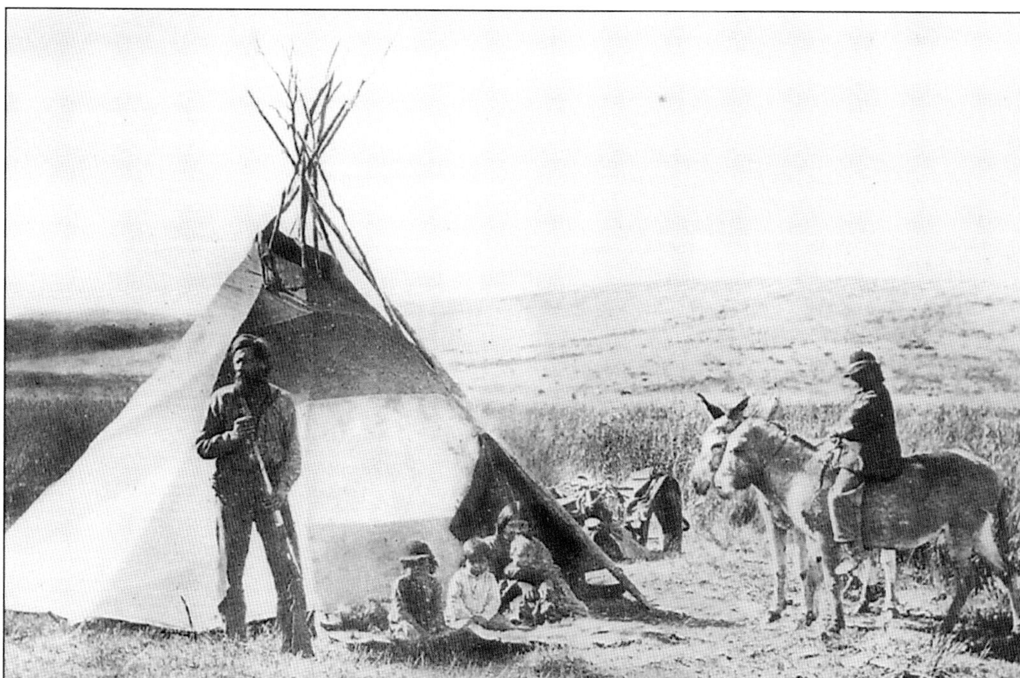

In 1876, tragically, Beaver Dick's Shoshone wife and six children died of smallpox. He later married Susan Tadpole, who had been promised to him 16 years earlier, and they lived northeast of Rexburg. He was a guide for Theodore Roosevelt when he bagged a trophy buffalo four miles north of Rexburg. (Courtesy of Upper Snake River Valley Historical Society.)

Two

Colonization

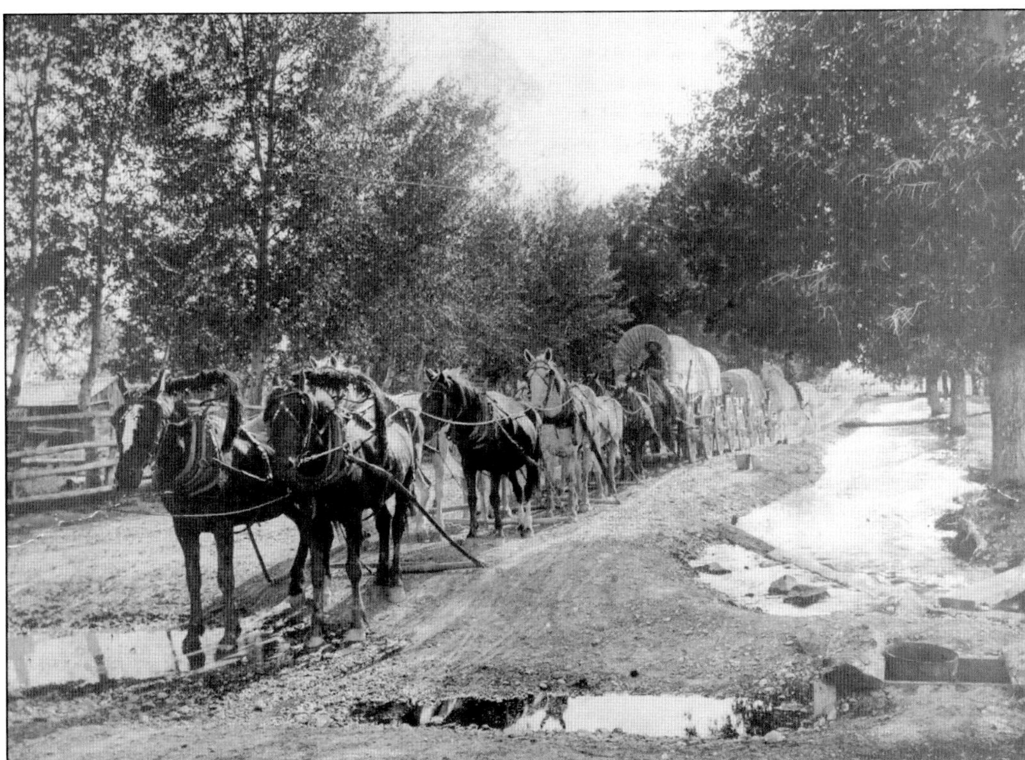

Early Mormon Church authority Brigham Henry Roberts noted that the success of Mormon colonization stemmed from "the loyalty of the people to their leaders and their unselfish and devoted personal sacrifice" in carrying out the calls from their church leaders. The colonizing time for Rexburg came on March 10, 1883, when a handful of men came into the Upper Snake River Valley to establish a community. (Courtesy of Diana Fuller.)

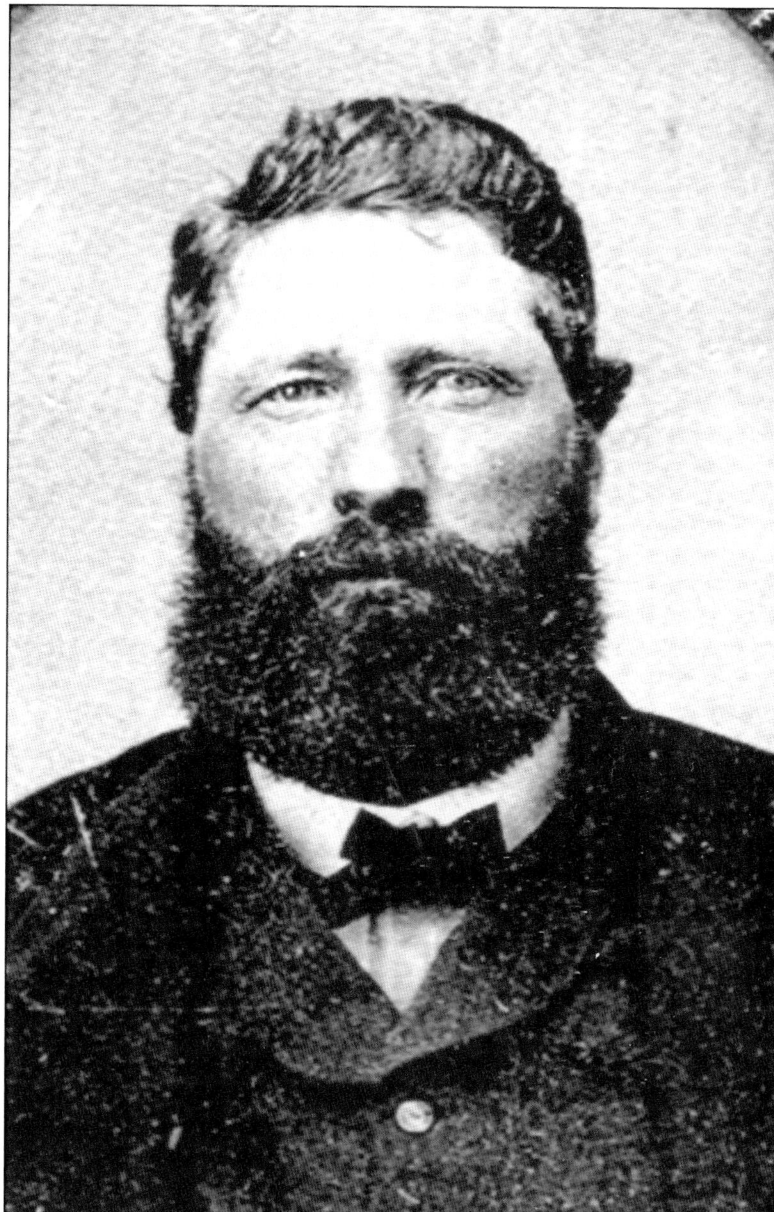

This picture of a young Thomas E. Ricks was taken from a small card portrait that was taken in Nebraska in 1866. Ricks was a man of great courage and a 19th-century visionary. According to Dr. Samuel Beal, "He achieved success in all phases of community building despite formidable obstacles and opposition. His capacity to analyze the everyday problems of pioneer life and his leadership ability to direct men in solving those problems is attested by the remarkable development of the Upper Snake River Valley, the true mark of the heritage he left the community of Rexburg." The colonization came in 1883 when Mormon Church authority William B. Preston visited the area and was so pleased that he sent a handful of men led by Ricks to develop the region as the "central point for religious, educational and commercial enterprises." On March 11, 1883, it was named Rexburg in honor of Thomas E. Ricks. Rexburg was nicknamed "Mosquito Flats" by many of the early settlers. (Courtesy of Val Hemming.)

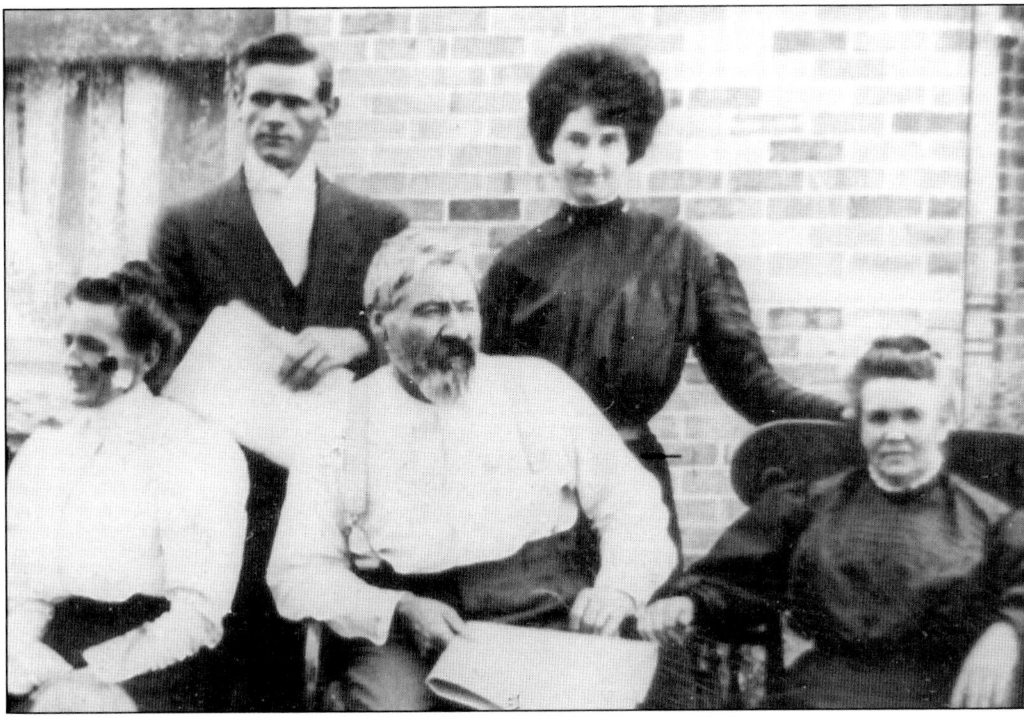

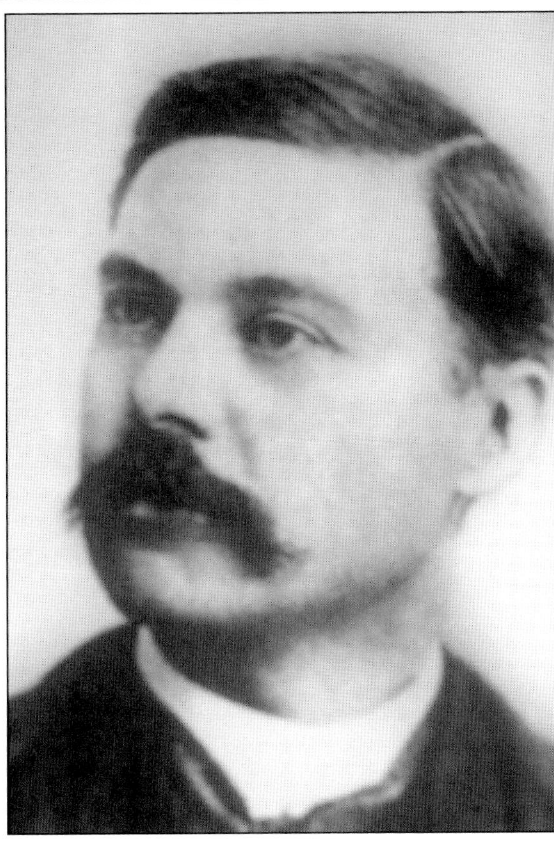

Polygamy was practiced by the Mormon Church from 1830 to 1887. This 1909 family portrait shows the polygamist family of Joseph Ricks, who is seated with second wife Sophia on his left and first wife Margaret on his right. Standing are son Peter J. and Peter's wife, Emily. Those outside the Mormon religion looked upon the practice of polygamy as a political institution that rivaled the power of the state. An anti-Mormon party was founded by Fred T. Dubois, pictured at right. A crusade was launched against all polygamists, and many raids on the city of Rexburg were conducted, with the men sentenced to serve months in the penitentiary and pay a fine of $300. Other polygamists were forced to stay underground in order to avoid apprehension. At one time, Sheriff Ed Winn went to the home of Thomas E. Ricks and was denied entrance. He told his deputies to break the door down. According to Dr. Beal, a deputy said, "Nothing doing, Old Tom has thirteen sons, and every one of them is armed with a shot gun." (Above, courtesy of Sherwood Ricks.)

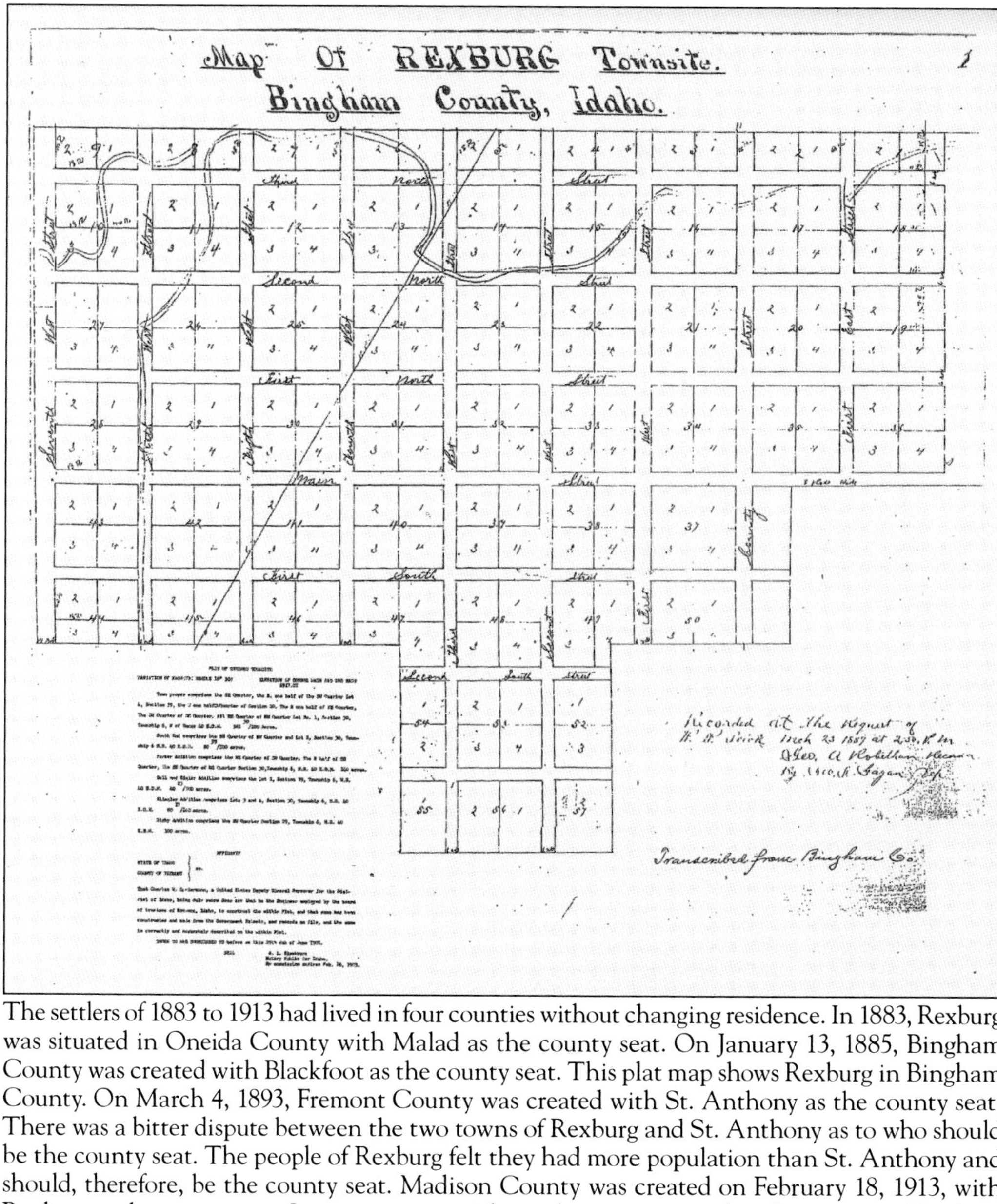

The settlers of 1883 to 1913 had lived in four counties without changing residence. In 1883, Rexburg was situated in Oneida County with Malad as the county seat. On January 13, 1885, Bingham County was created with Blackfoot as the county seat. This plat map shows Rexburg in Bingham County. On March 4, 1893, Fremont County was created with St. Anthony as the county seat. There was a bitter dispute between the two towns of Rexburg and St. Anthony as to who should be the county seat. The people of Rexburg felt they had more population than St. Anthony and should, therefore, be the county seat. Madison County was created on February 18, 1913, with Rexburg as the county seat. It was a common joke in the community that the citizens of Rexburg would go to bed in one county and wake up the next morning in another because of the multiple counties the city had existed in. (Courtesy of Terrell and Margaret Porter Arnold.)

Three

EDUCATION

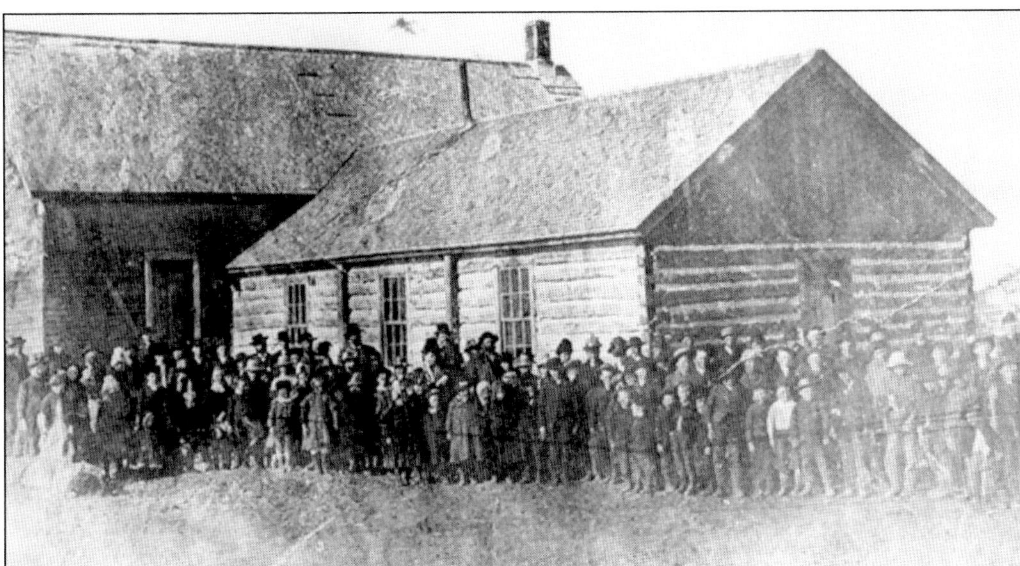

A public school was organized in 1885 and was held in this church building. On November 12, 1888, superintendent of the Mormon School system Carl G. Maeser officially opened the Bannock Stake Academy. In 1898, the name changed to Fremont Stake Academy; in January 1902, the name changed to Smith Academy; and on March 5, 1902, it was named Ricks Academy in honor of Thomas E. Ricks.

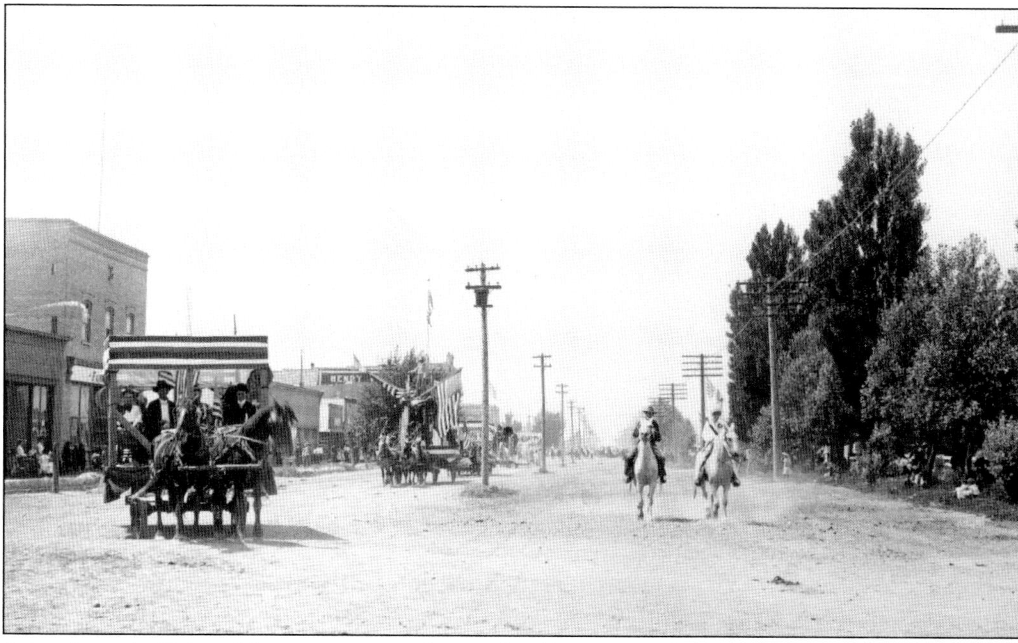

School was held in a Mormon meetinghouse for 10 years, and then it was moved to the Zions Cooperative Mercantile Institution (ZCMI) building at the corner of East Main Street and South Second East. This picture shows the two-story ZCMI building on the left behind the horse-drawn float. Tuition was paid by farm produce and chopped wood. Plans were made to construct a new two-story building at the end of South College Avenue. The cornerstone for that building was laid by George Q. Cannon on June 25, 1900. The cost of the construction was $40,000. The labor was all donated by Mormon Church members throughout the Snake River Valley. The Spori Building was completed in 1902 and stood for over 100 years until it was razed in 2003. (Both, courtesy of BYU–Idaho Special Collections and Archives.)

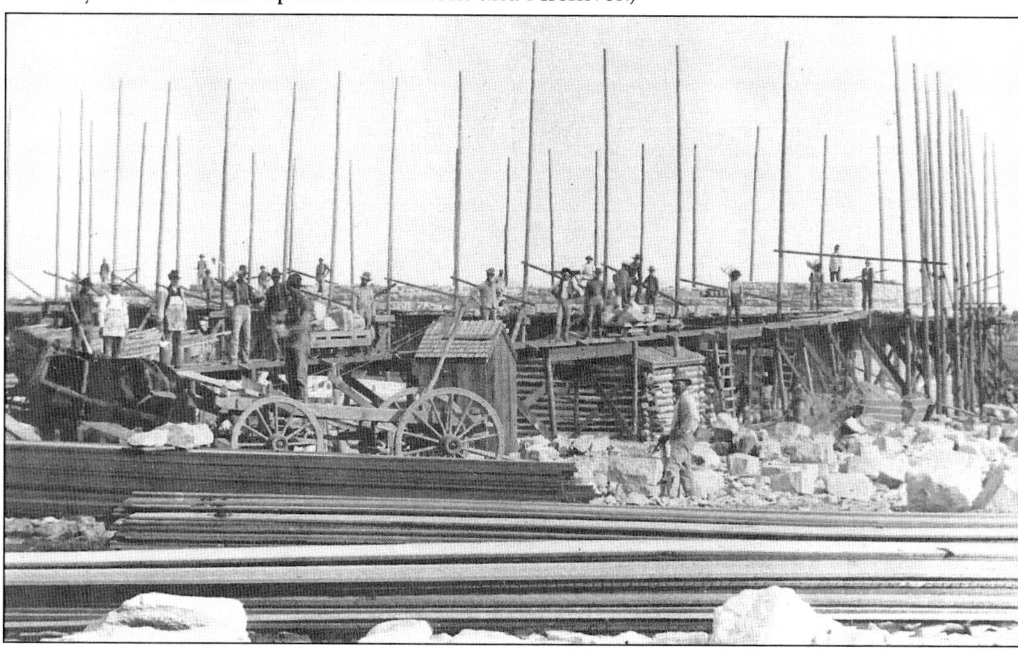

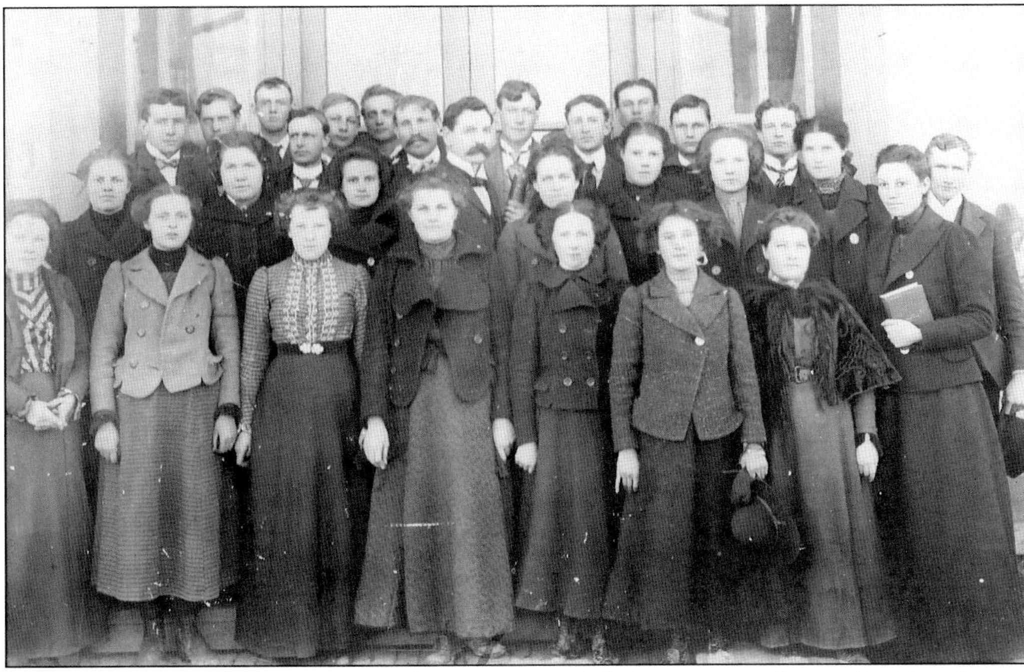

This 1911 photograph is a group of students that attended classes in the Thomas Building, located at the corner of East Main Street and South First East. The classes were held in a back room of the Ballif and Thatcher Clothier store. (Courtesy of Dona Bigler.)

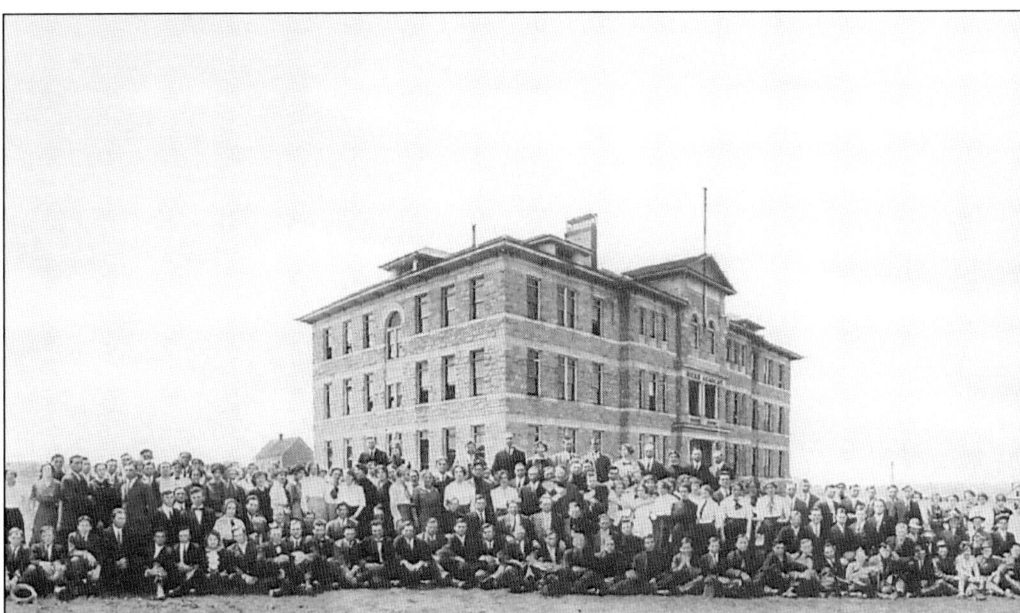

This building was called the Spori Building after Jacob Spori. Stake academies were established first as modern high schools, since public schools only offered an eighth-grade education. Ricks Academy survived when stake academies were discontinued because they added a year of college work to their curriculum, and it became known as Ricks Normal School. In 1923, it was renamed Ricks College and functioned as a two-year college. (Courtesy of Dean Rasmussen.)

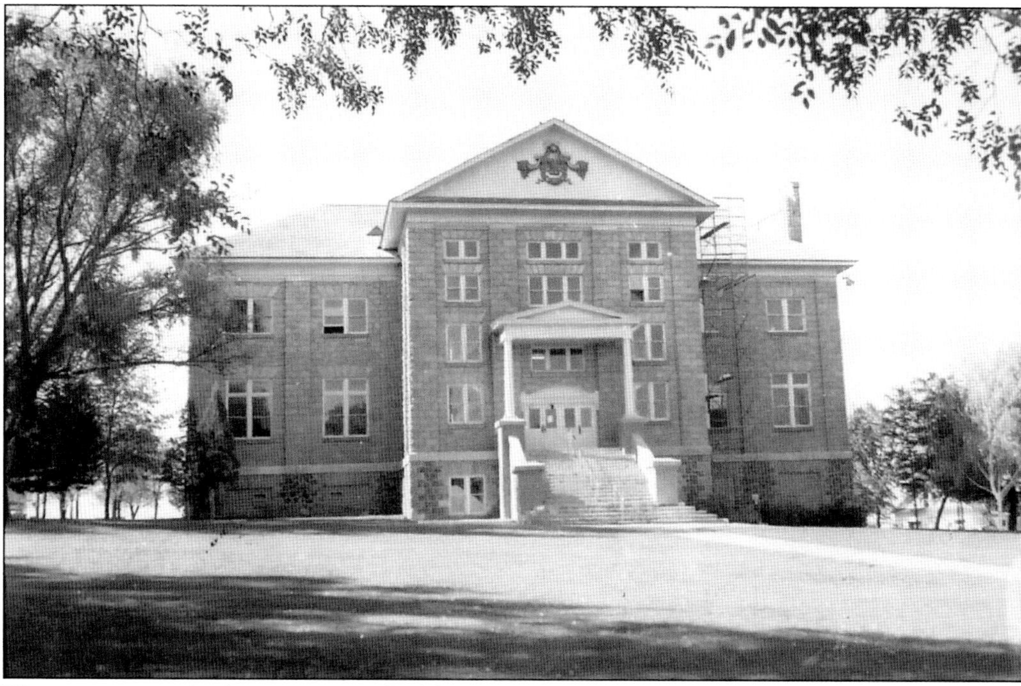

The cornerstone for the gymnasium building was laid by Nathan Ricks on June 16, 1916. The cost of the building was $60,000. It was dedicated on March 22, 1919, by the president of the Mormon Church George at the time, Albert Smith. There were classrooms on the main floor, a ballroom and a basketball court upstairs, and a swimming pool in the basement.

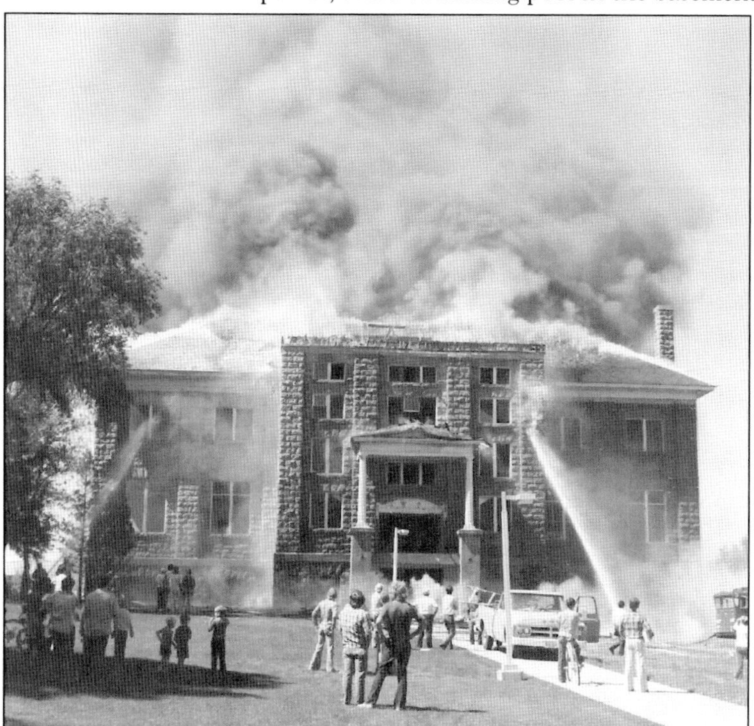

It was decided by the Mormon Church that the gymnasium building had outlived it use, and demolition began. The building was made of native rhyolite rock and was so well built that the wrecking balls could not demolish it, so it was burned to the ground on July 23, 1977.

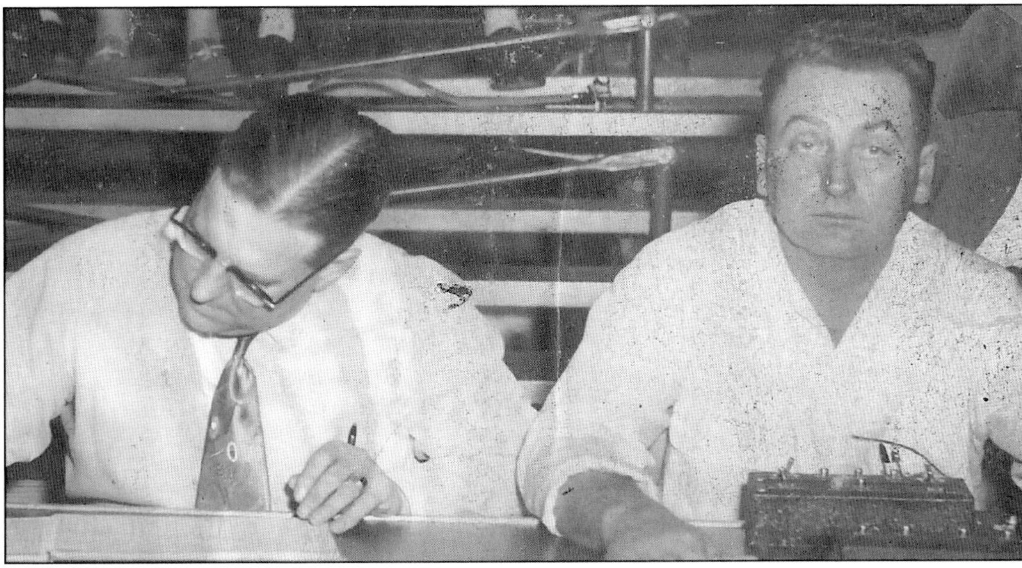

Rexburg was an athletic-oriented community. Football and basketball games at Ricks College were community events that the entire city would attend to socialize along with enjoying the games. The Ricks College girls' basketball team attended the Dairy Bowl basketball championships yearly and won almost every time it participated. Above, John Parkinson (left) and Jack Randall were the Ricks College basketball scorekeepers from 1952 to 1977. Below, the 1930–1931 Ricks College Men's basketball team stands on the steps of the gymnasium building. The team is made up of, from left to right, (first row) Eugene Manwaring, Noel Johnson, Howard Blackburn, George Swainston, Tenneth West, Boyd Reynolds, Albert Holman, and Roy Cole; (second row) Lenard Jensen, Joseph Erdley, Arthur Sylvester, Rulon Harris, Conley Watts, Alma Adams, and coach Clyde Packer.

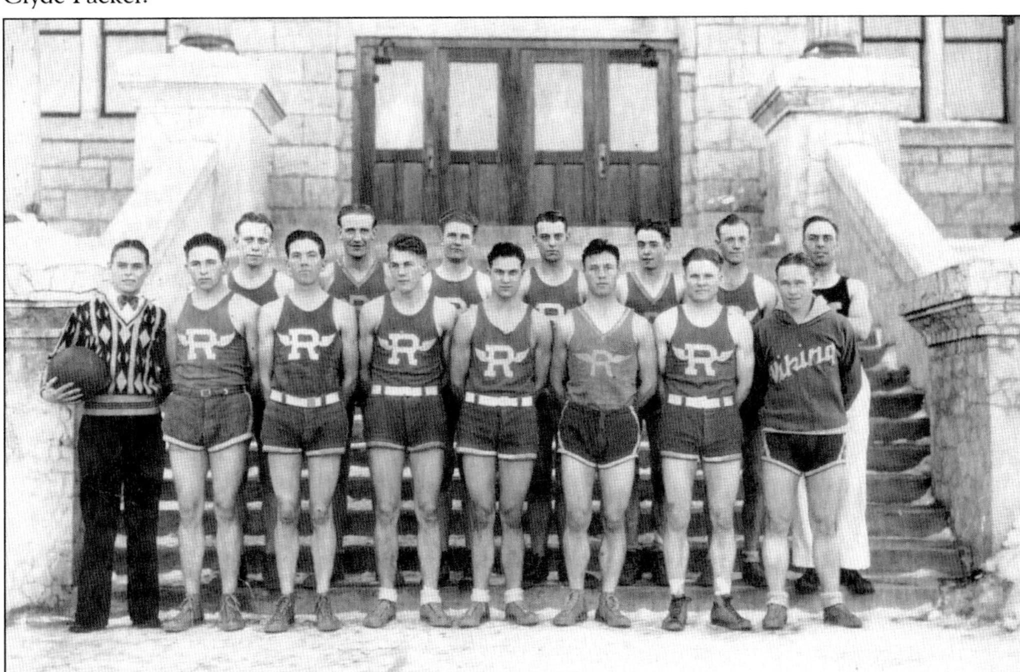

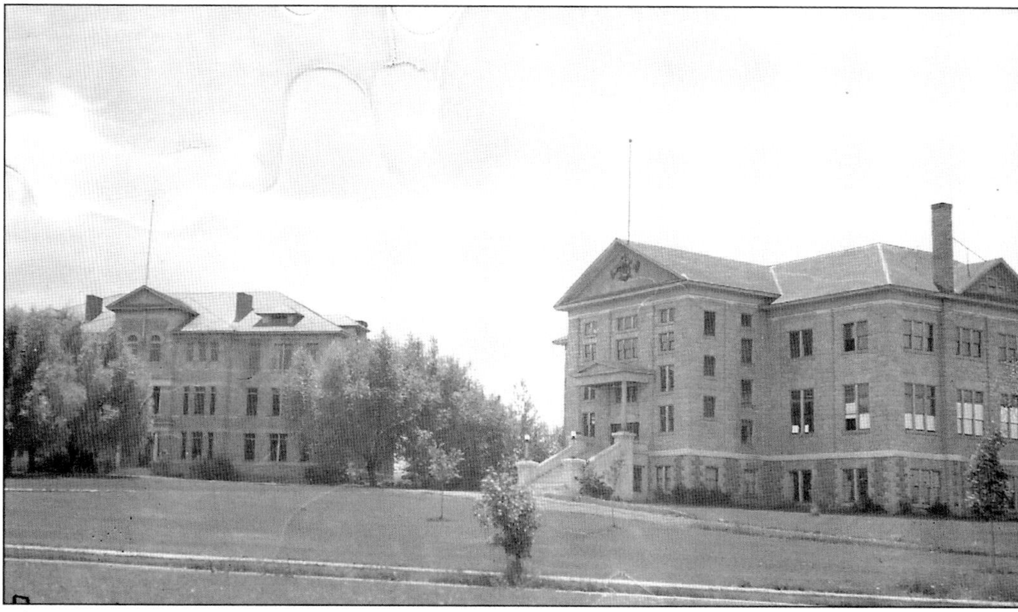

This is a panoramic view of the two major buildings on the Ricks College: the Jacob Spori Administration Building, erected in 1902 (left), and the 1916 Ricks College gymnasium.

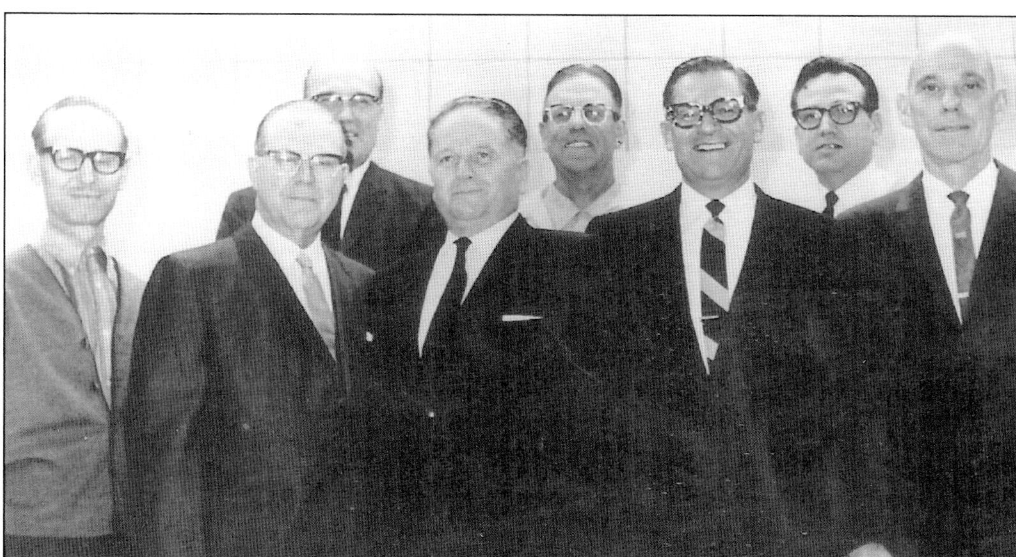

Dr. Leo Eugene Peterson was the inspiration behind the creation of the Ricks College Booster's Club. This club was a fundraising organization for athletic scholarships and, after 25 years, had raised $2.5 million. From left to right are (first row) Dr. Leo Peterson, Dr. Murland Rigby, Ricks College president John Clarke, Judge Mike Donahue, and Dr. Lowell Biddulph; (second row) Grover Hemming, John D. Parkinson, and Terrell Arnold.

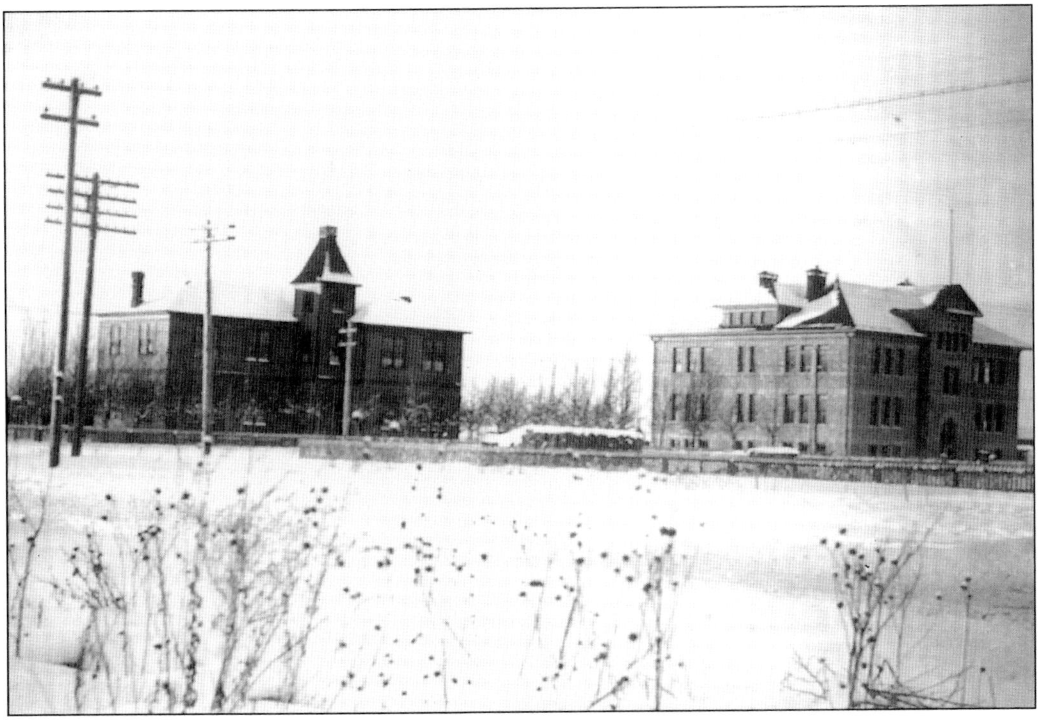

In this 1916 photograph, the building on the left was the first elementary school building constructed in Rexburg in 1897 and was known as the First District School for grades first through eighth. Eighth grade was usually the highest level of education that students attained during this period of time. This building was located on the corner of West Main Street and North First West. The building on the right was the second school erected in the city of Rexburg. It was built in 1904 and was made of native rhyolite sandstone. Named the Central Elementary School, it offered kindergarten through sixth-grade classes. The top floor was an open area used for dances and assemblies. The beautiful young woman pictured at right, Fredonia Josephine Jensen, had just completed the eighth grade and is seen holding her diploma.

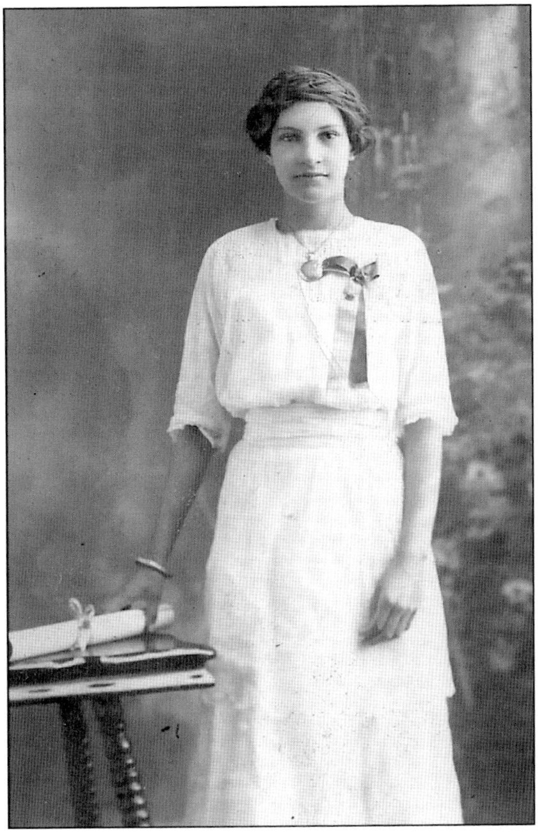

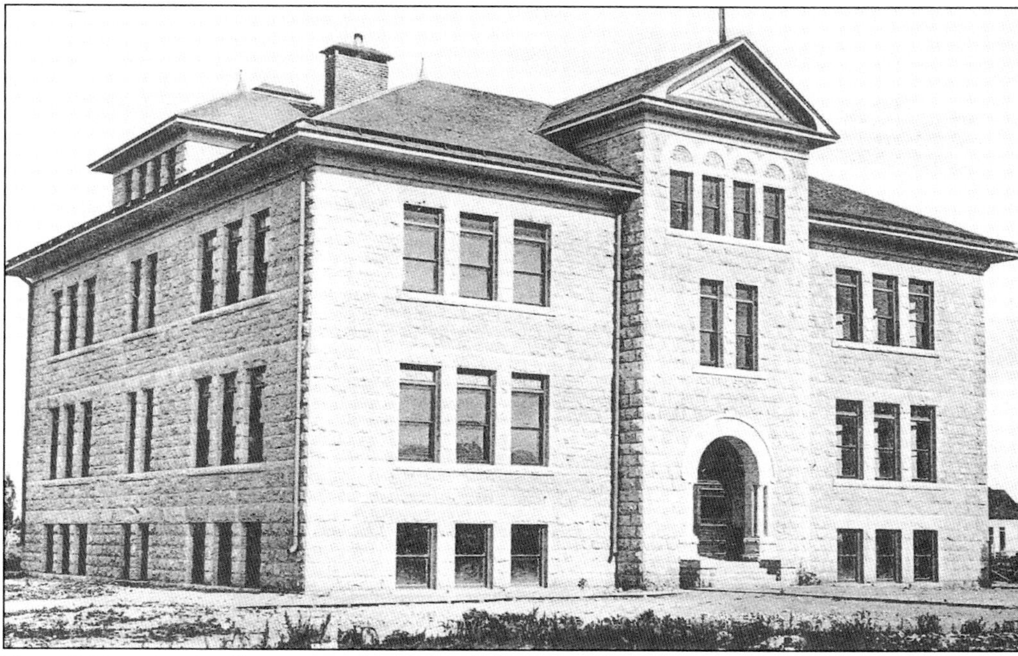

This 1904 rock schoolhouse was first named the Central Elementary School, but the name was later changed to the Washington Elementary School. The building stood and was in use in Rexburg for over 72 years but was sadly demolished by the floodwaters of the Teton Dam flood on June 5, 1976.

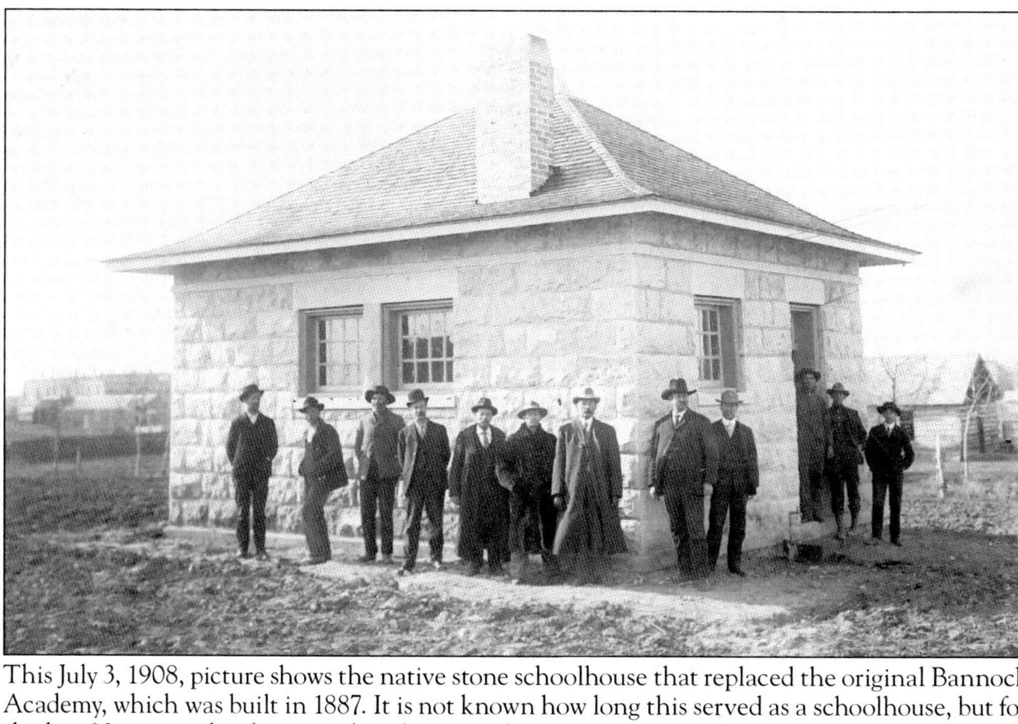

This July 3, 1908, picture shows the native stone schoolhouse that replaced the original Bannock Academy, which was built in 1887. It is not known how long this served as a schoolhouse, but for the last 90 years, it has been used as the City of Rexburg's pump house. The men in photograph are all unidentified. (Courtesy of BYU–Idaho Special Collections and Archives.)

The third elementary school in Rexburg, built in 1916, was the Adams School. The school was named after US president John Adams. The building was constructed of brick and native rhyolite sandstone. Located at the corner of North Second East and East First North, it housed first through sixth grades until it was severely damaged by the floodwaters of the Teton Dam.

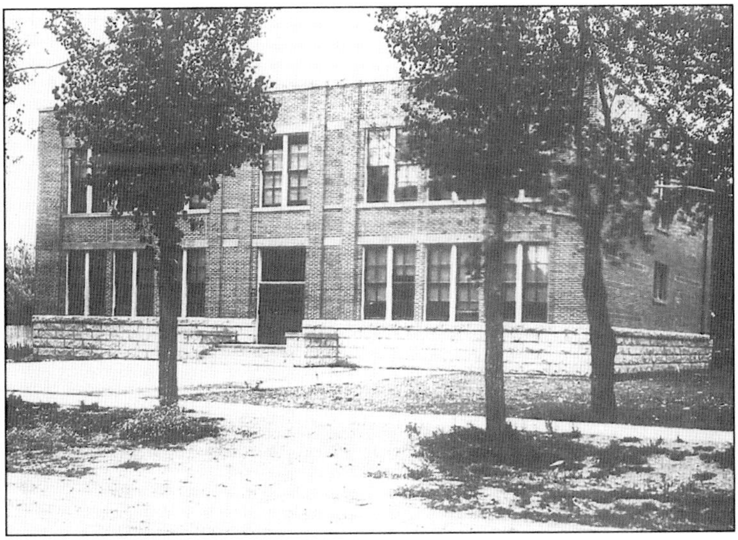

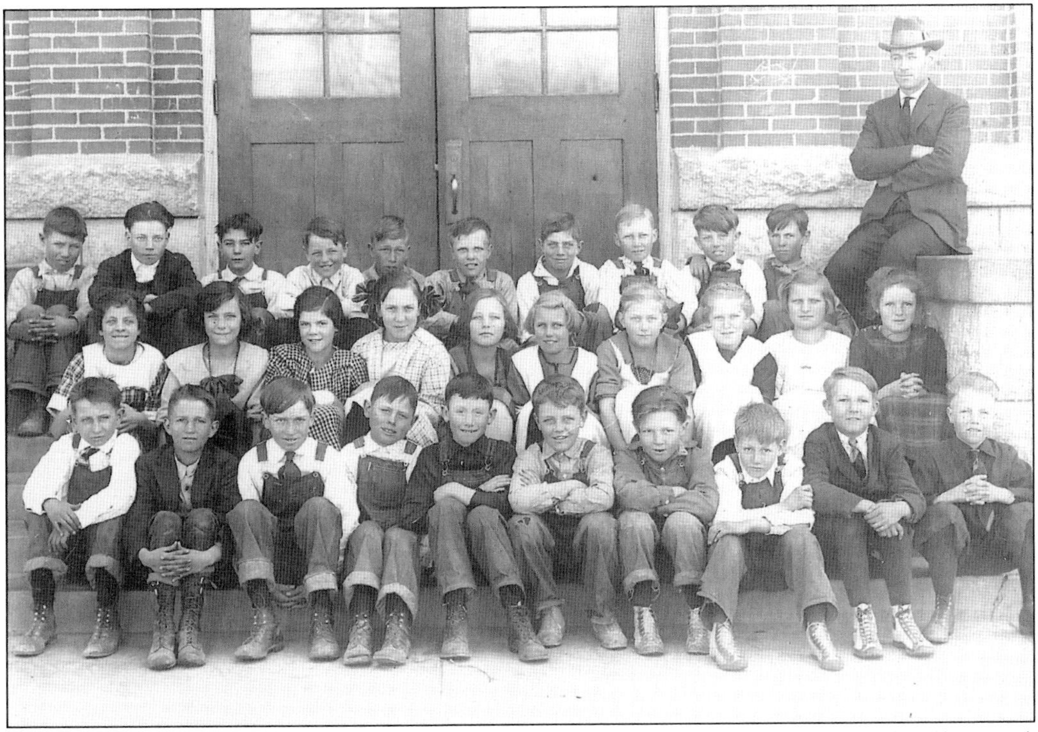

Pictured is the Adams School sixth grade of 1924–1925; they are, from left to right, (first row) Harry Markowski, Bill Blaser, Kenneth Blunck, Eugene Manwaring, Don Grover, Darrell Larsen, John Porter, Billy Oviatt, Eldon Dayley, and Reed Garner; (second row) Myrtle Flamm, Luella Ferro, Louise Archibald, Vera Bitter, Fanny Freeman, Pearl Krogue, Rhea Porter, Lula Hill, Vera Smith, and Bessie Hill; (third row) Arnold Wilding, Echlo Smith, Cleo Cooper, Ace Raymond, Vern Covington, Glen Stoddard, Edwin Flamm, Harold Bigler, Walter Odermatt, John Parkinson, and teacher Sterling Nelson.

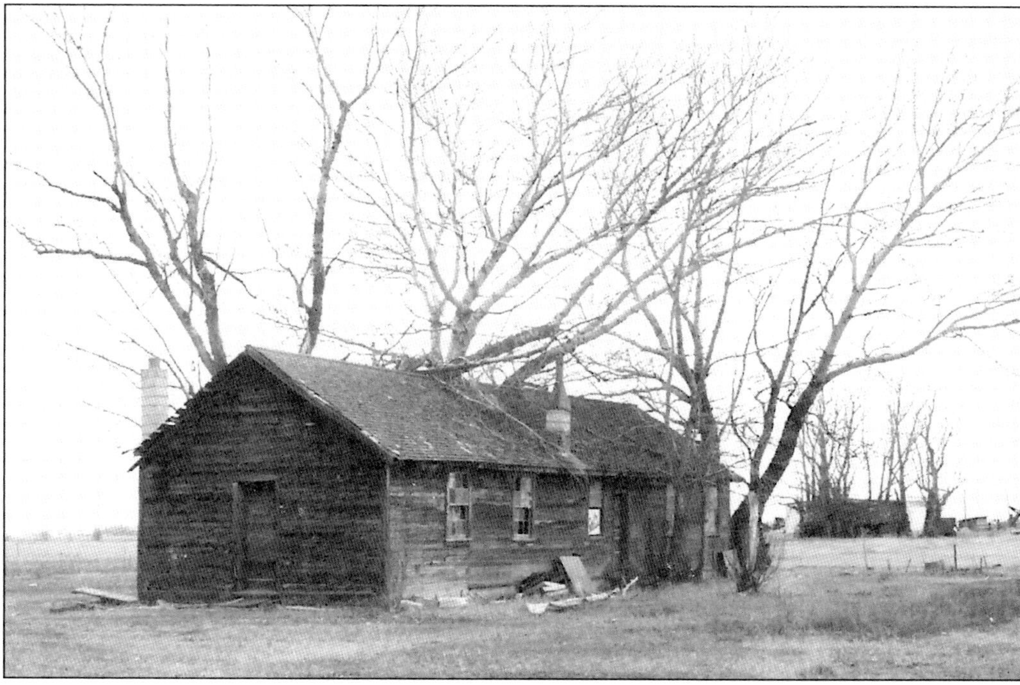

The American-Japanese Language School was built in 1924 and closed its doors on December 7, 1941. Seventy-five immigrant Japanese men were hired in 1899 by the Oregon Shortline Railroad to build tracks from Idaho Falls to Rexburg. After the tracks were completed, these men were out of work, so they hired on with the local sugar beet farmers in the surrounding area and began to raise their families in Rexburg. They realized their children were forgetting their culture, so they built this school to provide lessons in Japanese language and customs. The school was also used as a Buddhist temple. These families were very industrious people and went on to buy their own farms and became prominent in the sugar beet industry. The building was torn down in May 2008.

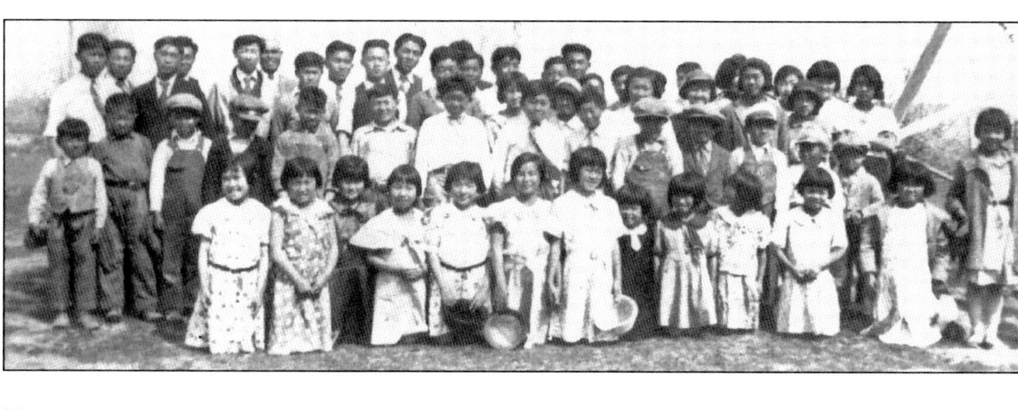

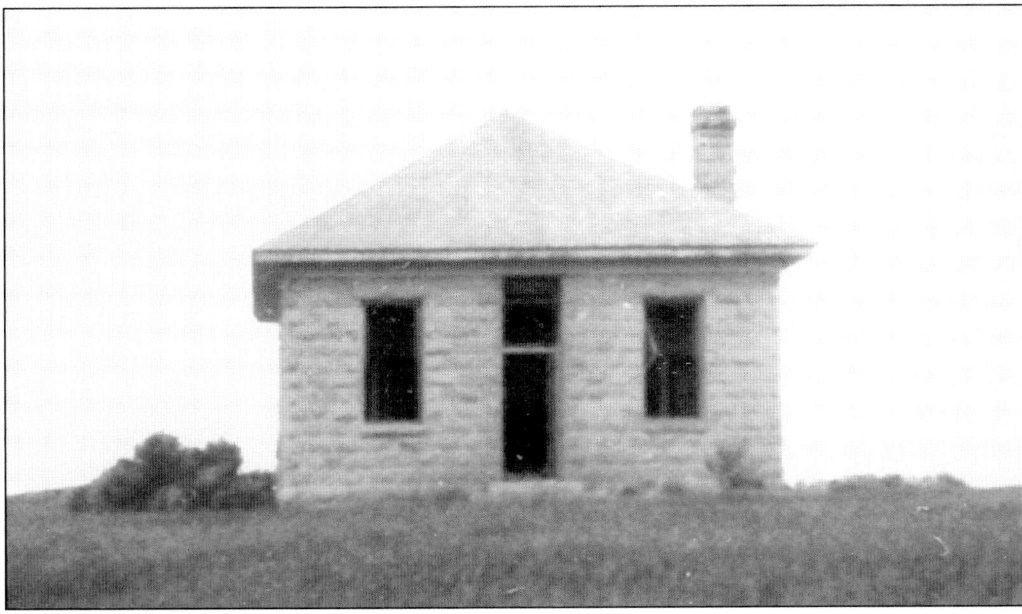

The 1913 Hawthorne School No. 44 was on the upper Rexburg bench and accommodated the children of the dry farmers in that area. None of the farmers lived on their farms in the harsh winters. This school opened in the middle of March, so the children could transfer from the Rexburg schools they attended in the winter to this school in the spring. The move allowed the children to help their families on the farms. The only farming families who attended this country schoolhouse were the Darley, Faucett, Parkinson, and Wood families. This school operated until 1933. This rare photograph shows what the classroom looked like inside this schoolhouse. The only two children identified are Edith and Sadie Parkinson (in the front far right) and school mistress Jenny Wood Brown. (Below, courtesy of Sharon Hinckley.)

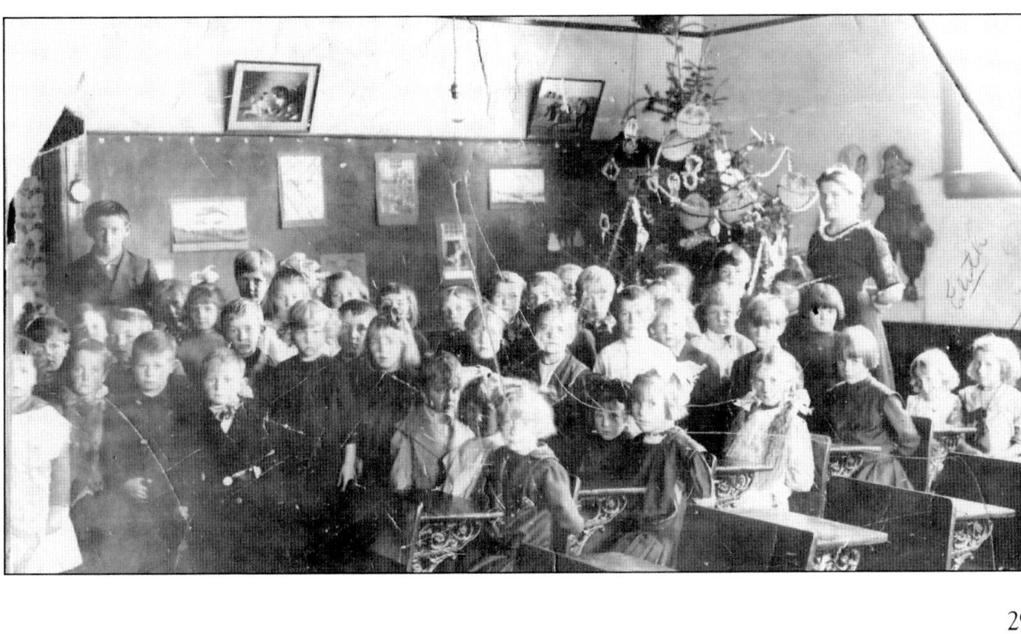

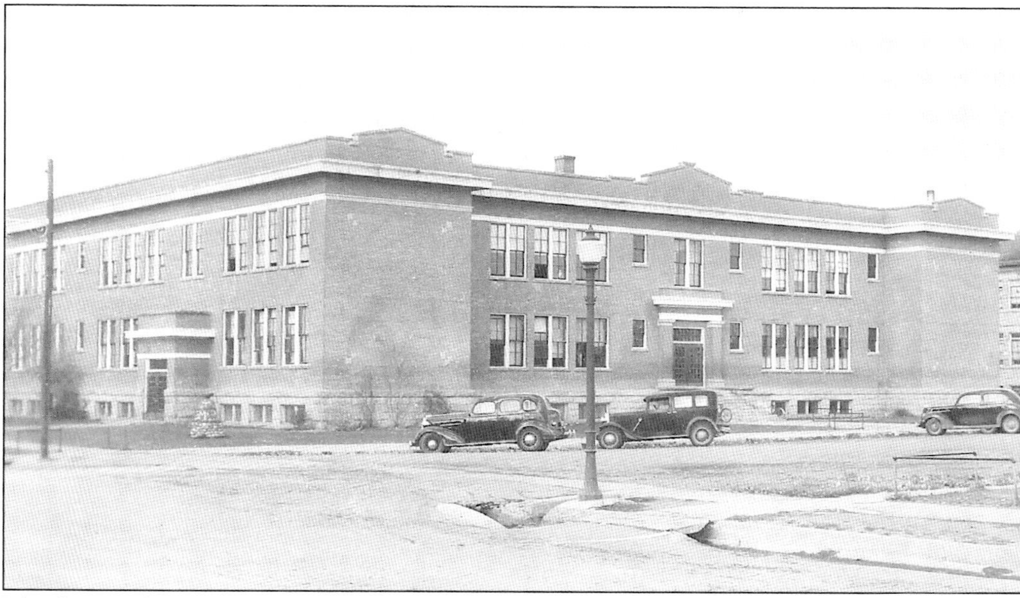

The first Madison High School was built in 1926–1927 on the location where the First District School once stood. The school accommodated freshman through senior high school students. It operated as a high school until 1956, when the second Madison High School was built a half block east on the same street. At that time, it was converted into the Madison Junior High School.

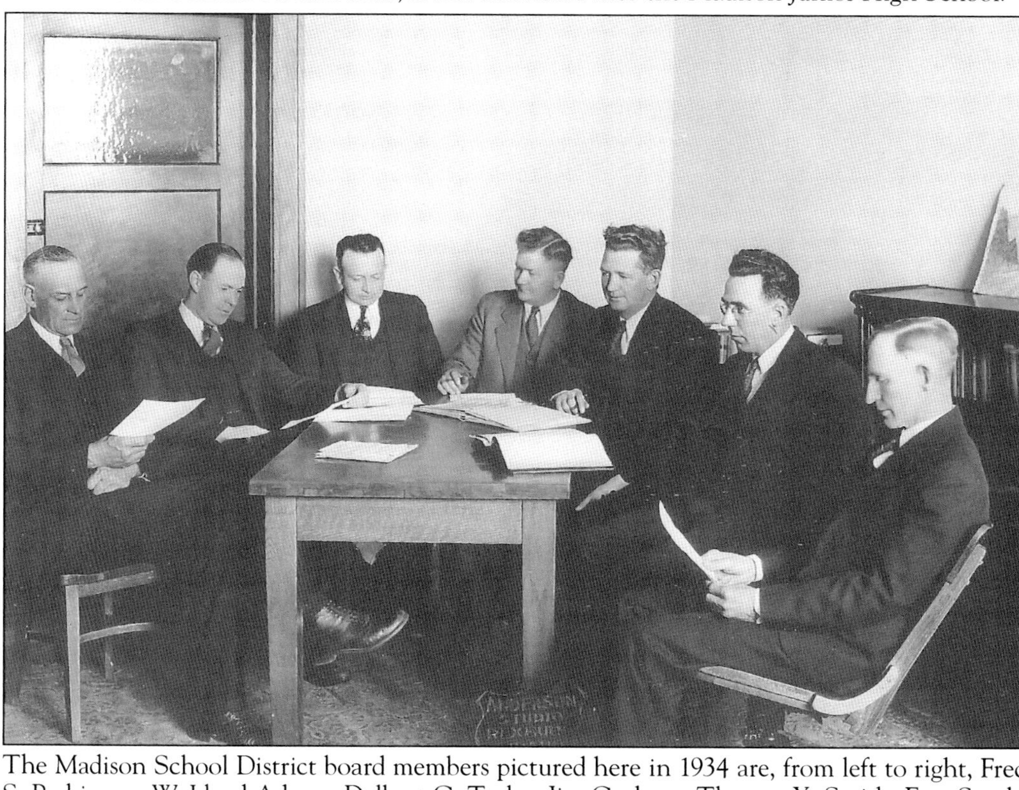

The Madison School District board members pictured here in 1934 are, from left to right, Fred S. Parkinson, W. Lloyd Adams, Delbert G. Taylor, Jim Graham, Thomas X. Smith, Ezra Stucki (superintendent), and Stephen Skelton (chairman of the board).

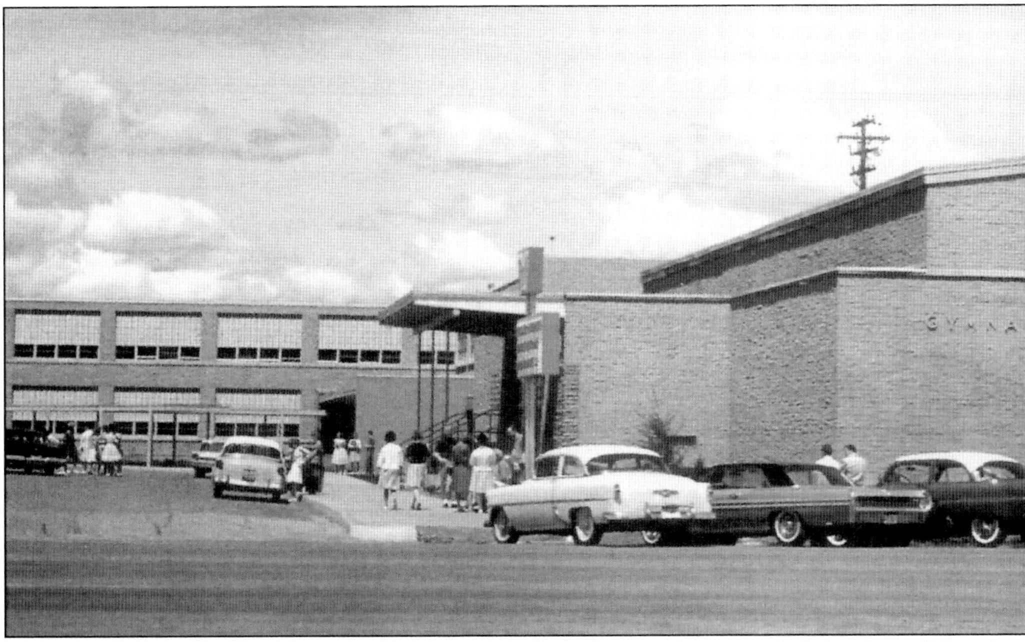

This school building was constructed in 1956 and used as Madison High School until the third Madison High School building was erected in 1972. This building then became Madison Junior High for grades eighth and ninth. It was used as the junior high until 2010.

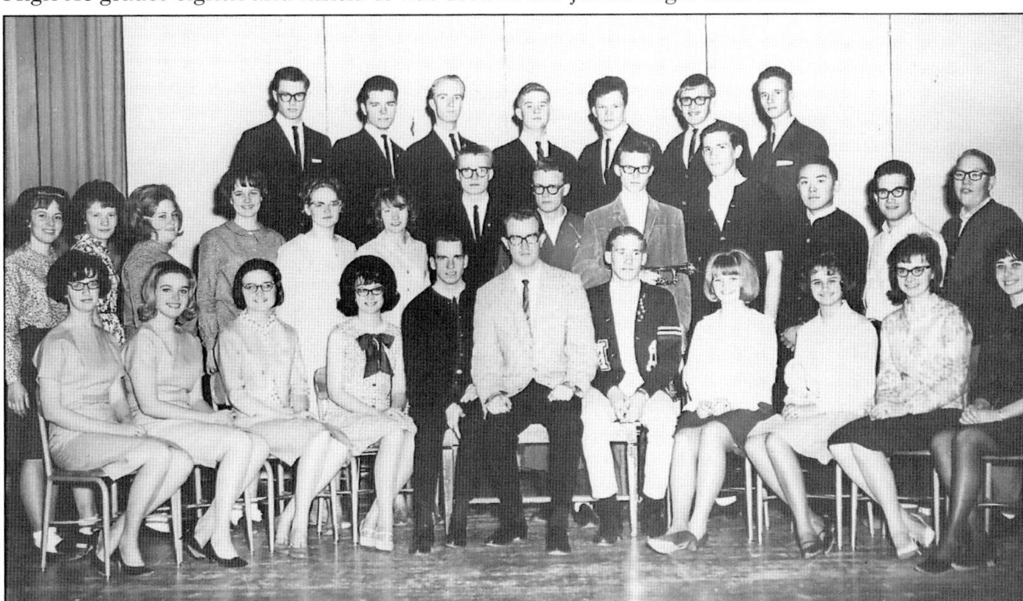

Exchange assembly is pictured here in 1965. From left to right are (first row) Jill Flamm, Rhonda Brown, Susan Passey, Evelyn Phillips, Lowell Parkinson, Lynn Skinner (advisor), Vaughn Mason, Joyce Rigby, Beverly Rigby, Ellen Davenport, and Cynthia Benson; (second row) Mary Patterson, Margaret Patterson, Carol McCain, Christine Moss, Carol Brown, Sandra Hathaway, Lynn Keeler, Stuart Agren, Brent Peterson, David Anderson, Bryan Fujimoto, Chris Jacob, and Bill Bean; (third row) Tom Matthews, Demar Merrill, Ronnie Allred, Steve Bunnell, Val Price, Keith Johnson, and Gordon Brown.

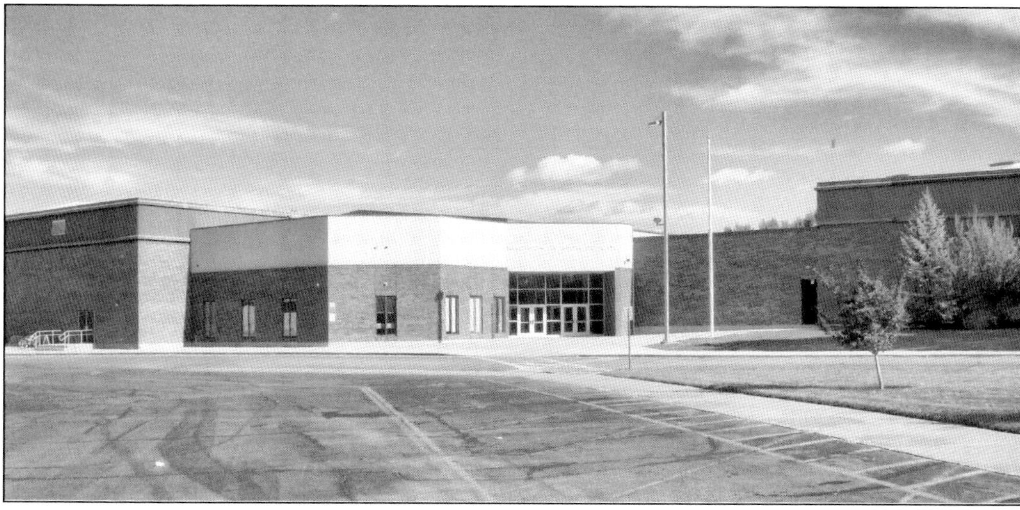

The third Madison High School was built on Madison Avenue in 1972, and doors opened for school in September 1973. In 2010, the current Madison High School was constructed, and this building became the Madison Junior High School; it is still in use today. (Courtesy of the *Rexburg Standard Journal.*)

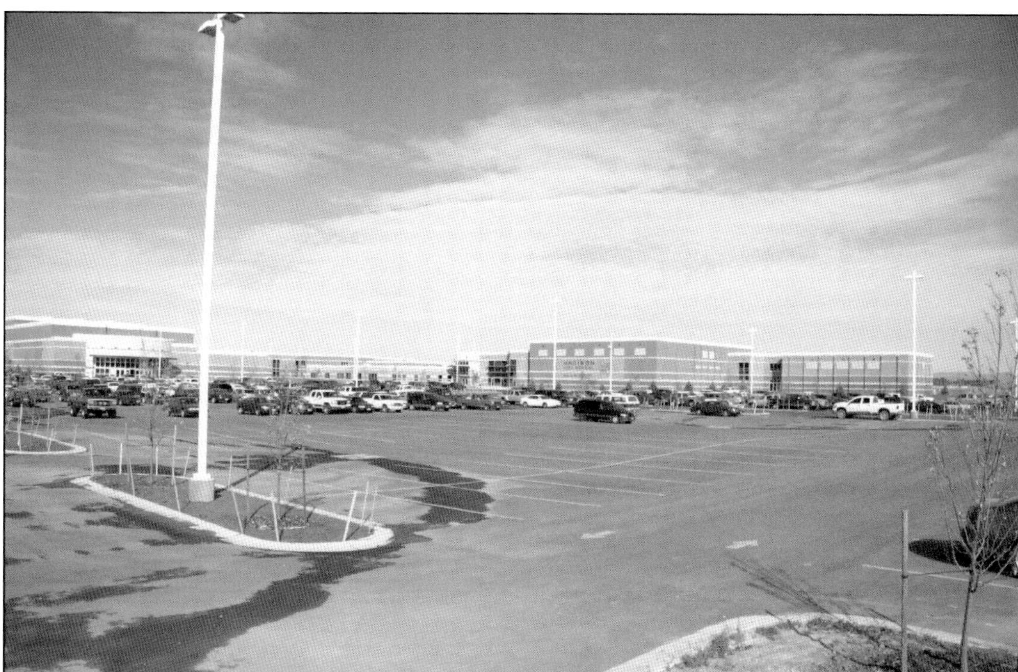

The fourth Madison High School was built at 2300 University Boulevard in the city of Rexburg and opened its doors in September 2010. It is a three-year public secondary school and the only traditional high school in Madison School District. It competes in the state's largest athletic division. (Courtesy of the *Rexburg Standard Journal.*)

Four

Commerce

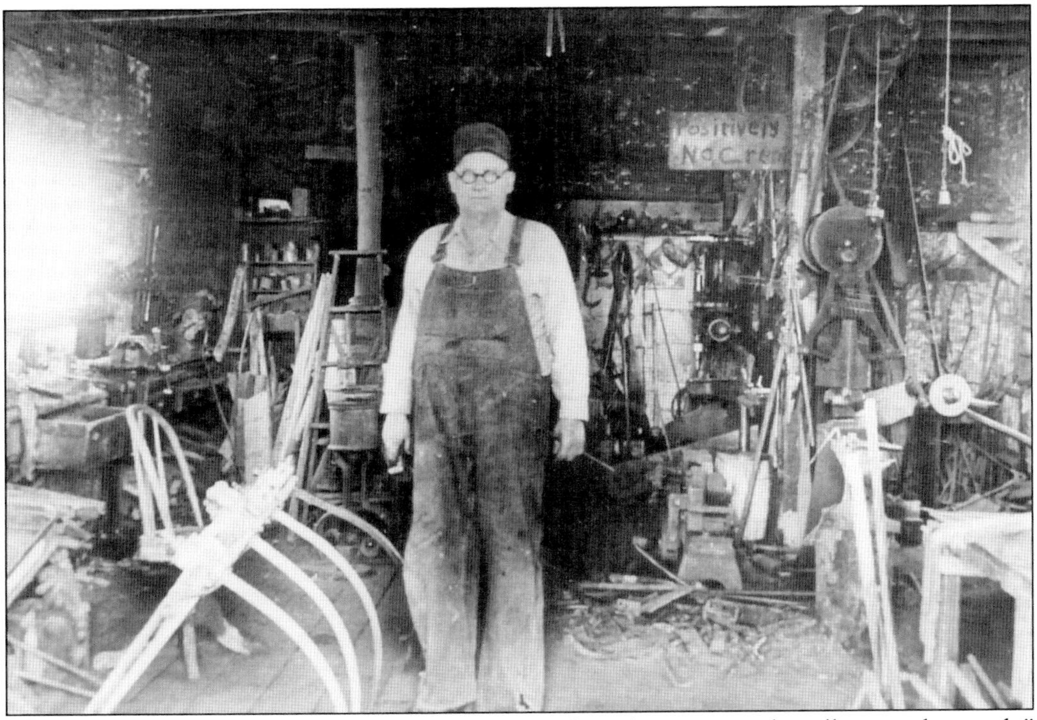

Henry Wadsworth Longfellow said, "Under the spreading chestnut tree the village smithy stands." The blacksmith shop was the nucleus of pioneer towns. Frederick J. Jensen was a blacksmith, justice of the peace, and constable in the little village of Thornton, located three miles outside of Rexburg. He held court in his office in the blacksmith shop and also performed several weddings. This blacksmith shop operated from 1918 to 1946.

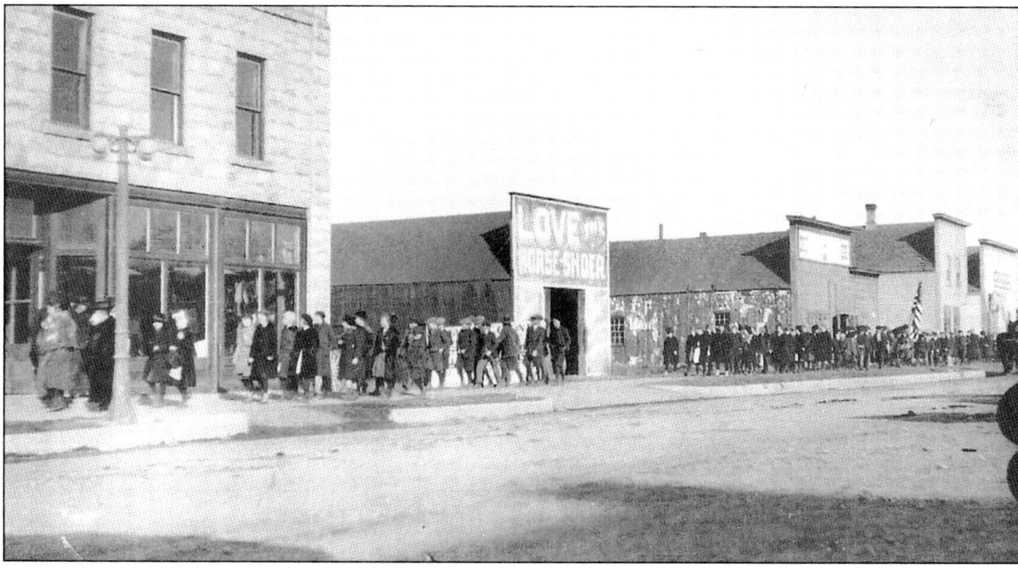

In this November 1918 photograph, note the "Love the Horse-Shoer" building. This was a specialty blacksmith shop where hand-forged horseshoes were made and fitted to the horse's hoofs with a hammer and horseshoe nails. The people are marching in celebration of the signing of the armistice ending World War I.

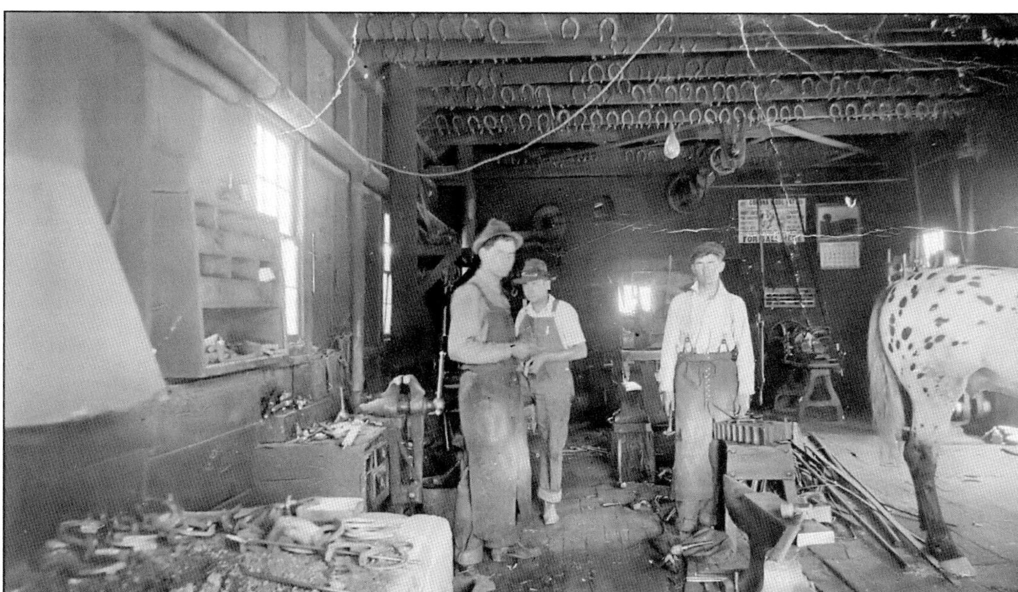

William A. "Billy" Bell came to Rexburg in 1883 at the age of 23 with some of the first settlers. He went into business in 1888, opening his blacksmith shop. He was a successful businessman and a valuable citizen. This photograph shows the inside of his blacksmith shop with, from left to right, Billy and Orvil Bell and Noah Dennis. (Courtesy of Diana Fuller.)

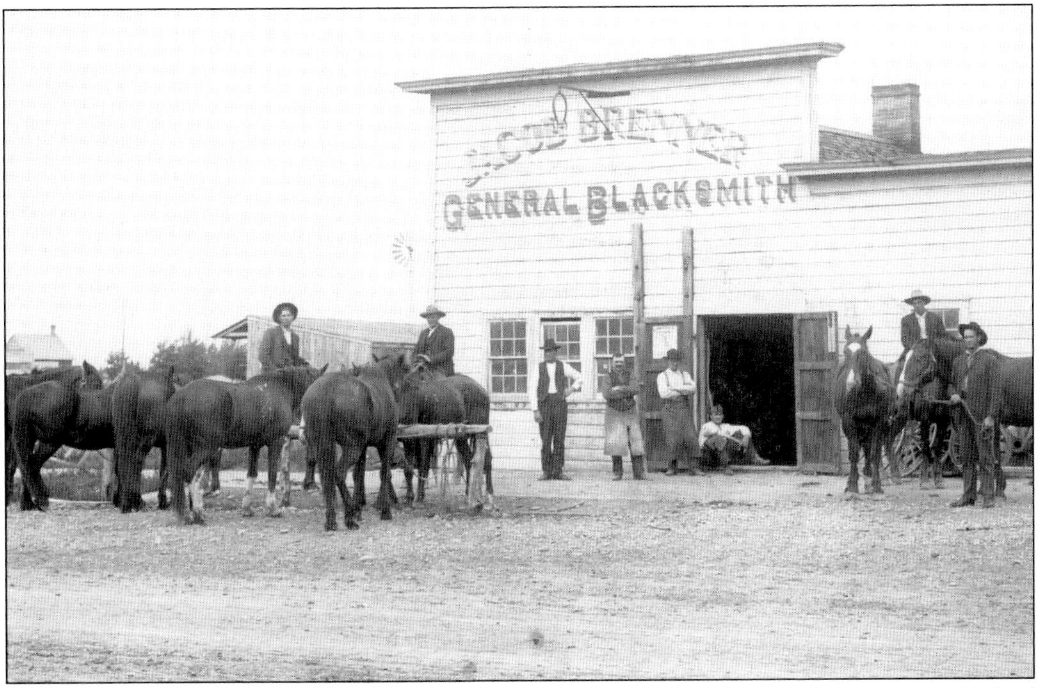

Jacob Brenner, a German immigrant, moved to Rexburg in 1888. That same year, he established a blacksmith shop on the north side of East Main Street. He also built one of the most elegant native rock homes in Rexburg. He held positions on the city council and the school board and served as a bishop in the Mormon Church. He sold the business in 1919 to the Cole family.

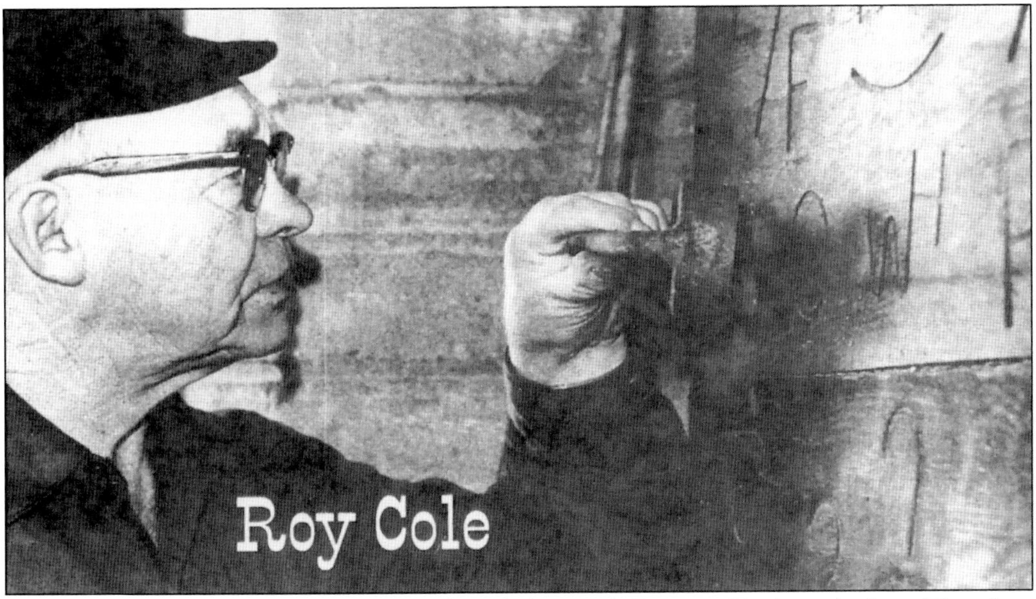

In 1919, George Cole and his sons purchased the Jacob Brenner blacksmith shop. This shop specialized in forging shears for plows, and George created the majority of the branding irons used by ranchers and farmers in the Rexburg area. The business closed, the property was sold to the Madison County commissioners, and the building was demolished on November 23, 1995. (Courtesy of Boyd Cole.)

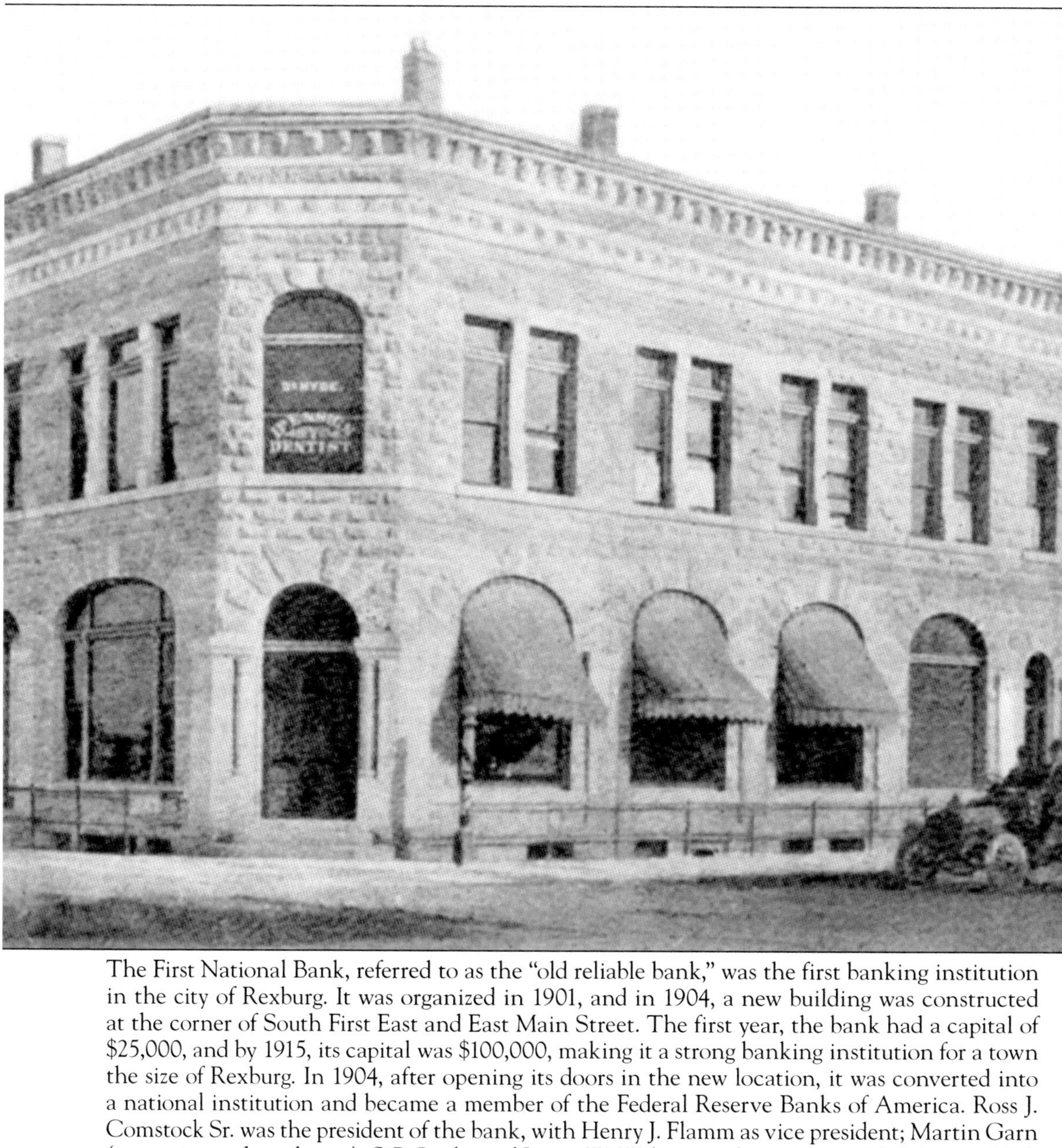

The First National Bank, referred to as the "old reliable bank," was the first banking institution in the city of Rexburg. It was organized in 1901, and in 1904, a new building was constructed at the corner of South First East and East Main Street. The first year, the bank had a capital of $25,000, and by 1915, its capital was $100,000, making it a strong banking institution for a town the size of Rexburg. In 1904, after opening its doors in the new location, it was converted into a national institution and became a member of the Federal Reserve Banks of America. Ross J. Comstock Sr. was the president of the bank, with Henry J. Flamm as vice president; Martin Garn (a prominent sheep baron), O.P. Soule, and James W. Webster as the major stockholders; and R.J. Comstock Jr. as the cashier.

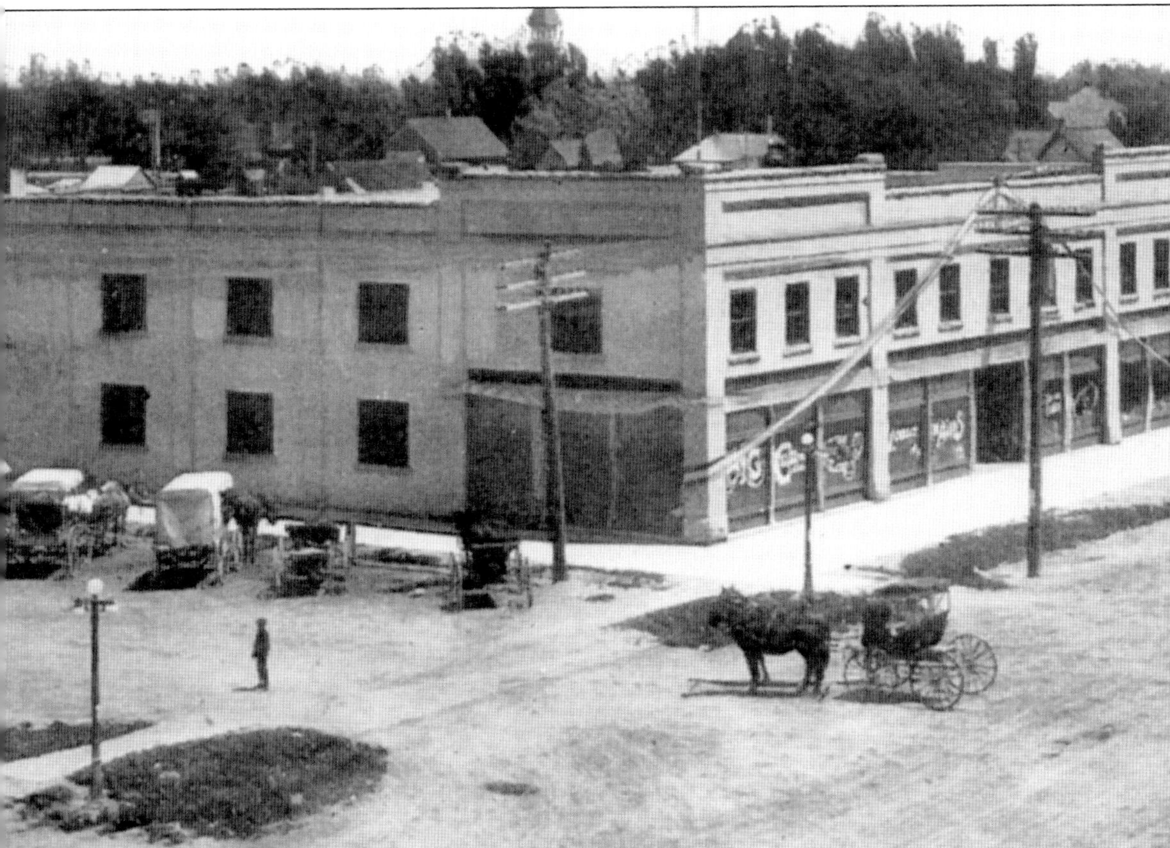

The Farmers and Merchants Bank was organized and opened for business on September 20, 1915, with a capital of $50,000. Its stockholders were over 40 of the most successful men in the entire valley. These men were not only recognized as successes in a financial way but also as men who had done big things for the county. The vice presidents were Nathan Ricks, Alfred Ricks, and James W. Webster, and William E. Gee was the bank cashier. The bank was located in a well-furnished room in the corner of the Consolidated Wagon and Machine Company building. It was an ideal location, as it was on one of the main corners of Main Street. The bank's motto claimed "to promise the public every courtesy and consideration consistent with sound banking." Sadly, this bank was forced to close its doors during the Great Depression.

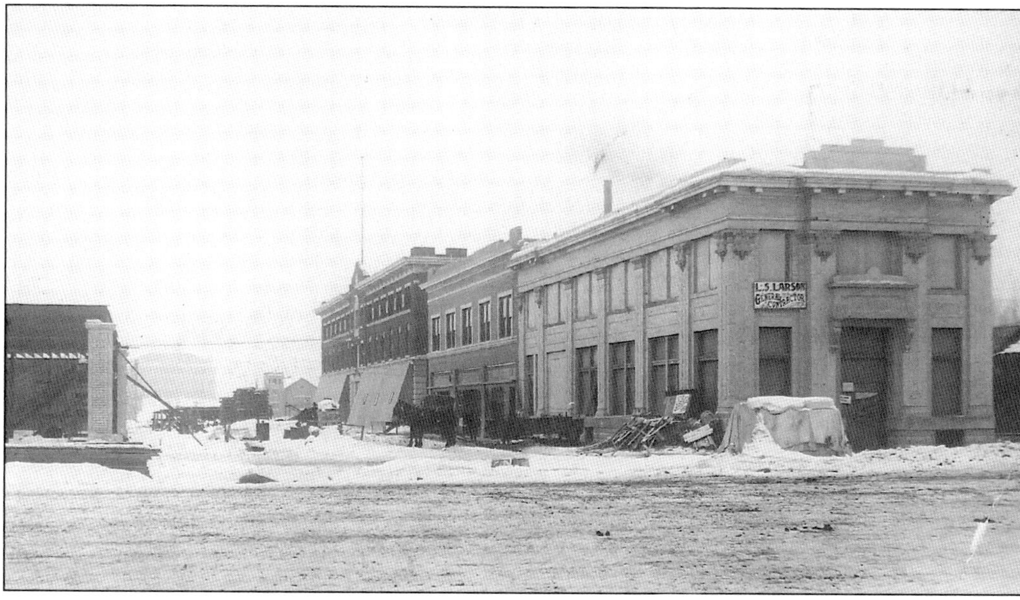

In 1905, the Rexburg State Bank opened its doors with a capital of $20,000. By 1915, the capital was $40,000. The officers of the bank were R. Steve Hunt, president; J.E. Cosgriff, vice president; J.R. Wright, cashier; and Harry N. Wright, assistant cashier. This bank was one of a chain of the Cosgriff Banks that operated in Utah, Wyoming, Nevada, Colorado, and Idaho. In 1918, a new bank building was constructed at North College Avenue and Main Street. The interior of this bank was made from quality marble and mahogany wood. Hunt was a local sheep baron; his honesty and integrity inspired confidence, and his word was considered as good as gold. This bank was the only bank in the county that remained open during the Great Depression.

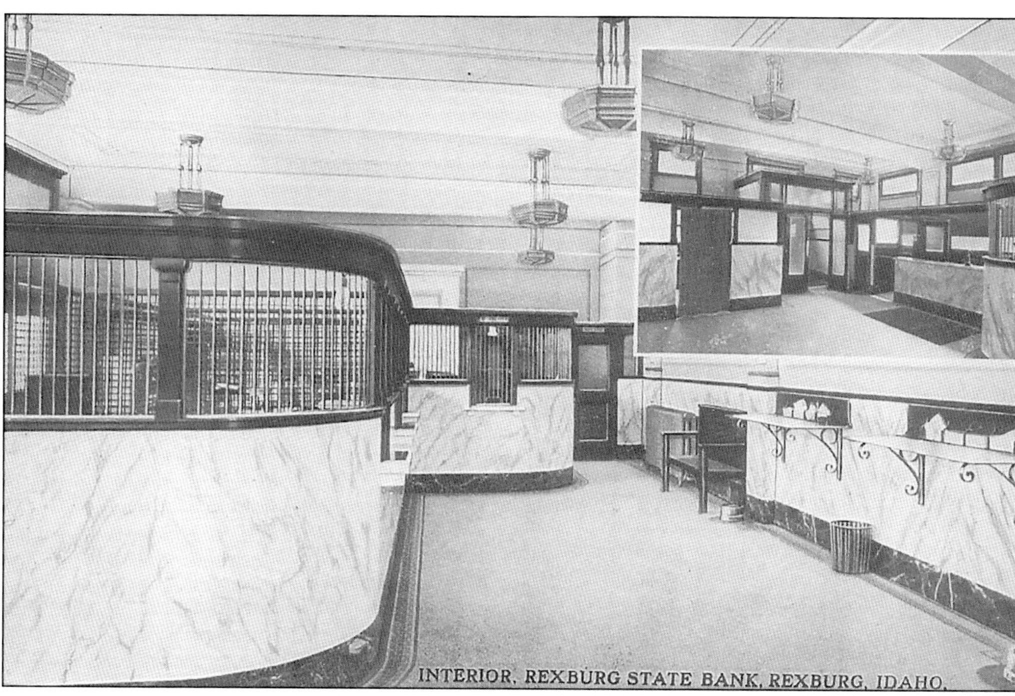

INTERIOR, REXBURG STATE BANK, REXBURG, IDAHO.

Rexburg Commercial Hotel, built in 1897, was located on Main Street west of the Idaho Hotel. Henry Jacob Bigler was the owner and proprietor. He and his family stand on the balcony. The hotel featured a general merchandise store as well as the hotel. (Courtesy of Dona Bigler.)

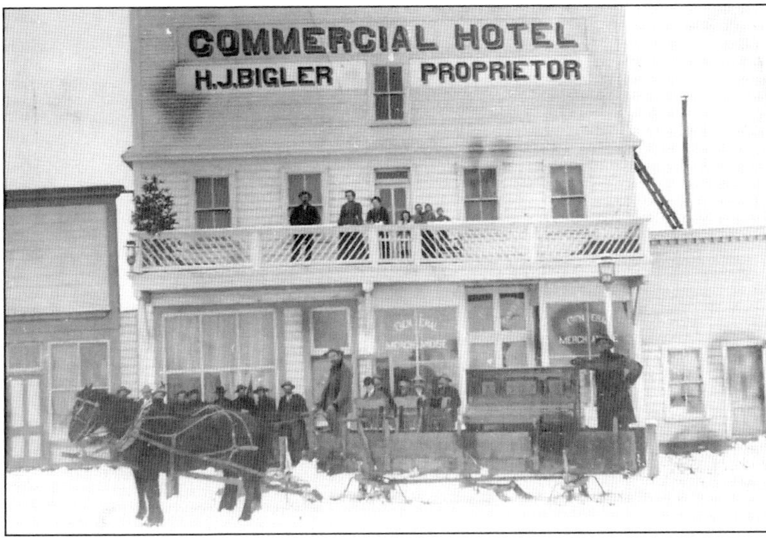

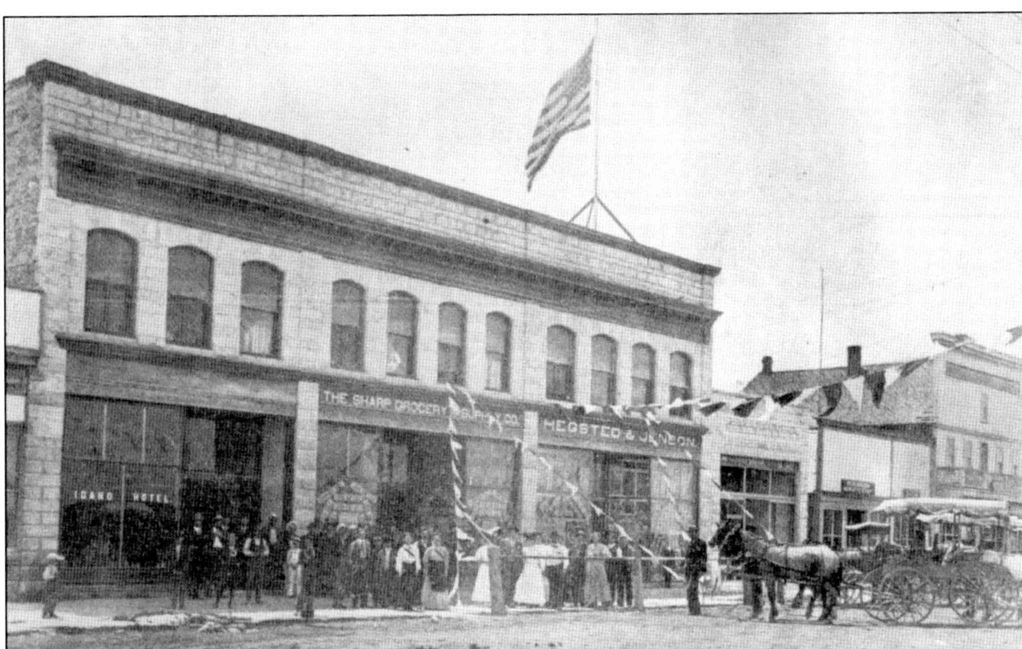

The Idaho Hotel was owned and operated by B.M. Shields. This was the second hotel on Main Street, built in 1905. The bottom floor was shared by Sharp Grocery and Supply Company and Hegsted and Jenson General Merchandise. The store was later occupied by Flamm furniture and mortuary. Bingham and Son's Furniture and Appliance store has occupied this historic building for over 50 years.

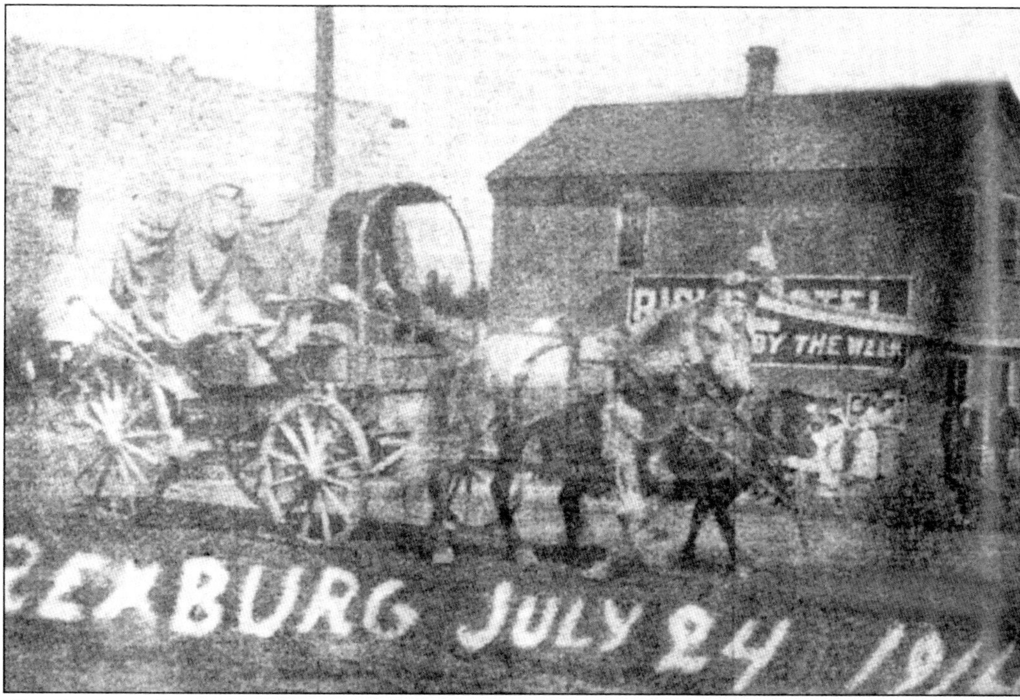

The Rexburg House Hotel, seen in this rare 1914 photograph, was built in 1888 by a Mr. Rand. The hotel, located on the north side of Main Street at the corner of Main and North First East, was sold to Thomas George in February 1906 and torn down in February 1917. The scene in this picture is a 24th of July parade.

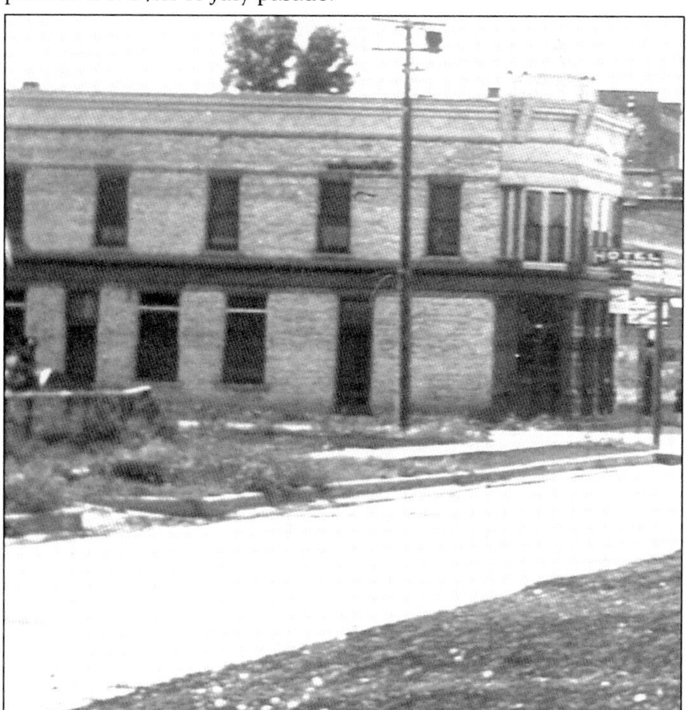

This building was erected on February 23, 1893, by the Mormon Church. It was the first two-story redbrick building on East Main Street and South Second East. It served as an apartment house for college students and was later used as a hospital for a Dr. Hyde before becoming a hotel. The name of the hotel has been lost to time.

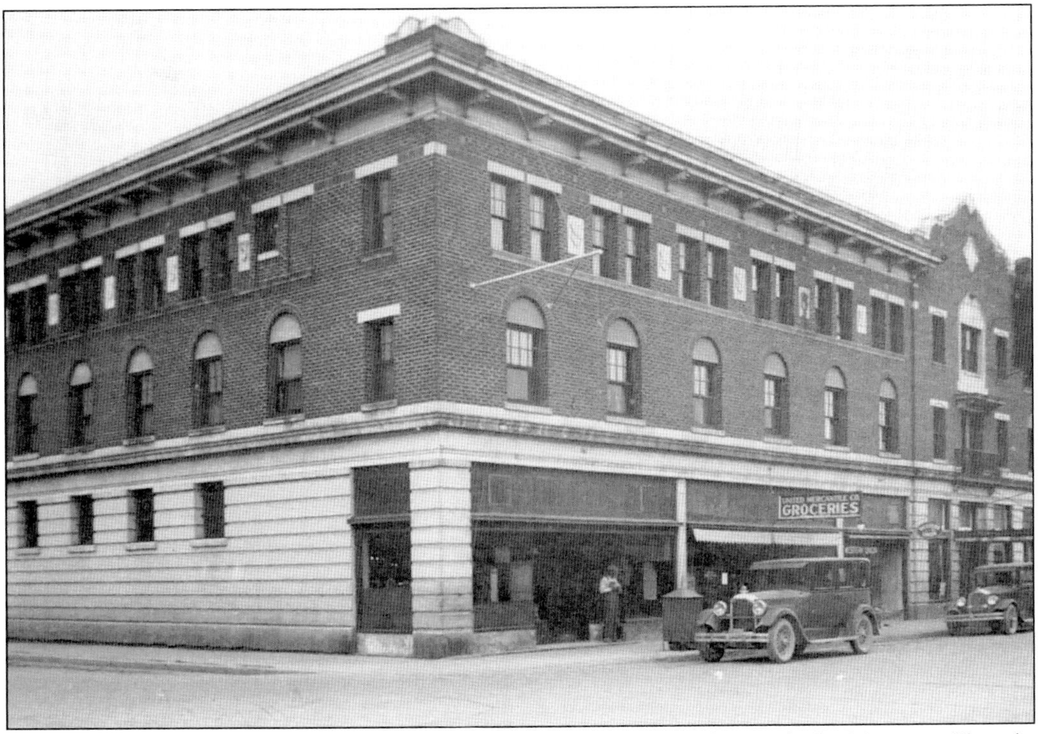

The Eccles Hotel was built in 1912 by the Eccles family in partnership with the Mormon Church. The hotel served as an overnight stop for train passengers en route to West Yellowstone. The building housed a post office, grocery store, café, bakery, and meat market as well as hotel rooms. The name was changed to the Idamont Hotel, and the building still stands today on College Avenue. (Courtesy of Dean Rasmussen.)

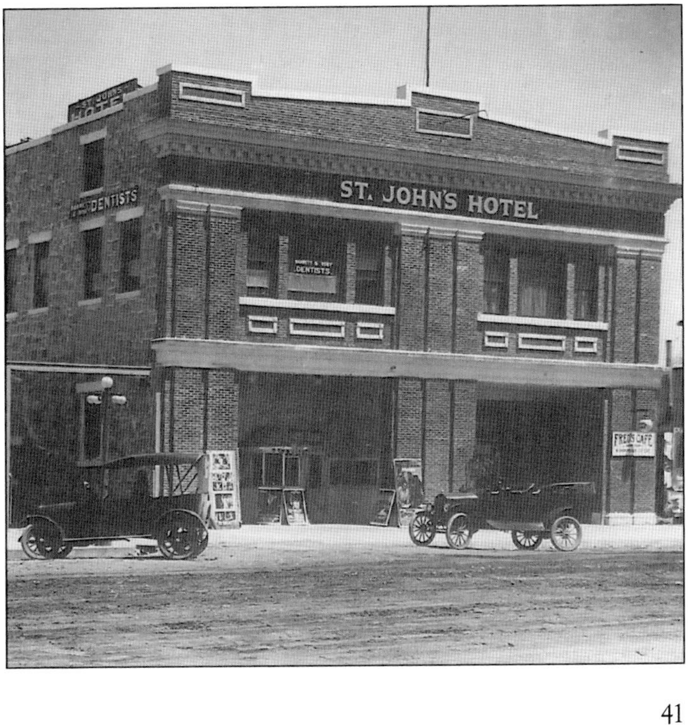

This building was constructed in 1915 by the Jones family. The bottom floor housed the Elk Theater, and the upstairs was shared by Dr. Bert Gill Dentistry and the St. John's Hotel, which was more of a boardinghouse than a hotel. The hotel's name was later changed to the Lincoln Hotel, and the building remained a hotel and theater until it was torn down in 1963. (Courtesy of Dean Rasmussen.)

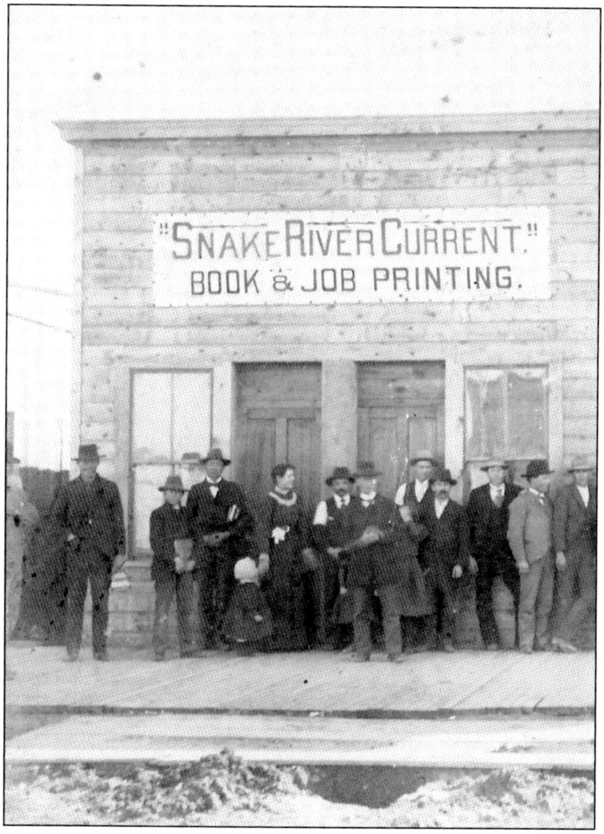

The local newspaper was considered the heartbeat of the community. In 1883, there were only four newspapers in Southeastern Idaho. Phineas Tempest was a pioneer newspaperman who founded the *Rexburg Press* in 1887. This paper was succeeded by the *Silver Hammer* with Ben Rich (pictured below) as editor. Then came the *Fremont County Journal* in 1898, and later, the *Snake River Current*, a Democratic Party newspaper. These two newspapers later evolved into the *Current-Journal*. In 1906, Arthur Porter obtained control of the *Current-Journal*, and it became the *Rexburg Journal* in 1917. Another newspaper, the *Rexburg Standard*, was the major Republican newspaper. It was started by William and Joseph Adams in 1907, and later, they partnered with James H. Wallace, who operated the *Enterprise*. The three men formed a corporation. In 1909, the newspaper was purchased by William Lloyd Adams.

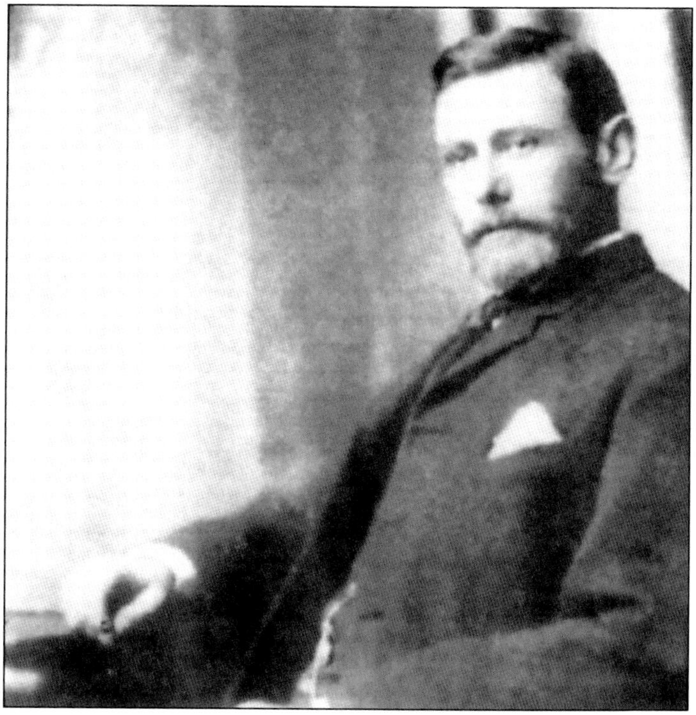

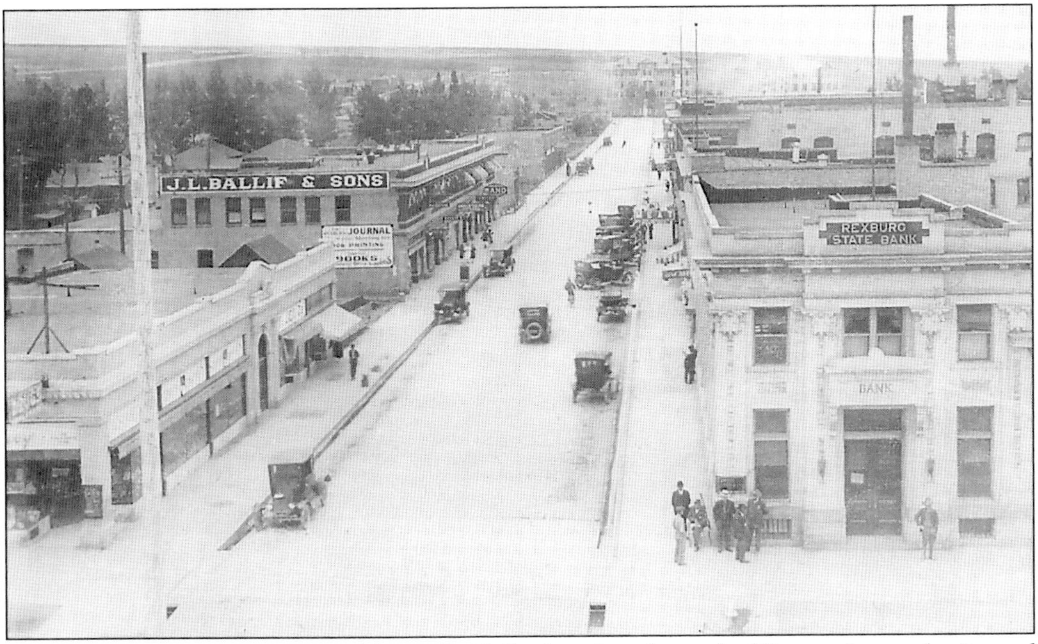

Early in 1916, Arthur Porter and his wife, Nelle, bought a larger building to house the *Journal* on Main Street, and then they moved to a building on College Avenue that would house not only the newspaper business but also several other businesses. He bought Squires Book Store, renamed it Porter's Book Store, and then expanded into selling merchandise such as toys, books, and Mormon Church publications.

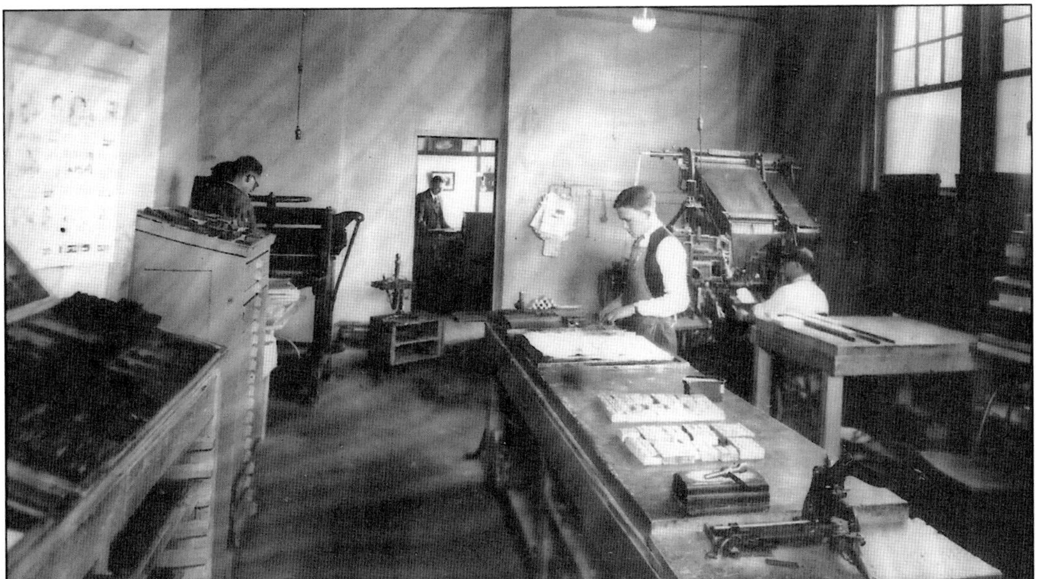

This picture shows the printing office of the *Rexburg Journal*, located at the back of Porter's Book Store on College Avenue. Arthur Porter (in the doorway) is seen in his office, John C. Porter stands at the table, and Marriner Morrell is seated at the cutting machine. The man at left is unidentified. Arthur Porter's son Art C. opened a printing business in the same office. ARTCO Printing later evolved from that printing business. (Courtesy of Arthur Porter.)

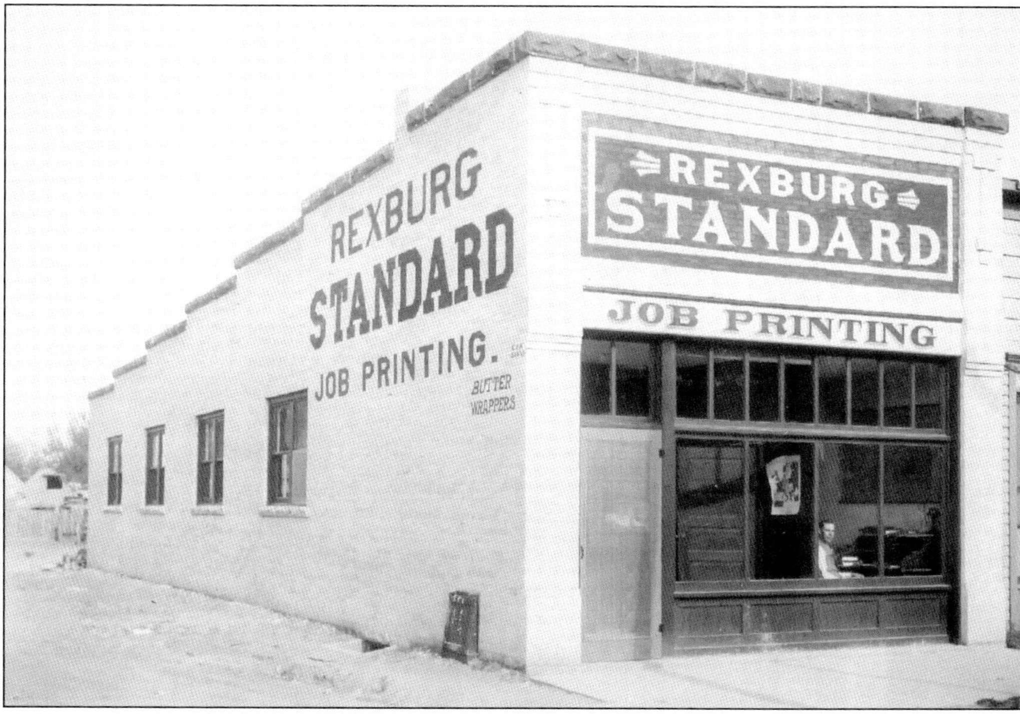

William and Joseph Adams of Ogden, Utah, opened a newspaper business called the *Rexburg Standard* in 1907, and in 1908, a new building was constructed at 23 South First East. The *Standard* was the Republican newspaper, and Arthur Porter owned the *Rexburg Journal*, a Democratic newspaper. In 1909, William Lloyd Adams, son of William Adams, came to Rexburg and purchased the *Rexburg Standard*. He had previously published several newspapers. William sold the newspaper to Burton L. Moore in 1938. Moore published the paper until January 1942, when he sold it to John C. and Art C. Porter. At that time the *Rexburg Standard* and the *Rexburg Journal* became one and the same newspaper published as the *Standard Journal*. The photograph below shows Lloyd Adams standing in doorway with Nettie Garner on right; the man in the center is unidentified. (Both, courtesy of Lloyd Miller.)

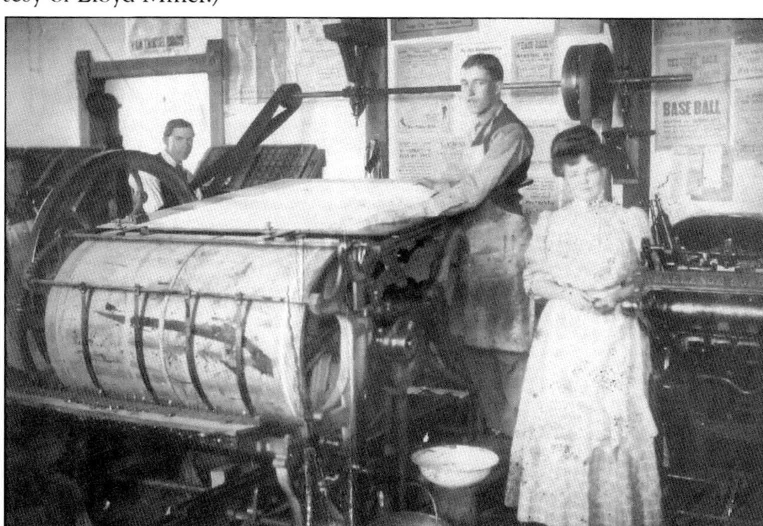

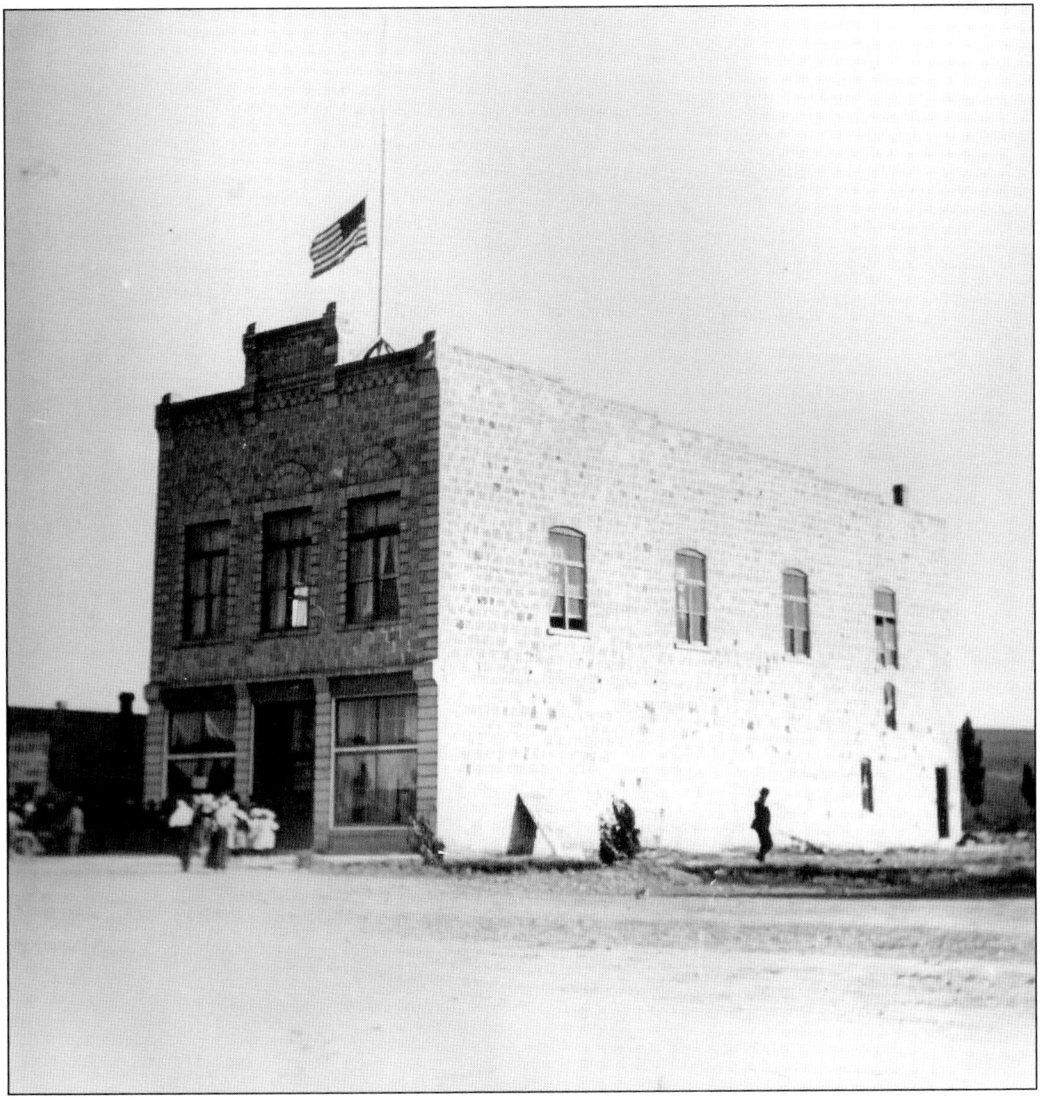

During the early part of 1883, merchandise was dispensed to the public by Jane Ricks, Thomas E. Rick's third wife, in her home located where the courthouse now stands. In 1886, Henry Flamm and his son-in-law John Jacobs established the Flamm Company. In 1888, they moved into this newly constructed building. The bottom floor consisted of the mercantile with dry goods, seed for crops, material for sewing clothes, kitchen utensils, and furniture. The back room was Flamm's Mortuary. Inside the store was a coffin suspended from the ceiling with a sign that read, "We will accommodate you from the cradle to the grave." Upstairs housed the Flamm Opera House with a stage and balcony. It served as the only social center for the Upper Snake River Valley.

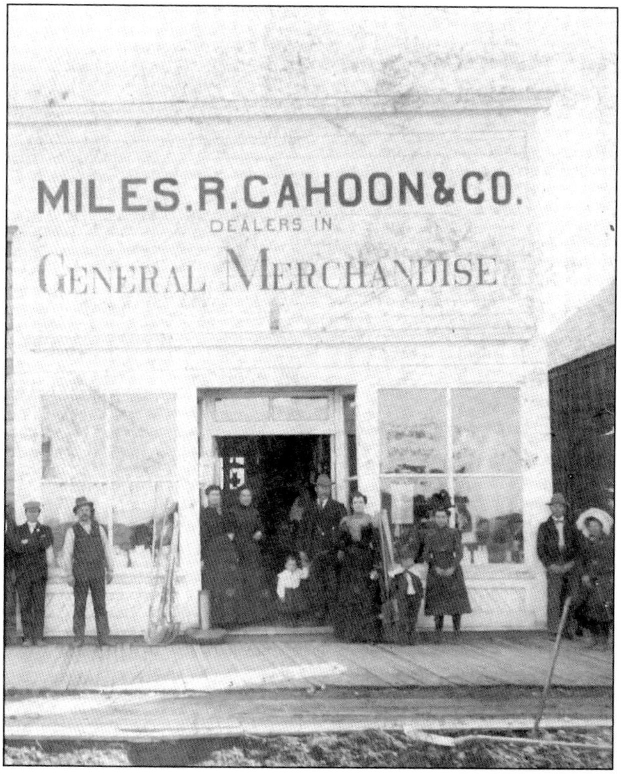

The Miles R. Cahoon and Company store was built in 1898 on Main Street. This business was a one-stop shop for anything needed in the late 19th century. The Cahoon family also owned and operated a dance hall on the edge of town known as Cahoon Park. Cahoon served as a probate judge and superintendent of schools. The John R. Winter & Co. building was located at the corner of South First East and Main Street. It was built some time between 1895 and 1900, and at that time, James W. Webster became a partner, so the structure became known as the Winter-Webster Building. In 1900, a second floor was added and occupied by the commercial club, forerunner to the chamber of commerce. In 1914, Rexburg's first courthouse occupied the top floor. (Left, courtesy of Dona Bigler.)

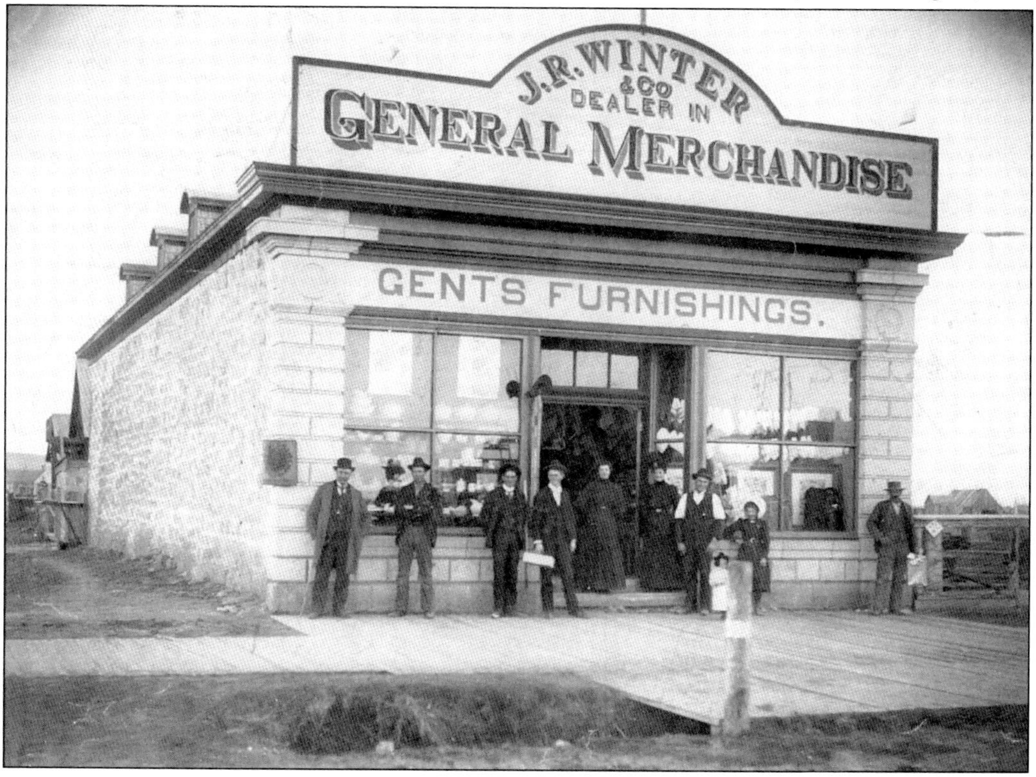

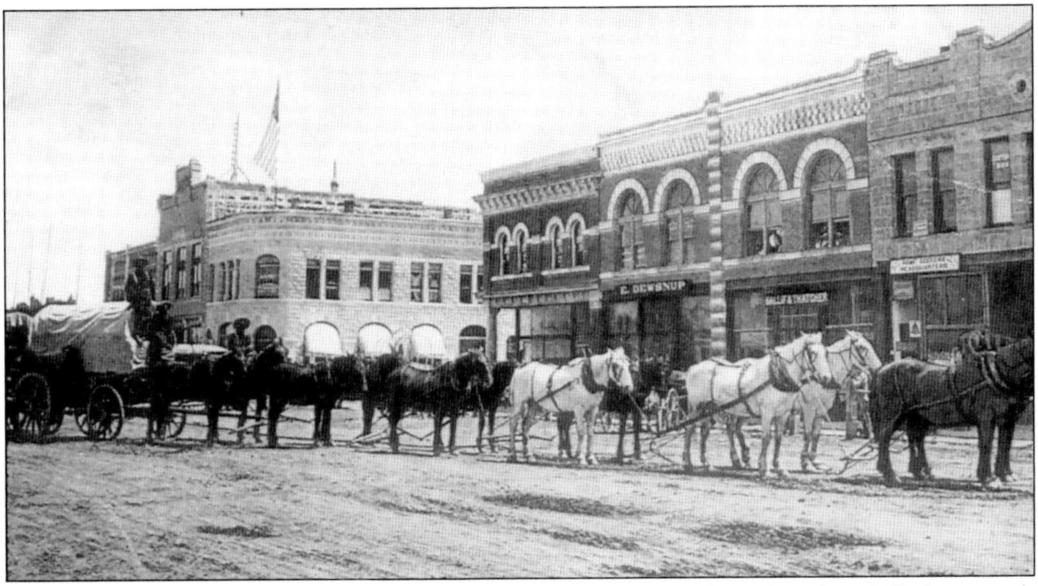

The building in the background housed John R. Dewsnup's Merchantile. This 1907 photograph shows a two-wagon, 12-horse team delivering goods to the store. A teamster accepted a bet that he could make the turn at the end of Main Street with a wagon and a large team of horses. The next morning, when the bet was won, the gambler should have counted the horses because the team was two horses short. (Courtesy of Dean Rasmussen.)

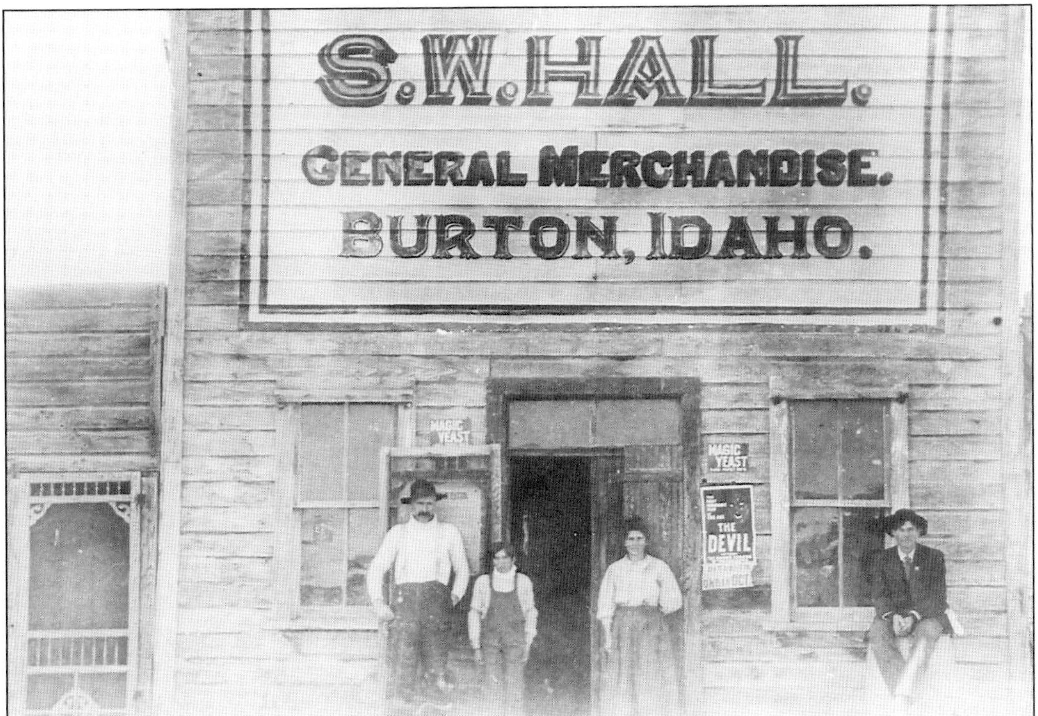

Sam W. Hall's general merchandise store was located five miles outside of Rexburg in the Burton area. Standing in this 1907 photograph are storeowner Sam W. Hall, his son Earl, and Sam's wife; seated in front of the window is Harvey Jones Summers.

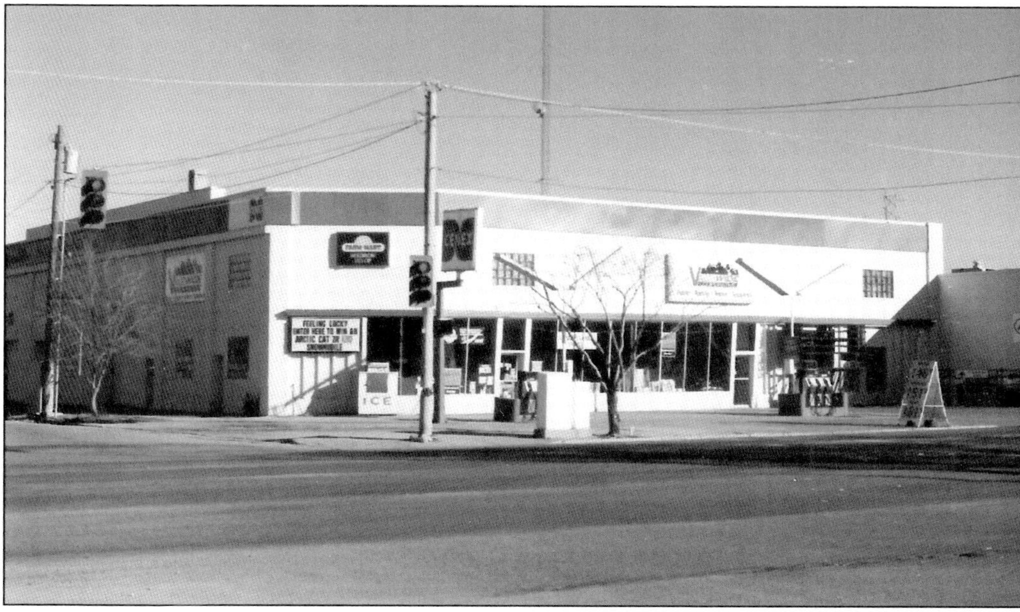

The building in this 1930 photograph, located on the corner of North First East and East Main Street, was erected in 1905. It was the Consolidated Wagon and Machine (CW&M) Company. This company was probably considered the first department store in Rexburg. It was an all-inclusive store for farmers. (Courtesy of Dean Rasmussen.)

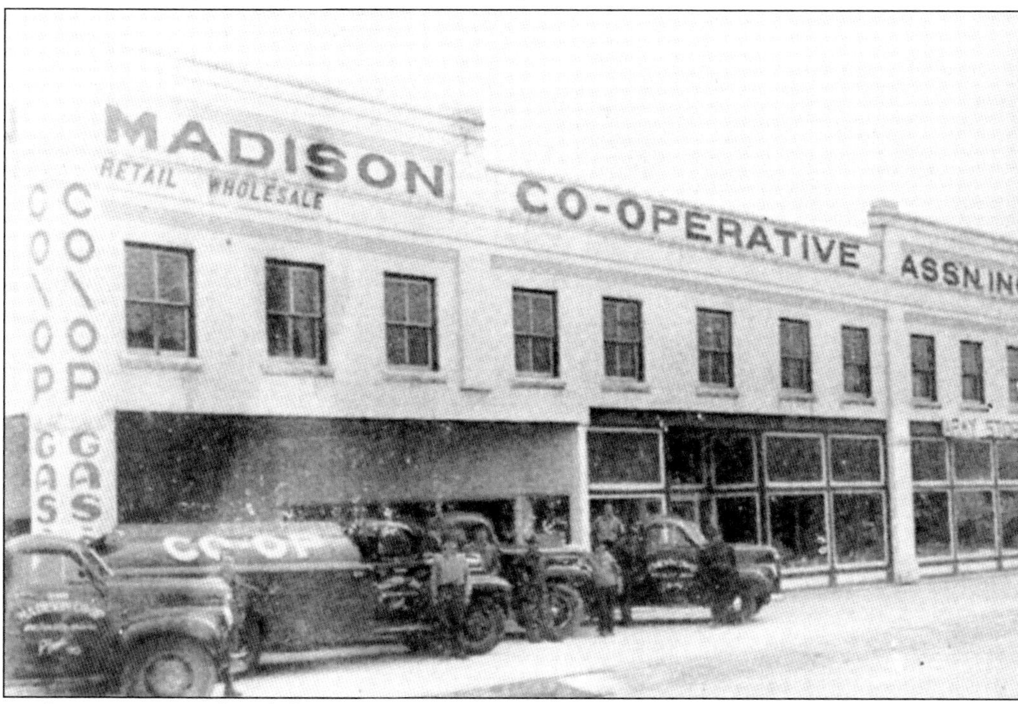

Madison Co-Op replaced the CW&M Company some time in the 1930s. The co-op furnished furnace oil, diesel, gas, coal, and supplies needed to operate a farm to the outlying homes throughout Madison County. The co-op evolved at a new location and was renamed the Valley Wide Co-Op.

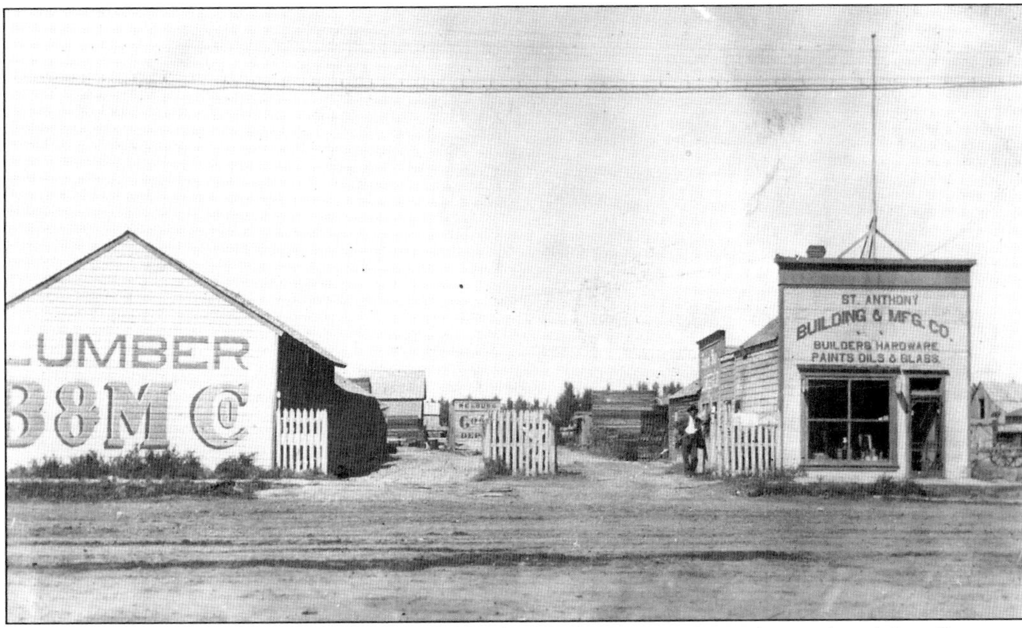

St. Anthony and Rexburg Building and Manufacturing Company was located on Main Street, as seen in this 1905 photograph. Peter Mickelsen Sr., standing to the side of the building, was owner and manager of this company. The business offered lumber and supplies needed to construct homes and barns, and it would deliver to the building site.

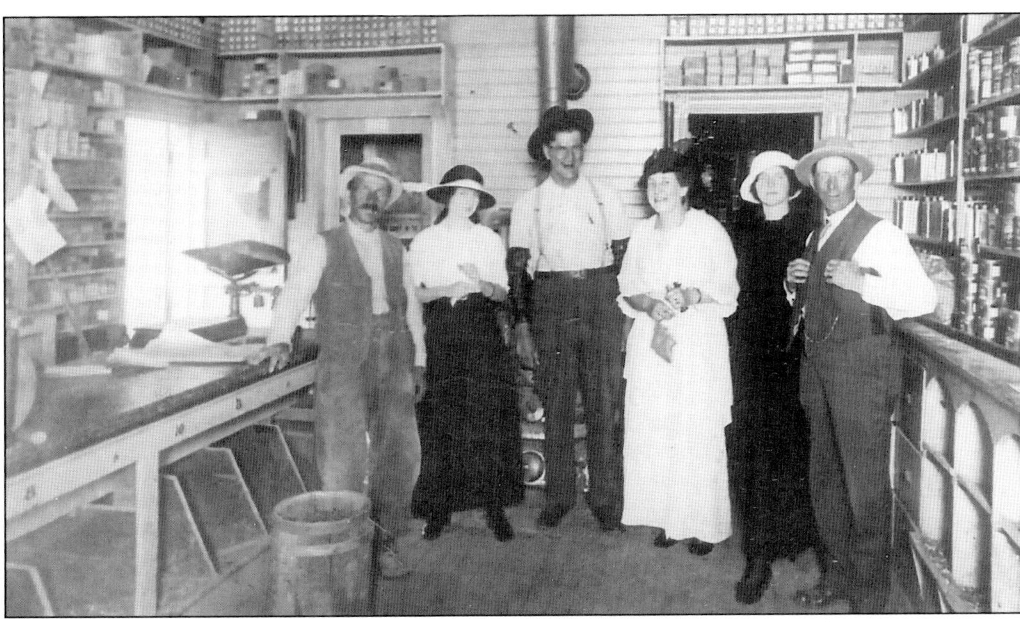

Here is an inside look of the St. Anthony and Rexburg Building and Manufacturing Company. Standing from left to right are Robert Blaser (contractor), Mrs. C.M. Smith, Peter Mickelsen Sr. (owner), Mrs. J.R. Young, Sarah Ann Barnes, and John Albert Garner Sr.

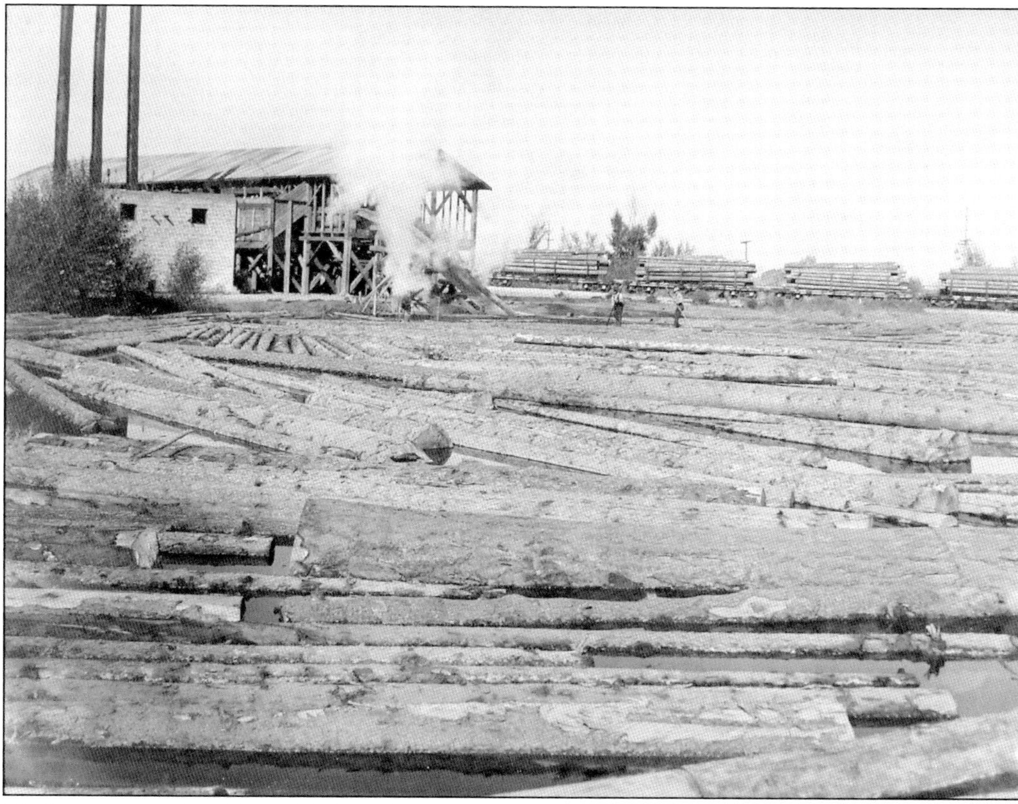

W. Burton Smead and David L. DaBell were owners of the Montana and Idaho Lumber Company. In 1949, the business was recognized as Rexburg's largest industry. It employed 40 workmen at its offices in Rexburg and an equal number in its logging operation near West Yellowstone, Montana. The company originated in 1922 as a railroad tie manufacturing concern at Guild, Idaho, near Mack's Inn, with W.H. Smead and his son W. Burton in charge. They had previously operated a sawmill at Pueblo, Montana, and in 1931, they moved to Ashton, followed by relocation to Rexburg in 1936. The company electrified and modernized its operation in 1949, and it was equipped with a steam plant and dry kiln for producing dry finished lumber. (Both, courtesy of Upper Snake River Valley Historical Society.)

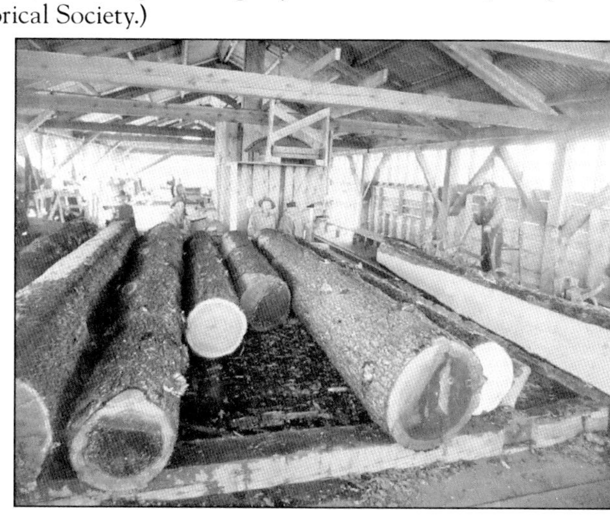

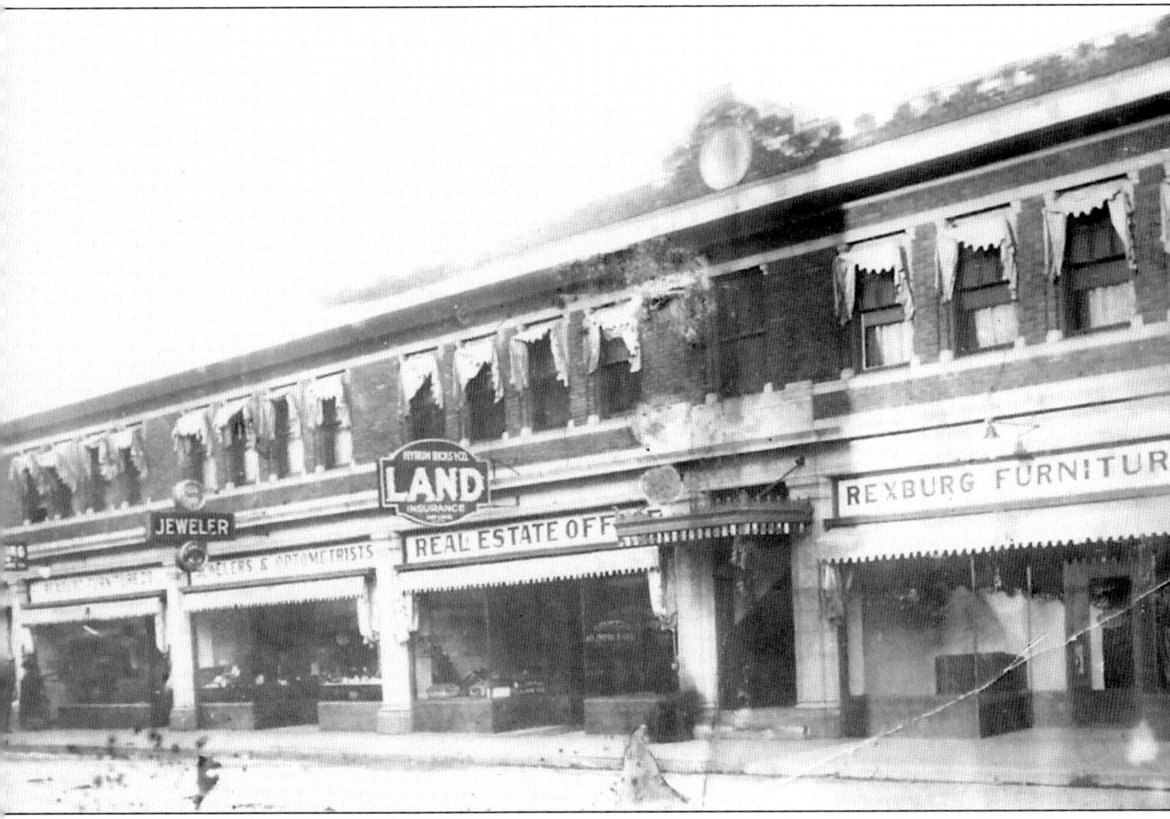

Arthur Porter was the renaissance businessman of Rexburg. In early 1916, he and his wife, Nelle, bought property for the *Current-Journal* newspaper on Main Street next to the Woodmen of the World building, but the Porters were not at that location for long. Arthur, along with Hyrum Ricks Jr., John L. Ballif Jr., and others, had a vision of opening a mini-mall on College Avenue. Not seen in the picture are Porter's Book Store, with the upstairs being used as apartments. The back of the store was the home of the *Current-Journal* newspaper. In front was Regal Cleaners, owned by Arnold Williams, who would later become governor of Idaho. The buildings shown in this 1925 photograph, from left to right, are: J.R. Young's Furniture and Undertaking, Widstein Jewelry, the office of optometrist Dr. Mack, Hyrum Ricks Jr.'s real estate office, and Rexburg Furniture, which appears closed.

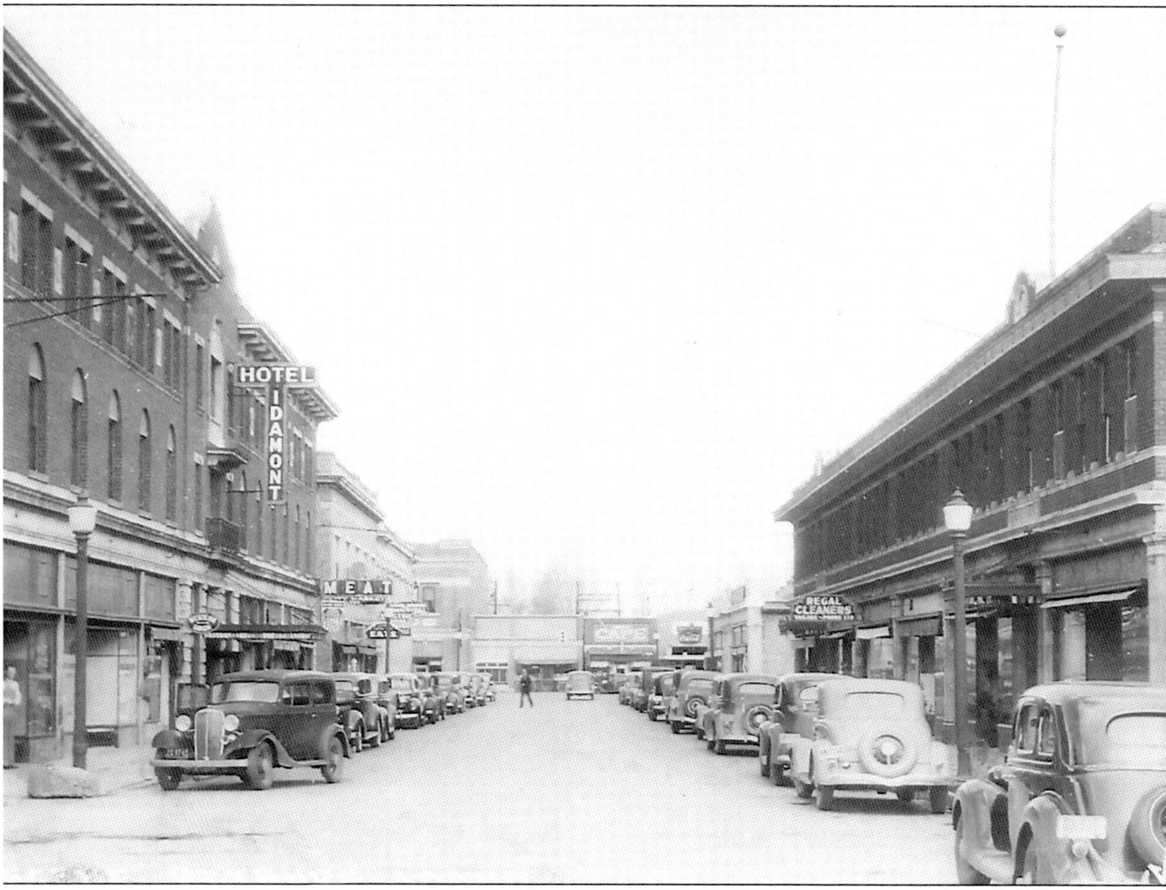

This 1935 view of College Avenue looking north shows the Eccles Hotel, built in 1912, on the left. Later, the hotel was renamed the Idamont Hotel. Inside the entrance of this building was a café operated by George and Ida Emery. At the corner of this building was the Rexburg Post Office. There was a Western Union office next to it, and Skelton's Meat Market with Al Brian's pool hall was at the end of the building. Across the street stood the Porter building. (Courtesy of Dean Rasmussen.)

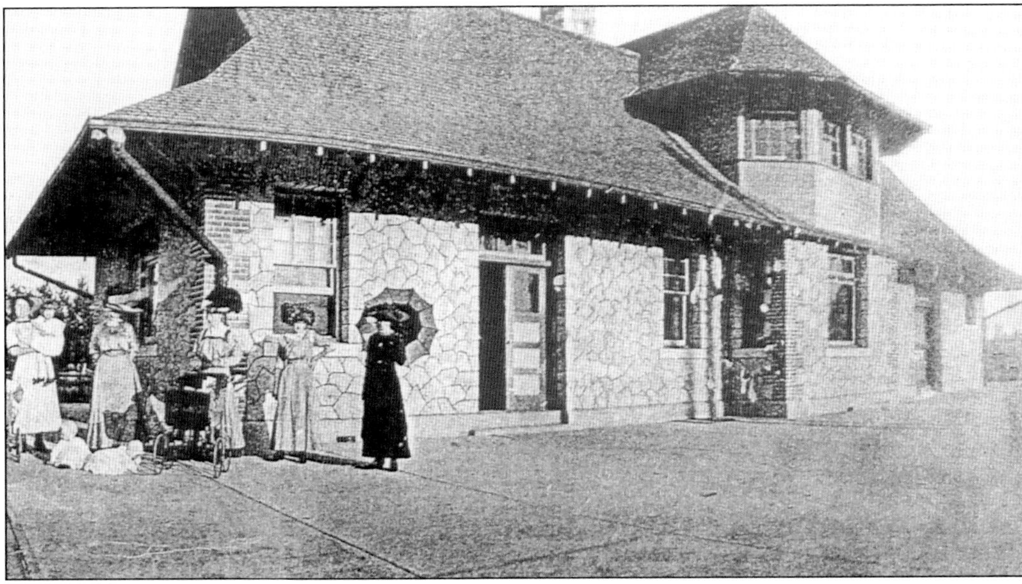

The first railroad built in Idaho was the Utah Northern, a narrow-gauge rail that reached Camas, Idaho, in 1879. The Oregon Shortline later bought this line, and a branch was constructed to reach Rexburg on November 22, 1899, later to St. Anthony, and then on to Teton Basin and West Yellowstone. The Oregon Shortline train depot in Rexburg was built in 1903. The only individual identified in the 1909 photograph above is Grace Woodmansee Beesley, wearing the black dress and holding a parasol, anxiously waiting for the train to arrive. The depot had a café that was operated by Kate Linderman, who served as manager, cook, and waitress. (Above, courtesy of Dean Rasmussen; below, courtesy of Donna Hall.)

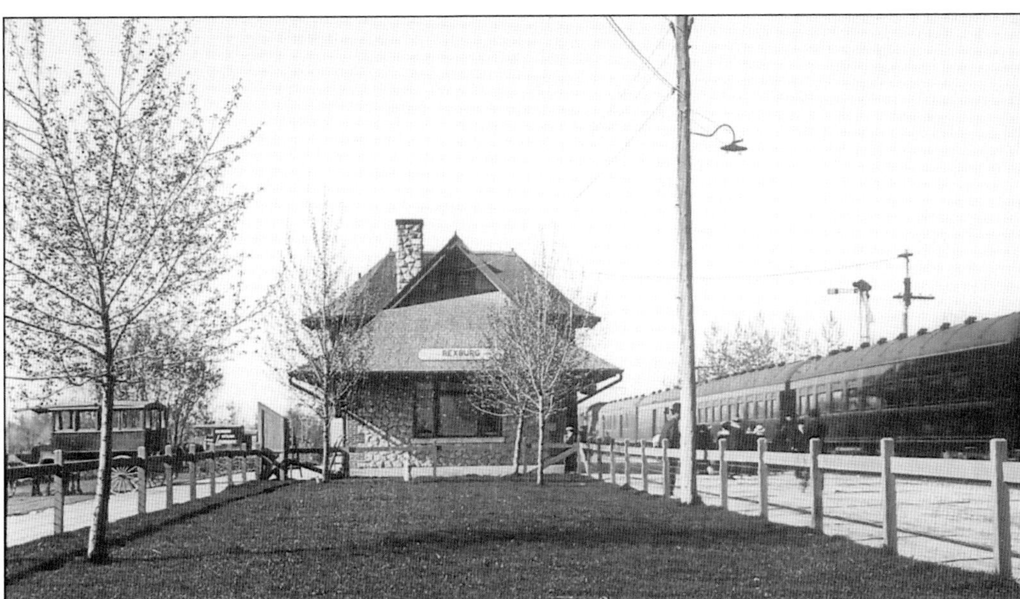

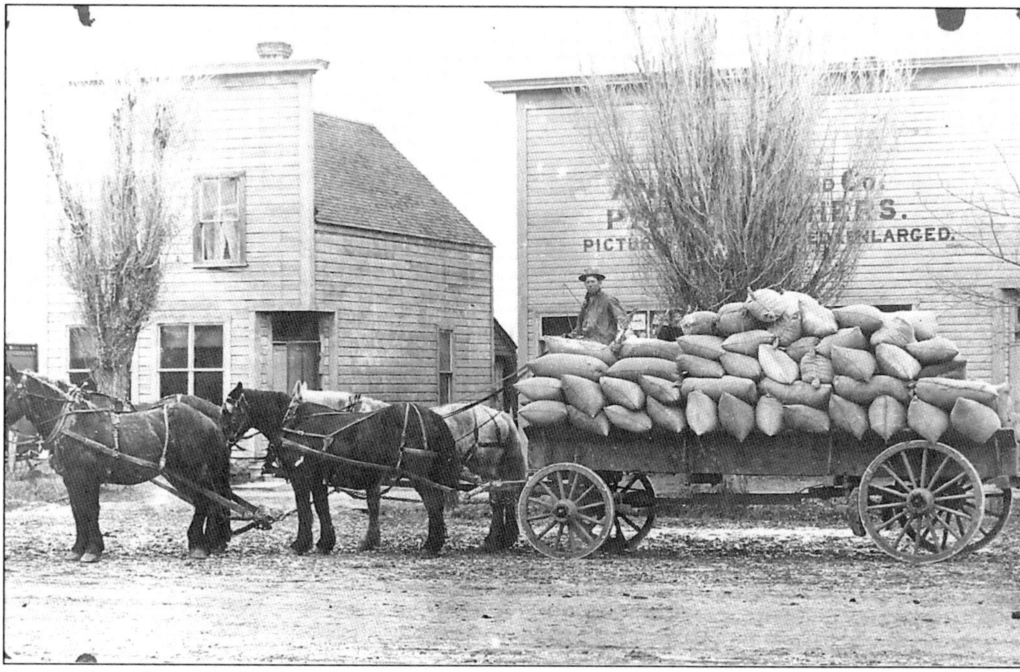

Henry Hunsaker, a hired man for Frederick Parkinson Sr., hauls a wagon loaded with hundred-pound sacks of wheat to be delivered to the Midland Elevators. This was the mode of transportation for farm produce from farm to market before a railroad line was built across the Rexburg bench. The Parkinson siding depot along the Oregon Shortline Railroad, and later, the Union Pacific Railroad, was located near the Dugway Road above Moody Canyon on the Rexburg bench. It was named in honor of Frederick Smart Parkinson, who sold the right-of-way to the Oregon Shortline so he could load his grain on boxcars to be shipped to Chicago.

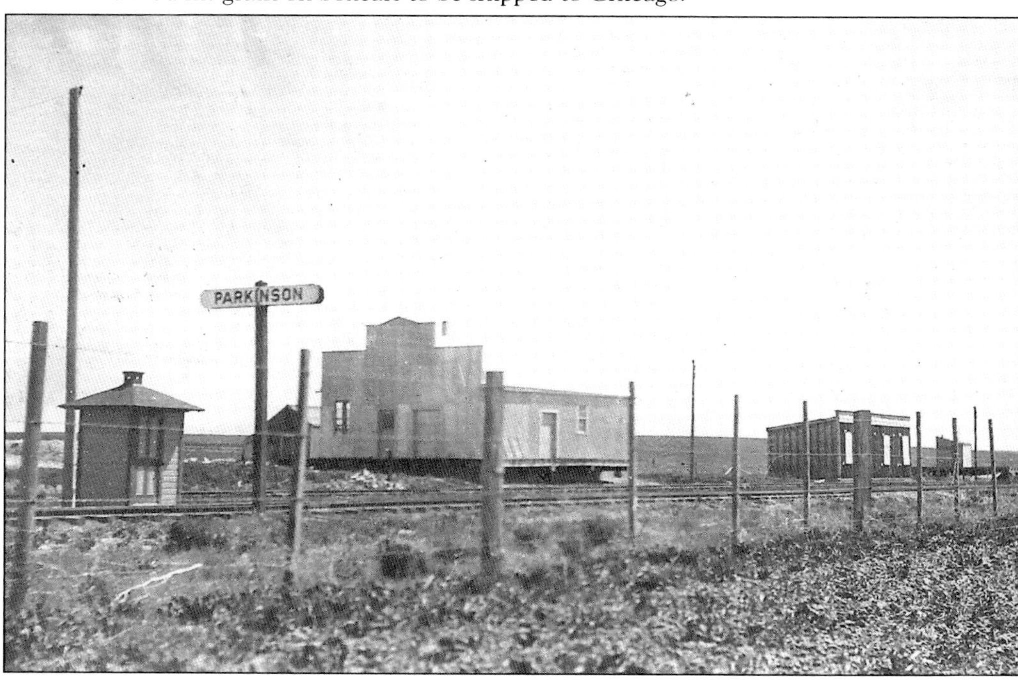

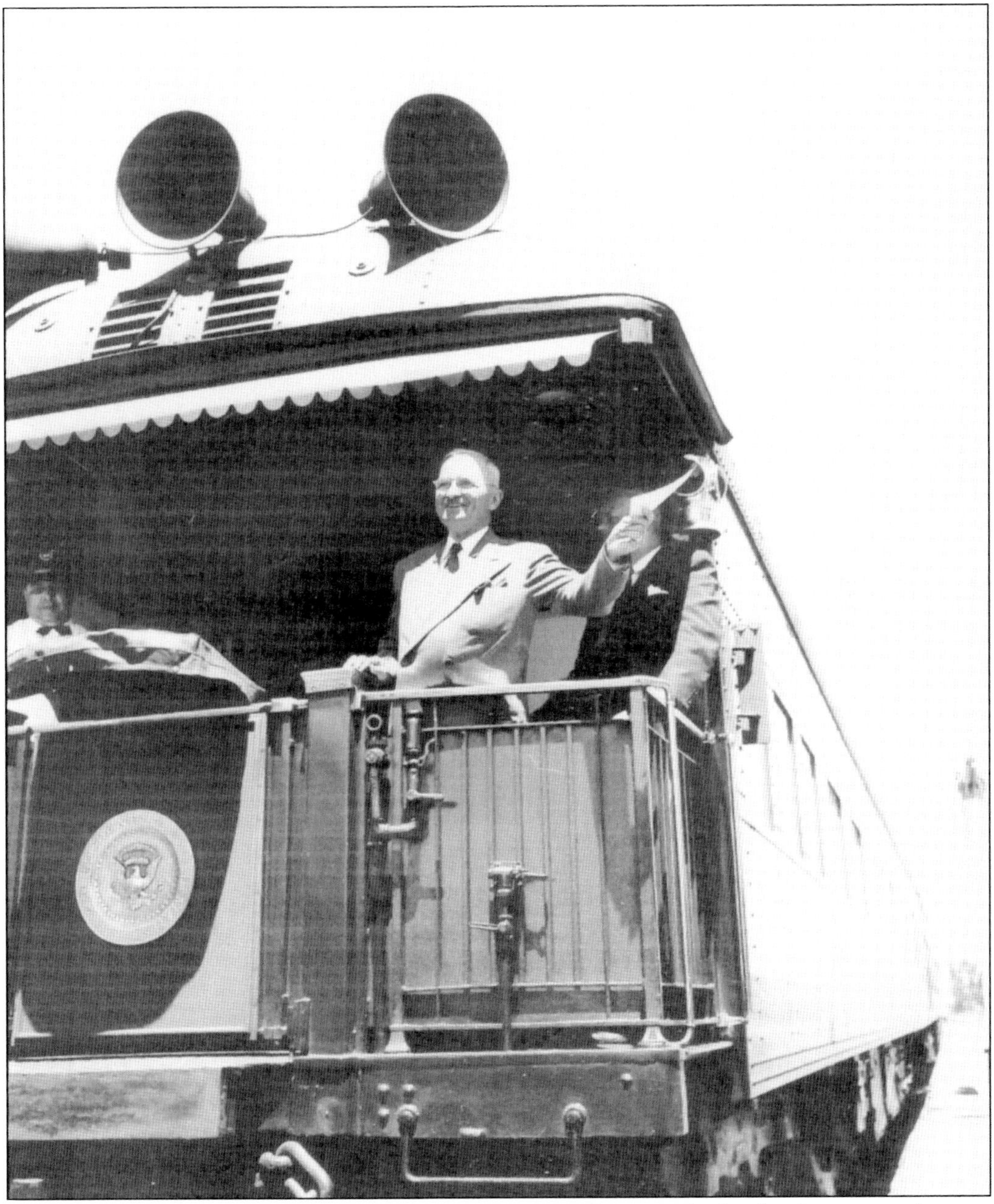

This is a 1948 picture of Pres. Harry S. Truman standing on the back of a train as he was campaigning for his second term as US president. President Truman was passing by Rexburg after giving a speech in Idaho Falls. The train didn't stop in Rexburg, but it passed slowly, allowing him to wave to the people. President Truman was not the only important person to pass through Eastern Idaho. Averill Harriman, the owner of Union Pacific Railroads, the Railroad Ranch in Island Park, and the Sun Valley Ski Resort and governor of New York stopped in Rexburg often to meet with Lloyd Adams, who served as the legal attorney for the Union Pacific Railroads in Idaho. In 1933, Hollywood actors Clarke Gable and Wallace Berry stepped off the train at the depot and walked a couple of blocks to Harry Houston's Commercial Grill on Main Street for dinner. (Courtesy of William Melville studio.)

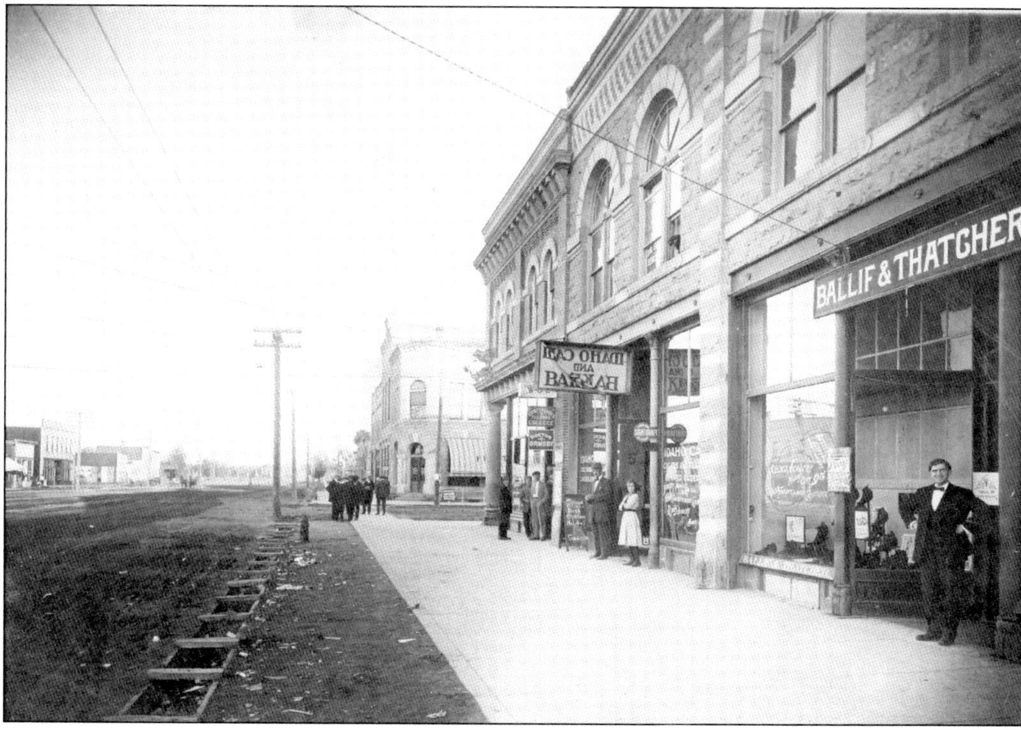

In the first two decades of the 20th century, Rexburg's Main Street was checkerboarded with many cafés. The Idaho Café and Bakery, located at the corner of South First East and East Main Street, was one of the more popular cafés during this time period. Urshel Bigler and his sister Gladys stand in front of the café. (Courtesy of Dona Bigler.)

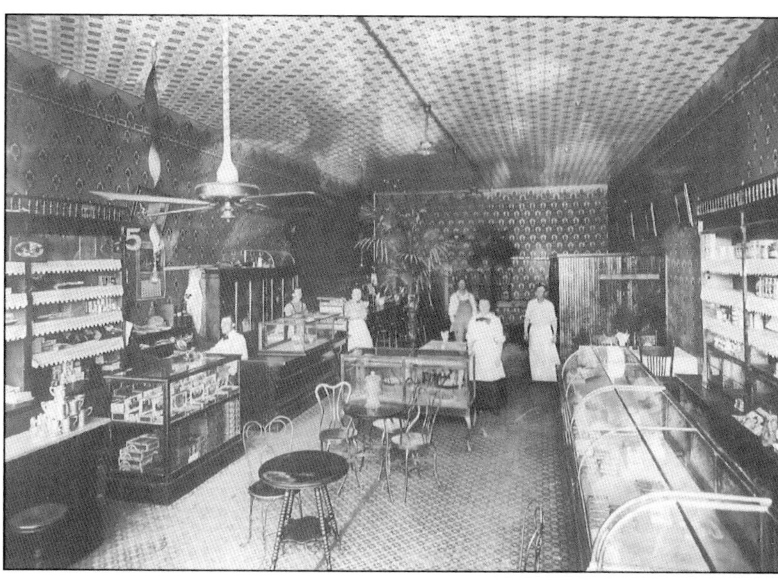

In this 1911 photography of the Idaho Café and Bakery, Urshel Bigler is seated at the desk as other members of his family serve as cooks and waitresses. The café was owned by Rexburg businessman Henry J. Bigler. (Courtesy of Dona Bigler.)

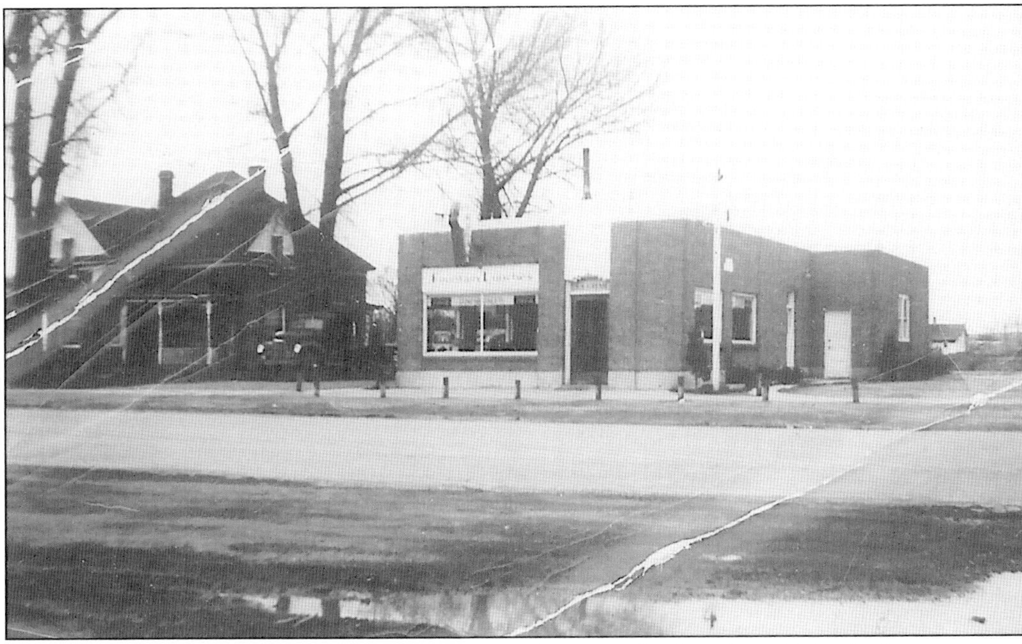

Evans Ice Cream Parlor and Drive Inn, owned and operated by Joseph and Martha Evans, opened in 1939 and was the first drive-in in Rexburg. It was located at 42 North Second East, and the original building still stands today. It specialized in hamburgers, fries, and shakes. (Courtesy of Joseph and Martha Evans.)

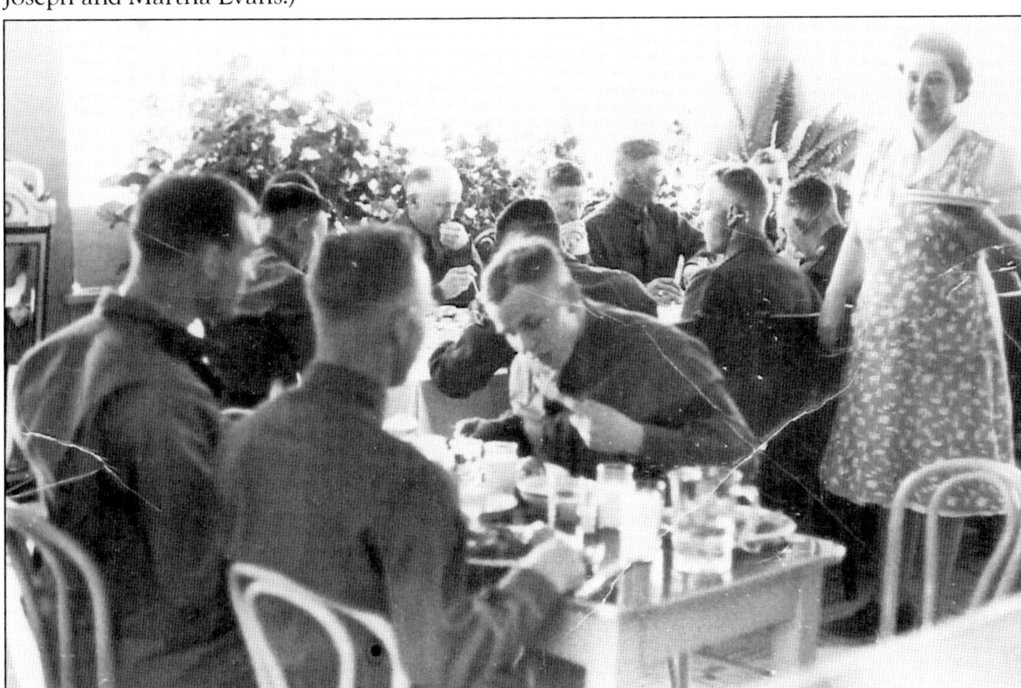

Martha Evans stands inside Evan's Ice Cream Parlor and Drive-In Café on December 7, 1941. Martha serves the Rexburg National Guard before they ship out for World War II. Art C. Porter, a member of the National Guard, took this picture. (Courtesy of Art C. Porter.)

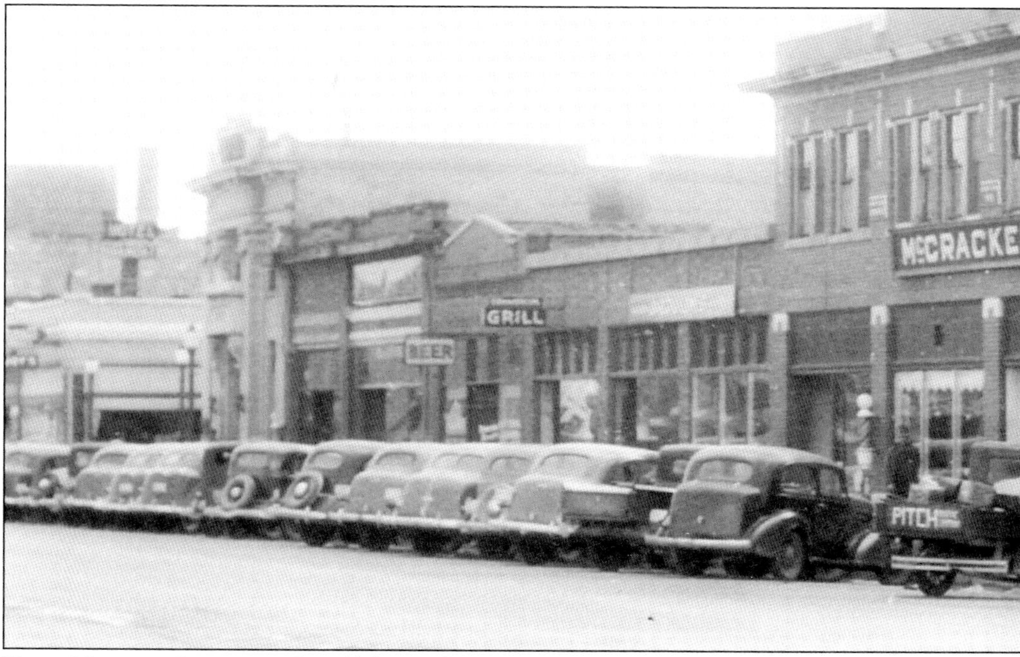

Harry Houston Commercial Grill, located on the south side of Main Street, was a popular eating establishment in the 1930s and 1940s. This restaurant catered to the downtown merchants and employees of Rexburg. The courthouse café was on the same side of the street and owned by Fred Shirley.

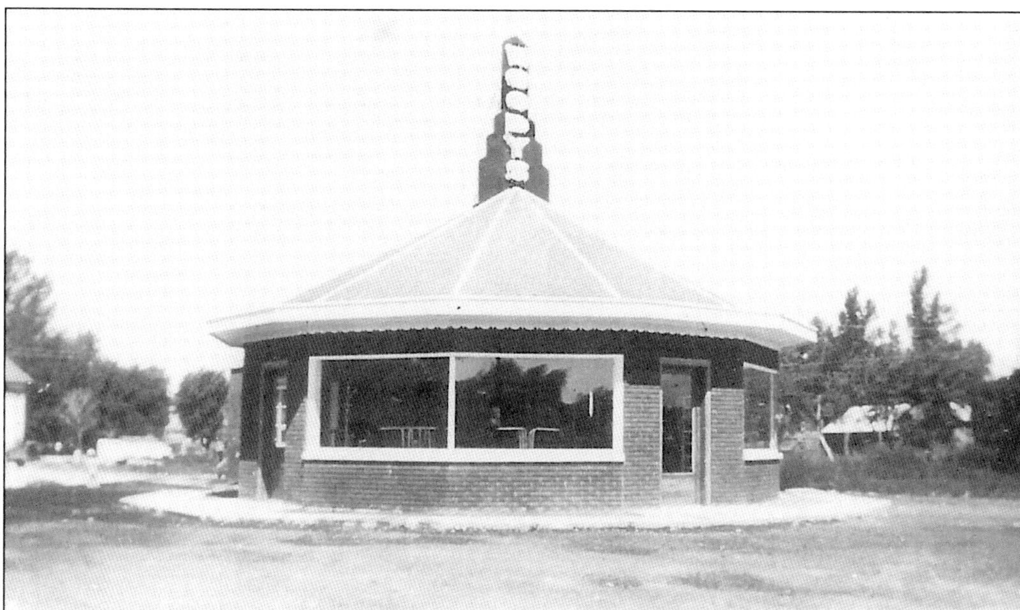

This octagon-shaped building was a popular drive-in and sit-down café in Rexburg. It was built by Terrell Woodmansee and Ferrel Wood in 1948. It was the first drive-in in Rexburg to offer carhop service. It was later sold to Bill Jockemson, and the name was changed to Bill's Drive-Inn. In 1969, the business was sold to Doyle Walker and became Walker's Restaurant. (Courtesy of Ferrel Wood.)

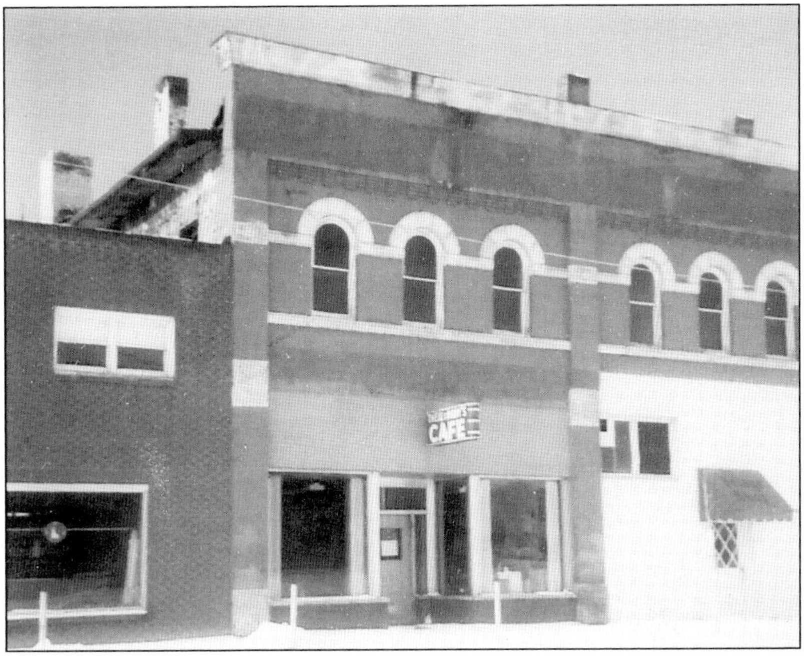

Thell and Mary's Café was opened in 1946 by Thell and Mary Bunnell. Thell was the cook, and Mary served the customers. Mary could carry five dinner plates full of food on each arm and deliver them without dropping a plate. They opened for breakfast at 6:00 a.m. and closed at 4:00 p.m. This café was a meeting place for farmers, merchants, and businessmen.

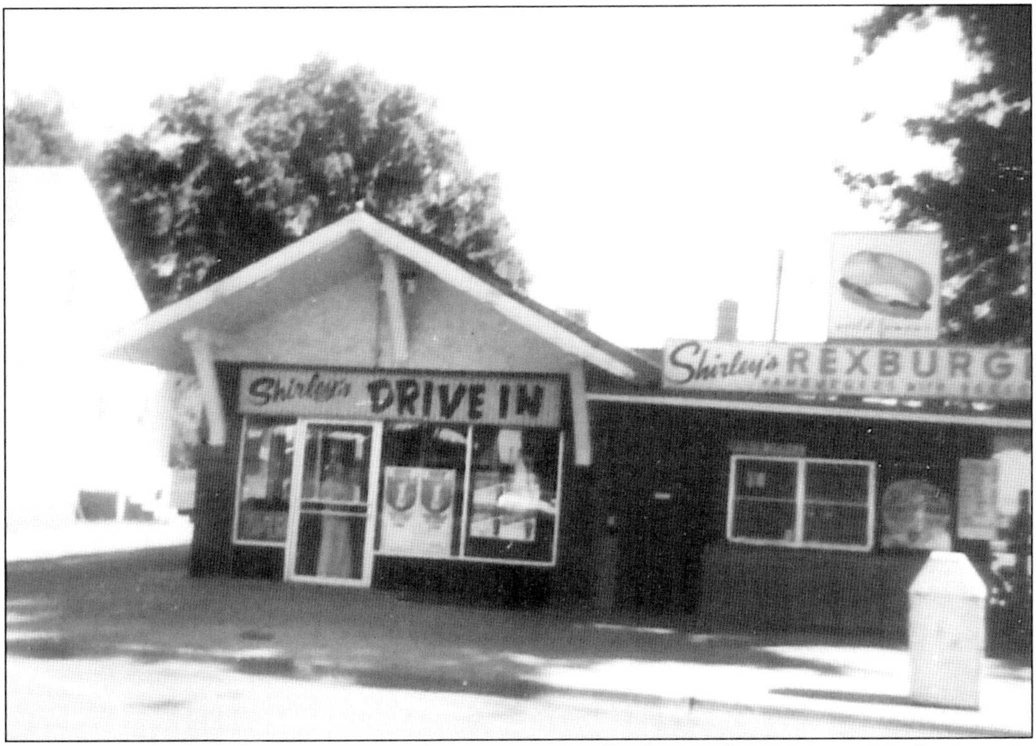

Shirley's Grocery and Drive-In, located on the south side of Main Street, opened for business in 1947. It was owned and operated by Fred Shirley and his son Henry. Henry managed the grocery store with the help of Floyd Keith and Verla Parkinson as cashier. Fred Shirley, along with his wife, and Rachel Brown ran the drive-in. Their hamburger was the famous "Rexburger." (Courtesy of Ann Shirley Merkley.)

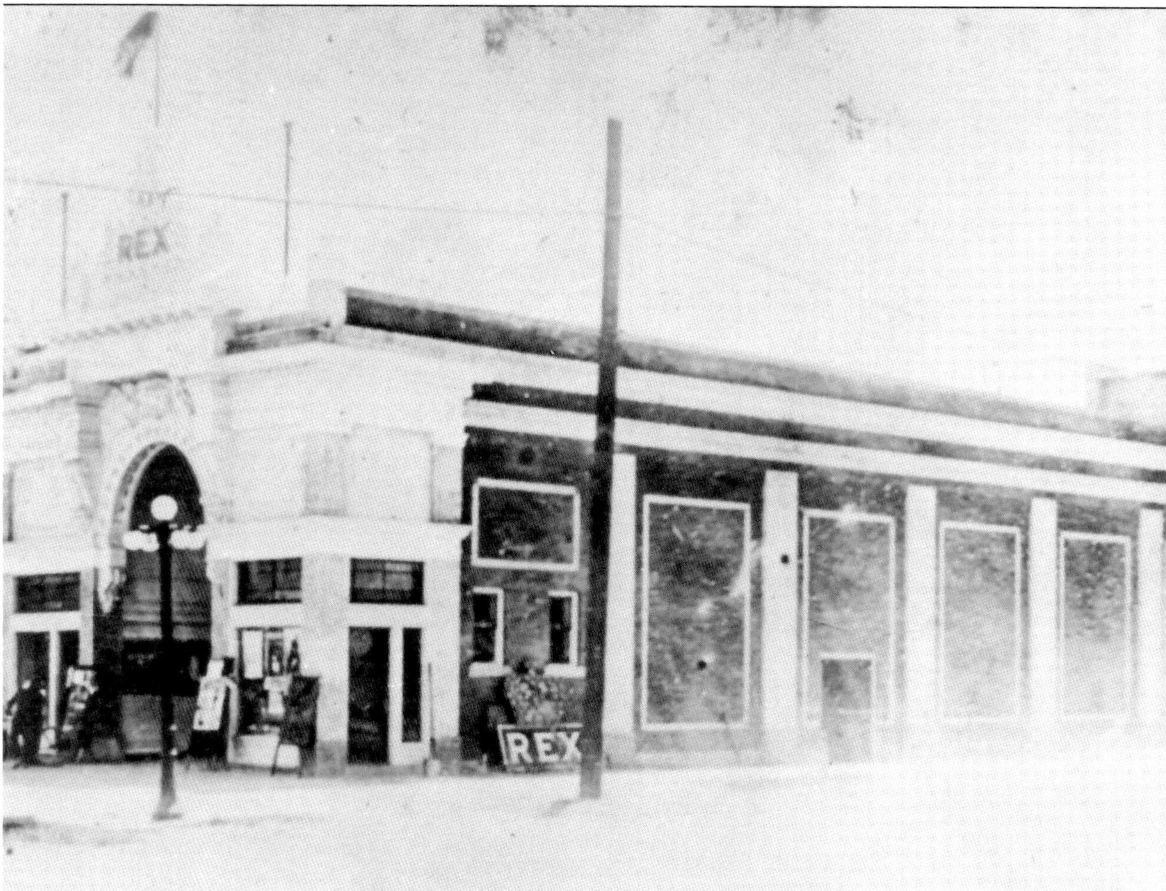

The Rex Theater, Rexburg's first theater, was built by Mark Madison, a Rexburg entrepreneur, in 1914. The building was located on the south side of Main Street and the corner of Center Street. It offered silent movies and traveling theatrical performances on stage. Recorded in the *Post Register* on October 16, 1914, was this tragic event: "Vaudeville actress Mona Delayn, known as the 'Bullet proof woman' was accidently shot to death by her partner and fellow performer, Mr. Hobbs, on the stage of the Rex Theater at Rexburg during a performance. Hobbs was arrested and is being held. He claimed it was his first accident in nine years." The Rex Theater became the Columbia Theater in the 1930s. In 1940, the name was changed to the Romance Theater.

In 1940, the once Rex Theater, then Columbia Theater, became the Romance Theater. The theater was severely damaged by the Teton flood on June 5, 1976, and a year later, it reopened under the name of the Westwood. The building was purchased by the City of Rexburg in 2004 and converted into a community center with the goal of the restoration of the building to make it look like it did in the 1940s. The renovation continues today. The Lincoln Hotel and Elk Theater, located at 33 East Main Street, was built in 1915 by the Jones family. An interesting feature of the theater was that it had fake bats hanging from the ceiling to add drama to the movies. As a prank, some young men snuck in real birds and released them at the climax of a movie.

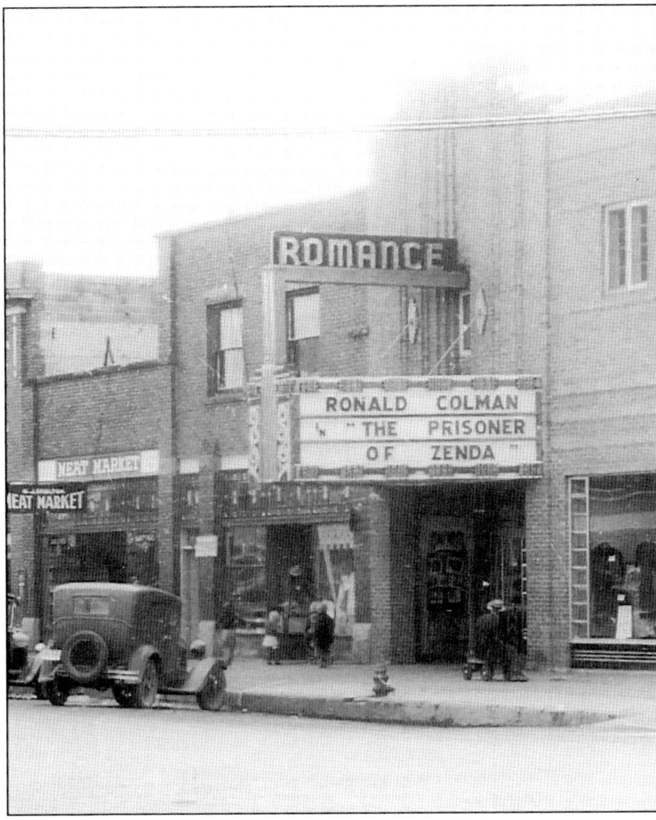

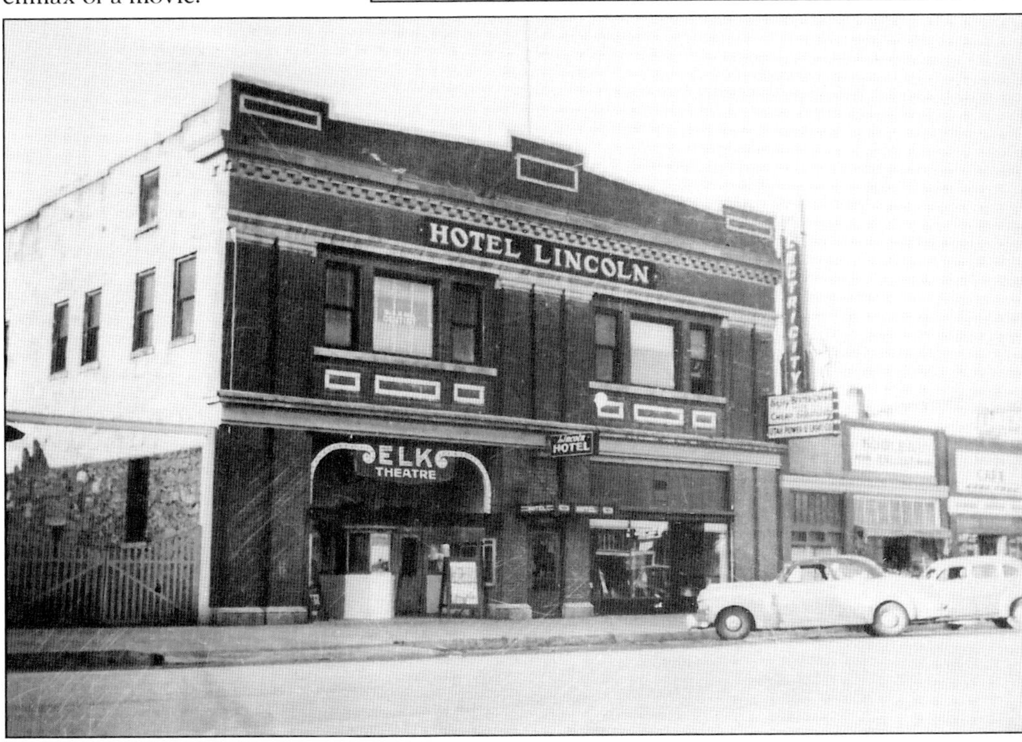

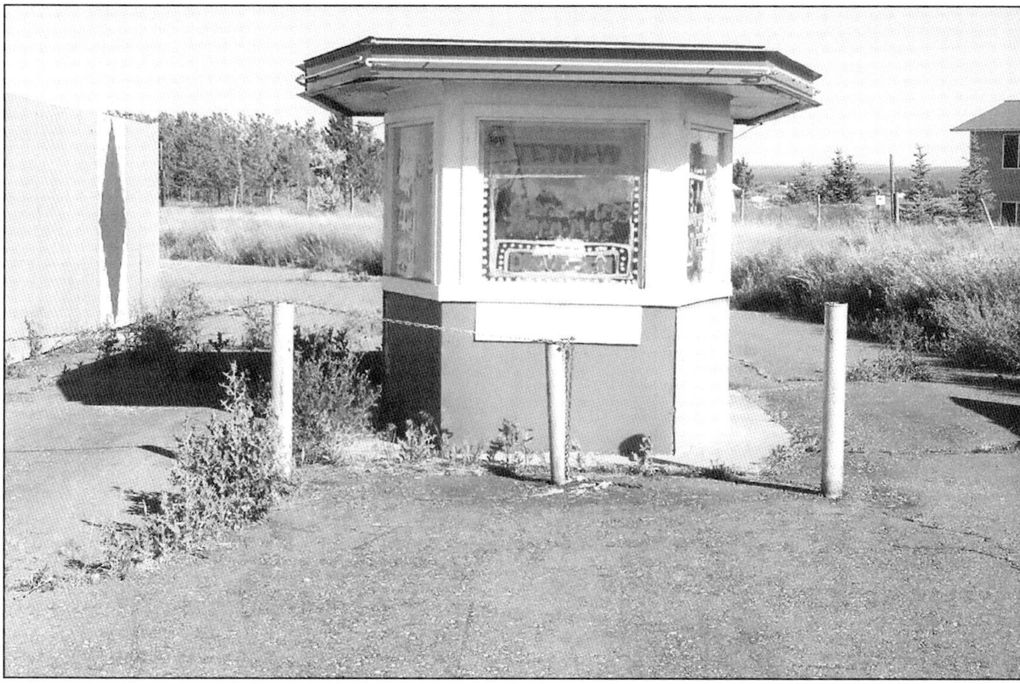

Teton View Motor-View Drive-In was one half-mile northeast of Rexburg. It was owned for over 30 years by Ralph Prestwich, who purchased it possibly in the late 1950s. It is one of a half-dozen outdoor theaters still in operation in Southeastern and Eastern Idaho. In the 1960s, the challenge was to see if people could get into the theater without paying the price of a ticket by sneaking as many teenagers as they could into the trunk of their car. Unfortunately, Prestwich had an eagle eye and was able to detect every teenager who tried to sneak into the theater. The theater has been used as a place for a swap meet and currently shows movies during the summer months.

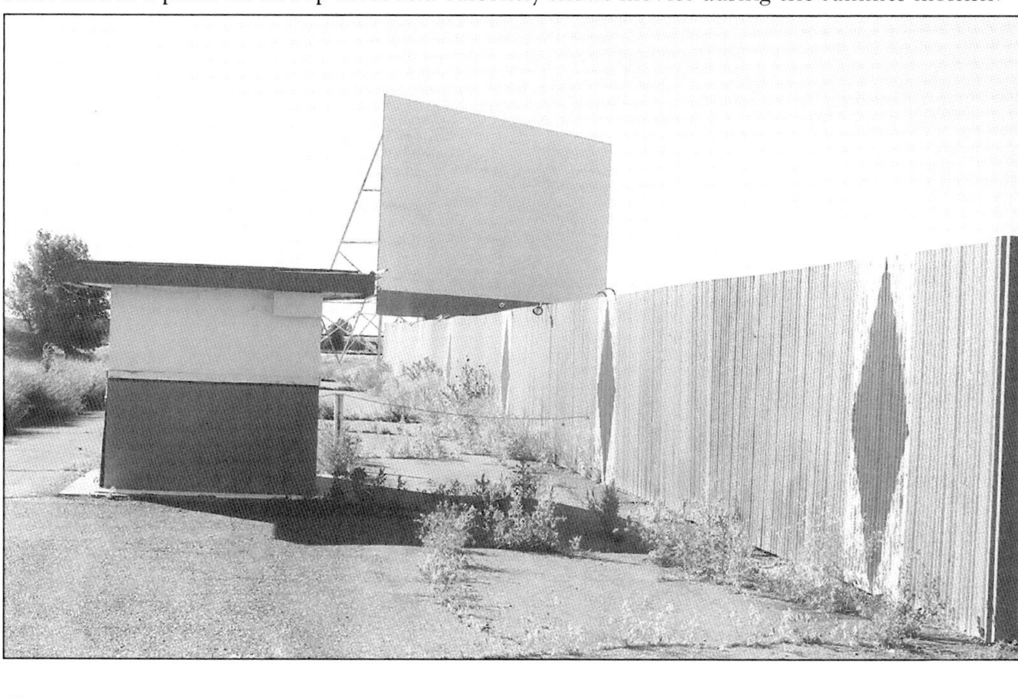

This scene was a familiar sight in Rexburg in 1905. This picture was taken along South First East and across the street from the present-day *Standard Journal* newspaper. The post office was located in the Winter-Webster Building. Men in the picture are unidentified; however, the man on the horse is thought to be Frank Watts, a Rexburg barber. (Courtesy of Frank Watts.)

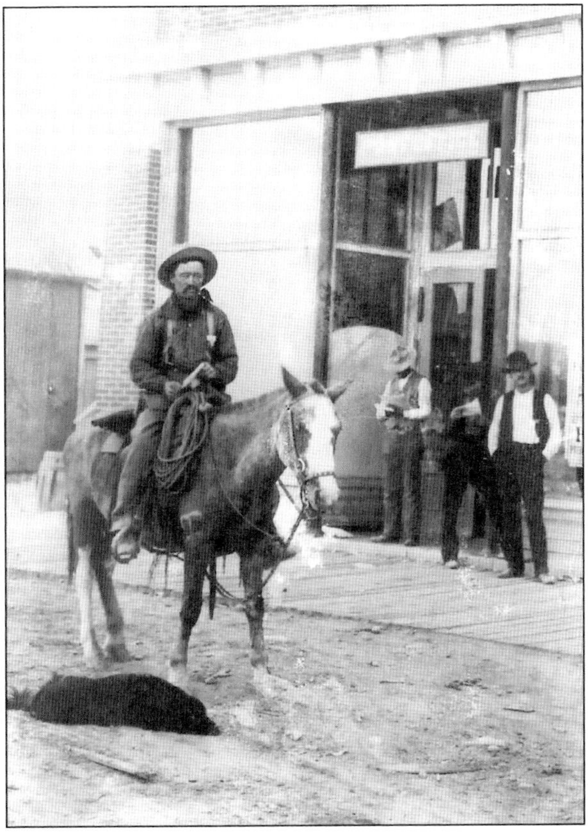

The first post office in the valley opened at Egin in 1880 with A. Parker as postmaster. The Rexburg office opened in 1884 with Thomas Bassett as postmaster. The mail was brought to Rexburg on horseback from Market Lake and then carried to other towns several times each week. This picture shows postmaster L.Y. Rigby standing in the door and Cy Watson at the window at left. The others are unidentified.

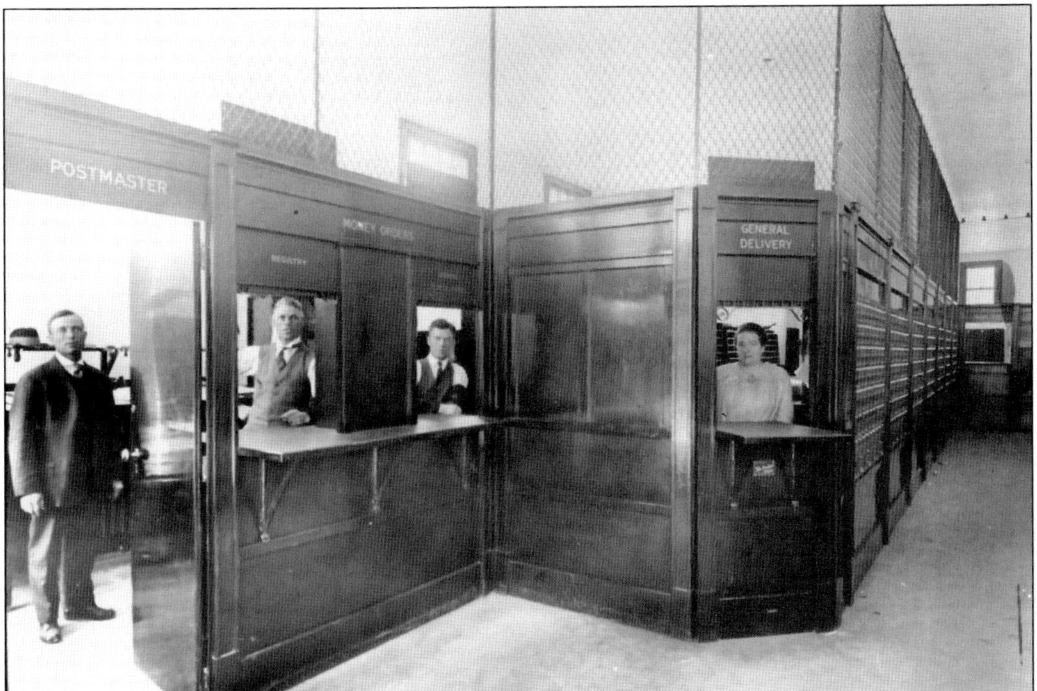

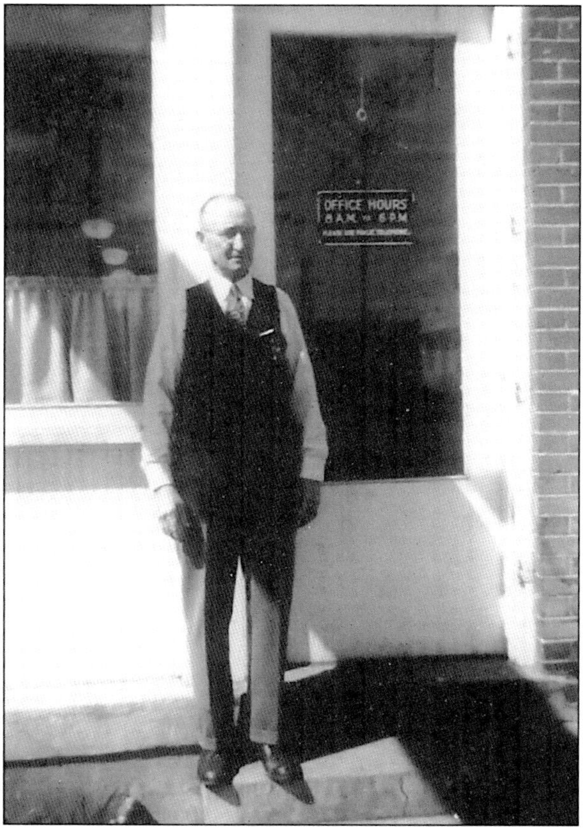

In 1897, the Snake River Telephone Company, under the direction of L. Rice, John Smellie, S. Carruthers, T. Hamer, and F. Bybee, constructed a line from Market Lake to St. Anthony. This line was absorbed by the Bell Telephone Company later the same year. Manager Herman Reed stands in front of the Rexburg Mountain States Telephone Company office in the photograph to the left. The image below was taken during a telephone office Christmas party in 1953. From left to right are (first row) Leon Whitehead, Nellis Garner, Carol Reese, Loa Leatham, James Clarke (manager), Ruth Perry, and Mary Shirley; (second row) Verla Parkinson (training manager), Elda Whitehead, Winney Leatham, Donetta Burns, Barbara Garner, Barbara Hirschi, and Janice Sharp; (third row) Shirley Bishoff, Patsy Oakey, Reneau Bohi, Norma Holley, Lavina Shelton, Catherine DaBell, Ruth Clark, Phyllis Hinckley, Nelda Evans, and Jean Hinckley. (Both, courtesy of Ruth Perry.)

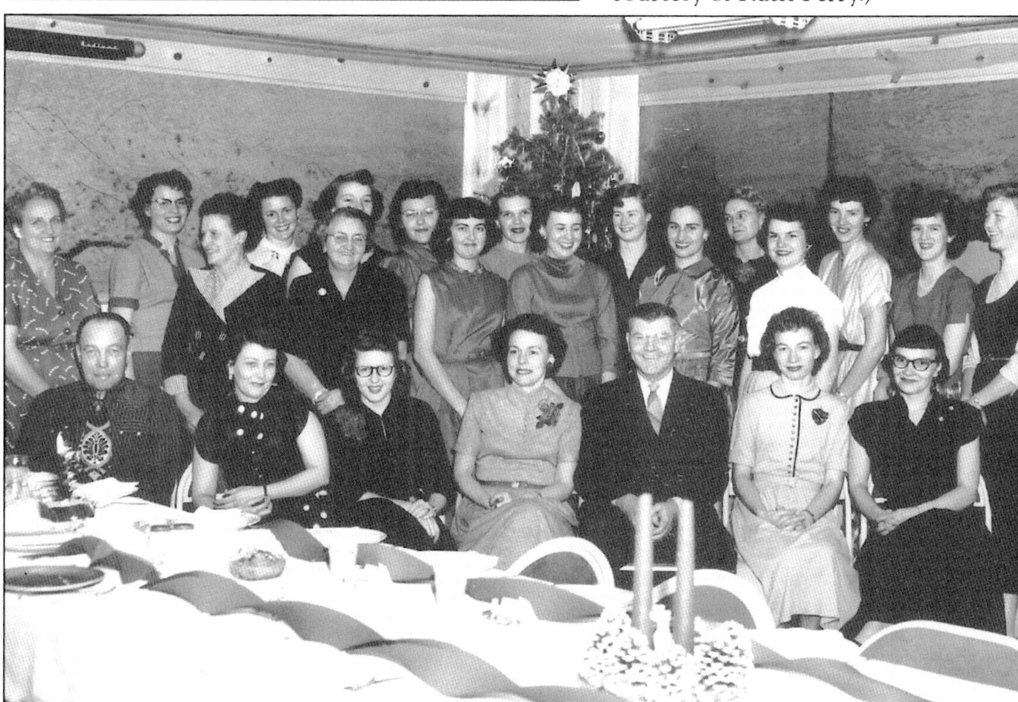

Pictured is the interior of Herman Layman's saloon, located on the south side of Main Street and the corner of North College Avenue. The bartender is a Mr. Lewis, and the other gentleman is unidentified, as are the two figures reflected in the mirror.

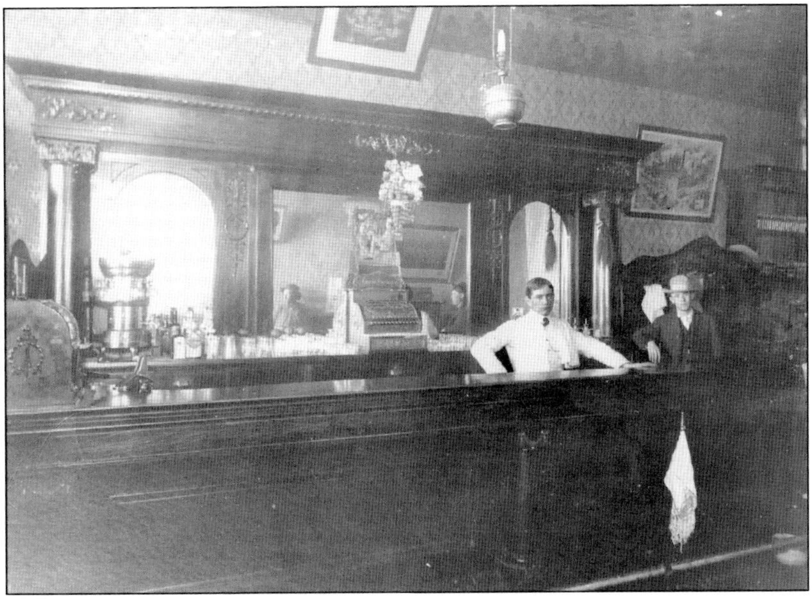

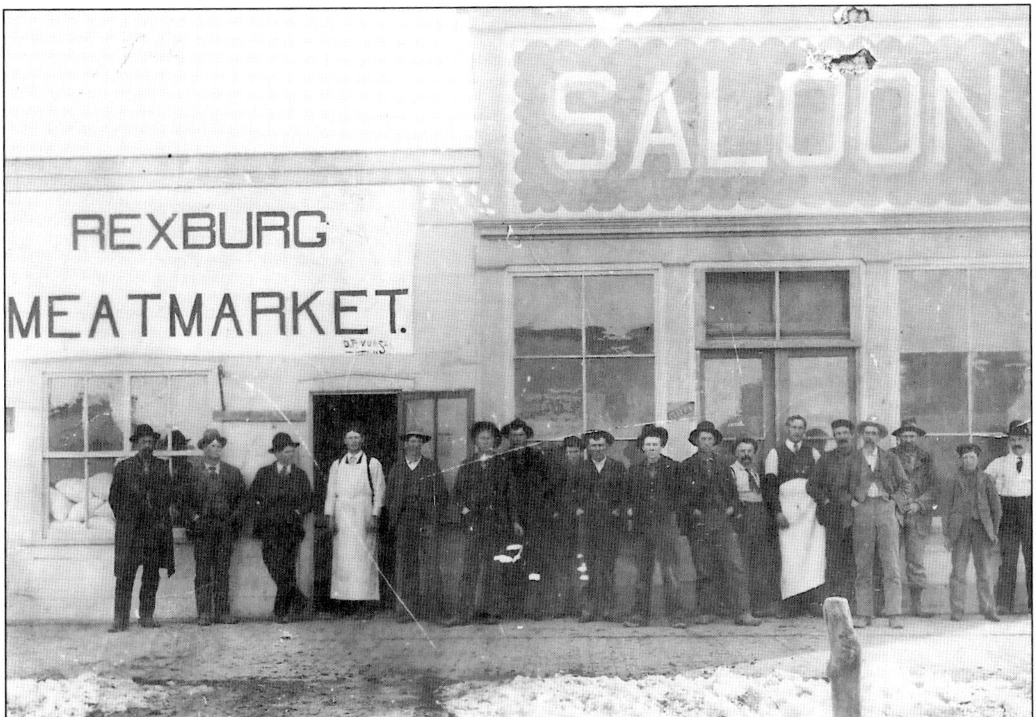

In this 1905 photograph, several men stand in front of the Rexburg Meat Market and Saloon, located at the corner of South Main Street and North College Avenue. Herman Layman was the owner, and Ed Walker was the manager of the meat market, with Herman Frank and Clyde Skelton as assistants. Walker stands in the doorway of the meat market.

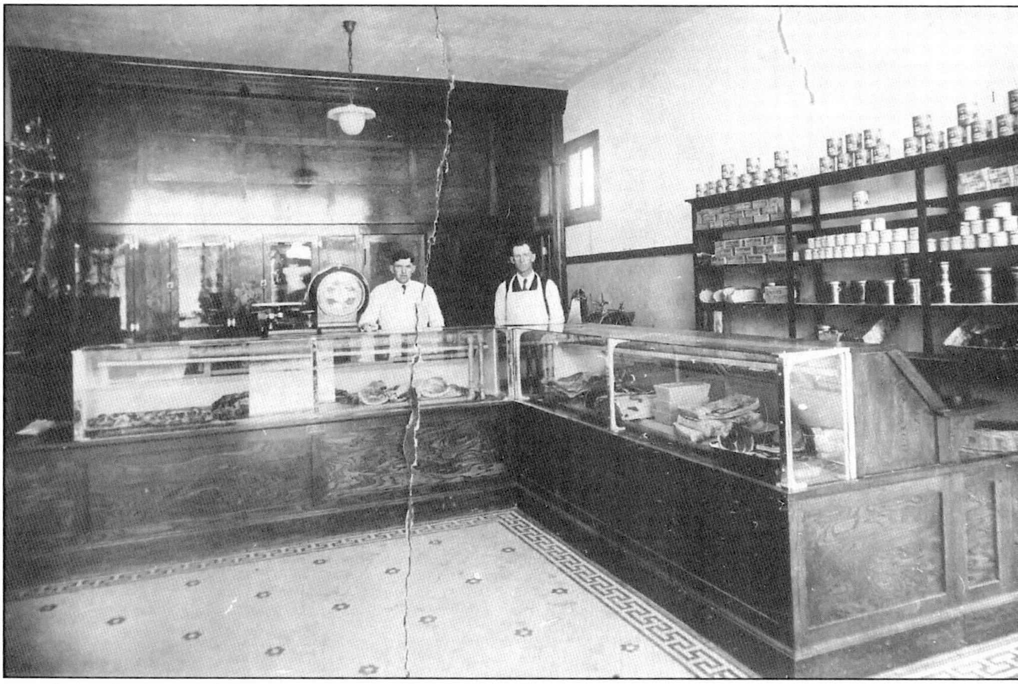

Local cattlemen and sheepmen would bring their slaughtered livestock to the meat markets to be processed. This picture of the interior of the City Meat Market, located on the main floor of the Eccles Hotel on College Avenue, shows the brothers Clyde (left) and Steve Skelton.

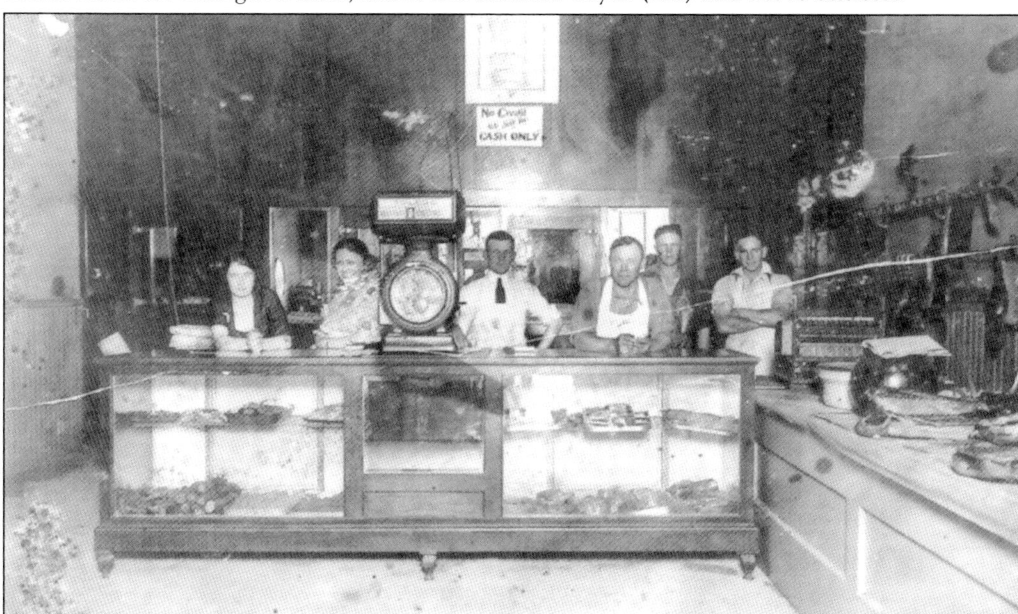

Pictured inside the Greuber Meat Market in this 1920 photograph is meat cutter Ross Jolley, the fourth man from the left leaning on the counter. The man on the far right is Oz Neeley, who lost his right hand while cutting meat at this market. The others are unidentified. (Courtesy of Upper Snake River Valley Historical Society.)

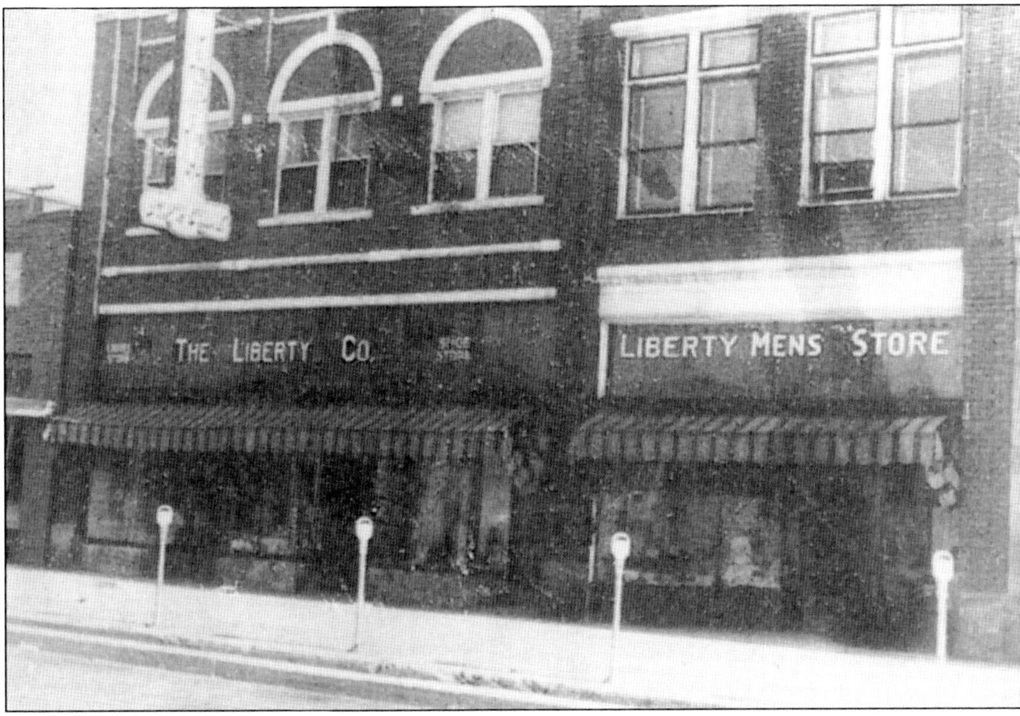

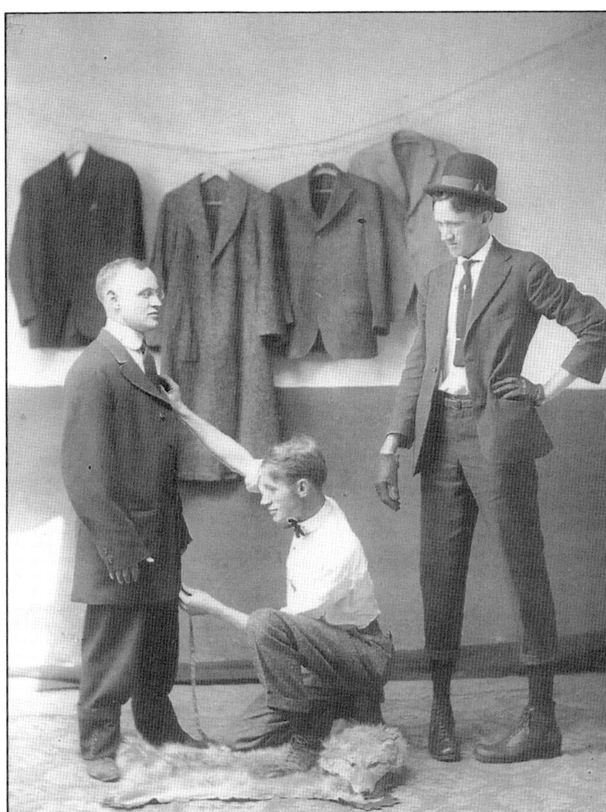

The Liberty Company was established in 1908 by Nathan and Sadie Levine. The company specialized in men's quality clothing but also carried women's clothing. Nathan would make trips to New York City and attend men's fashion shows to select the most up-to-date clothing. He had previously owned a clothing store in Kentucky prior to coming to Rexburg. He built a very impressive building on the north side of Main Street, and that building stands today. He bought the Walker Hospital and converted it into a beautiful home. Sadly, on Christmas Day in 1930, while the Levines were away, their home burned to the ground. The advertisement for the Liberty Store to the right shows Fred Shirley in the short pants. (Right, courtesy of Ann Merkley.)

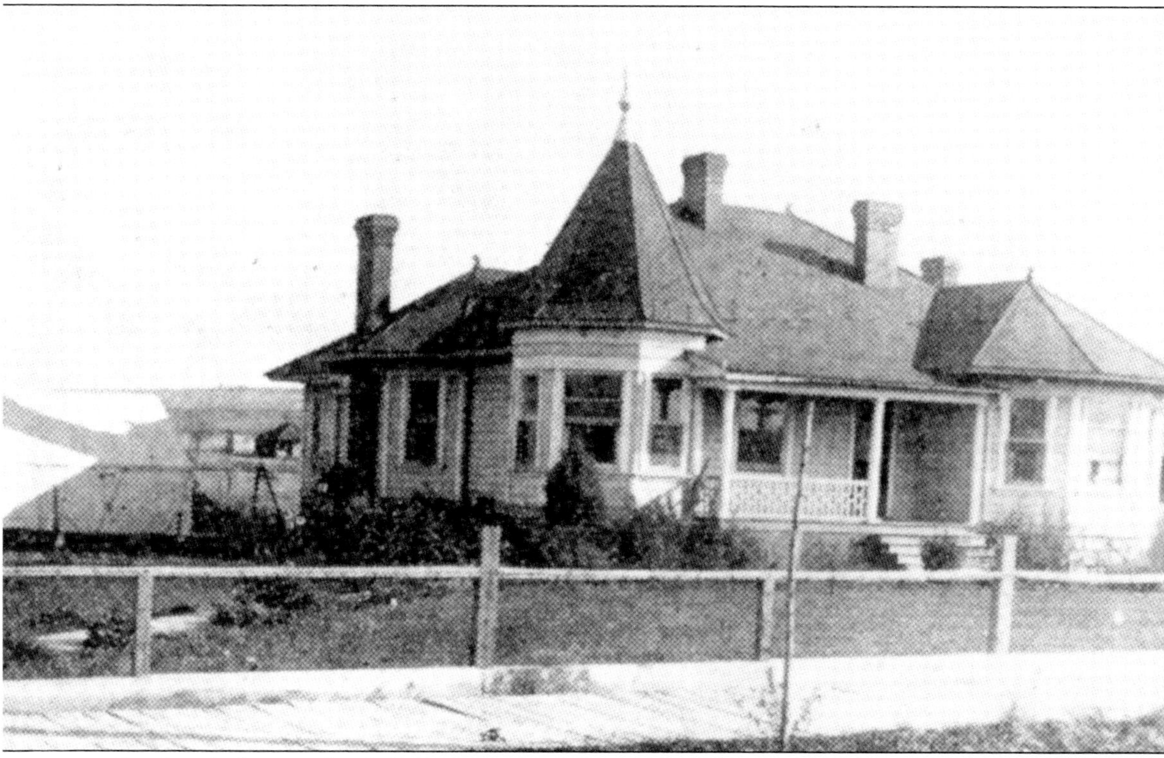

Rexburg's first medical doctor was a woman and midwife, Mrs. Watts, whose outstanding characteristic was that people believed in her. Dr. Joseph Walker built the first Rexburg hospital at 109 South Center Street some time between 1898 and 1903. The second hospital in Rexburg was owned by William L. Sutherland and located on the second floor of the Rexburg State Bank on the corner of College Avenue and Main Street. Dr. Sutherland was enticed to Rexburg in 1921 to go into partnership with Dr. Loren Rich. The third hospital was the Rigby Hospital, built by Dr. Harlo B. and Elsie Rigby in 1924. They ran this hospital for over 29 years and averaged 400 hospitalized patients per year. The Rigbys brought two generations into the world, including a set of triplets and 20 pairs of twins. The fourth hospital, Madison Memorial Hospital, opened its doors in 1953 at the east end of Main Street. That hospital was demolished, and a new hospital was built on the same site. It still operates today.

Five

Agriculture and Livestock

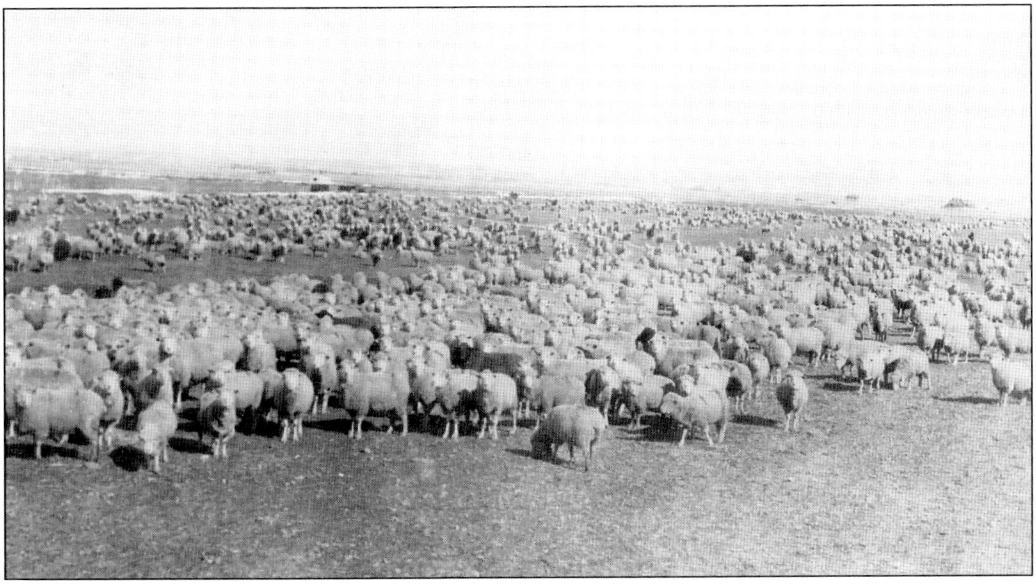

This 1910 picture shows three bands of sheep belonging to sheep baron Royal Raphael Garn grazing on top of White Owl Butte. Sheep raising was given particular emphasis by the pioneers. Grazing has always been good on the foothills and mountains above Rexburg because of the long, continued dryness of the summer atmosphere causing the nutritious grasses to cure as they grow. There were nine sheep barons in 1910.

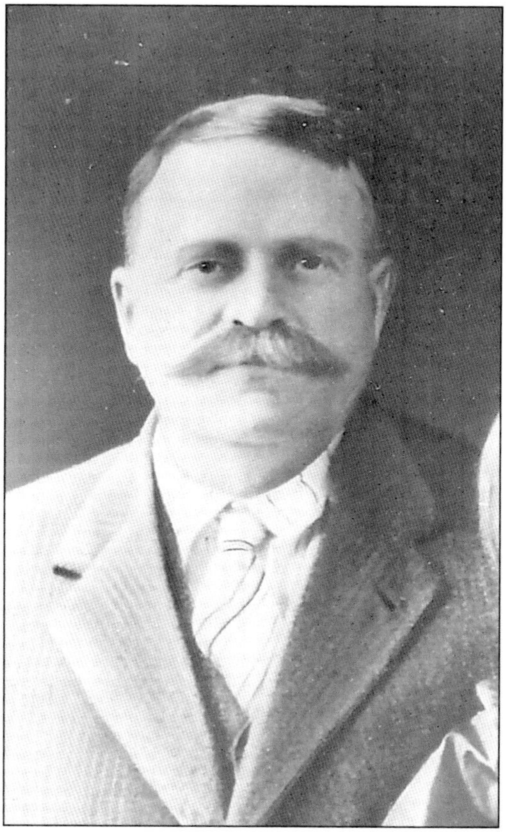

Ephriam Marning Davidson, a sheep baron in Utah, immigrated to Idaho in 1893. He ran three bands of sheep from Felt near Ashton, had headquarters at Wilford, and owned several thousand acres of grazing land in Madison County along Long Hollow Canyon. As a young man, he became a successful kickboxer, traveling to various fairs and pool halls in Utah, Nevada, and Idaho.

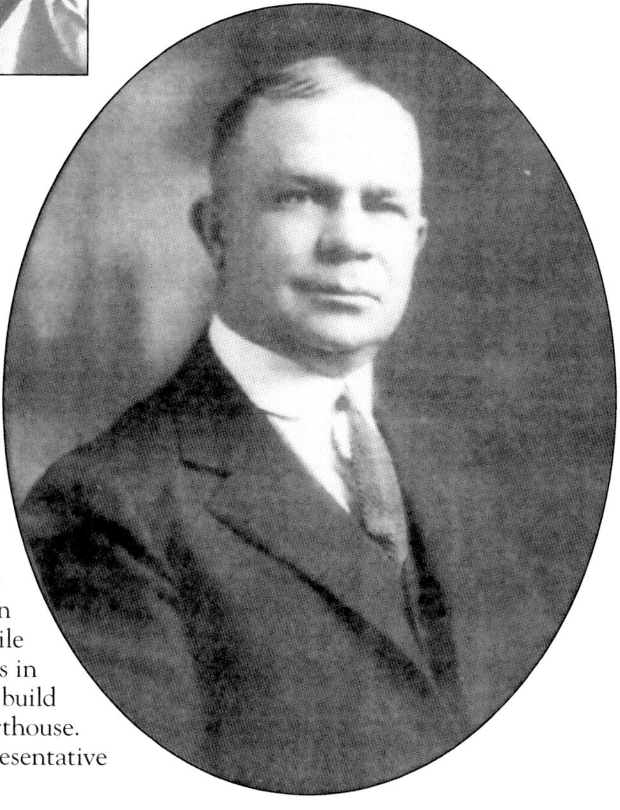

Royal Raphael Garn came from a prominent sheep family. His father, Martin Garn, was one of the first sheep barons in the Rexburg area, and Garn Mountain was named after him. While chairman of the county commissioners in 1919, he was able to secure a grant to build the present-day Madison County Courthouse. He also served two terms as a state representative for Madison County.

John Earl Garner Jr. migrated with his family to Rexburg in 1883. As a young boy, he watched the Indians camp near his home, where they would shoot rock chucks with a bow and arrow, throw the entire animal into a bonfire, and eat them entrails and all. He entered the sheep business in 1908, acquiring the Three Pines Ranch and, later, the Jacobi Ranch, where he ran his sheep.

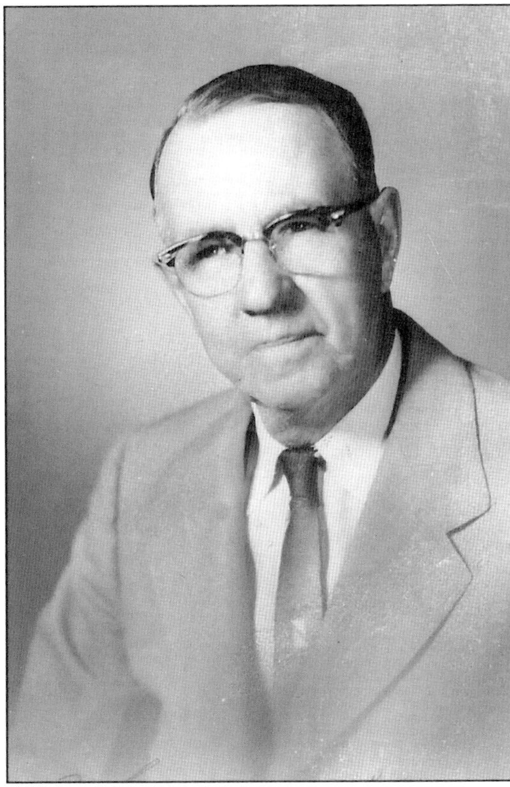

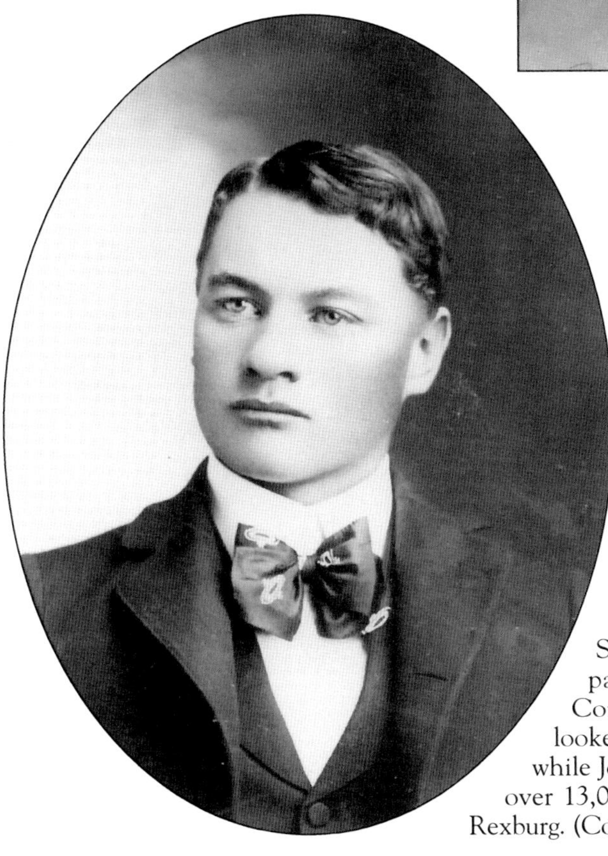

Sheep baron John J. Hunt was the active partner in the Hunt Brothers Sheep Company with his brother Steve. Steve looked after the banking and investments, while John managed the sheep. They operated over 13,000 acres in the Hibbard area west of Rexburg. (Courtesy of Diana Fuller.)

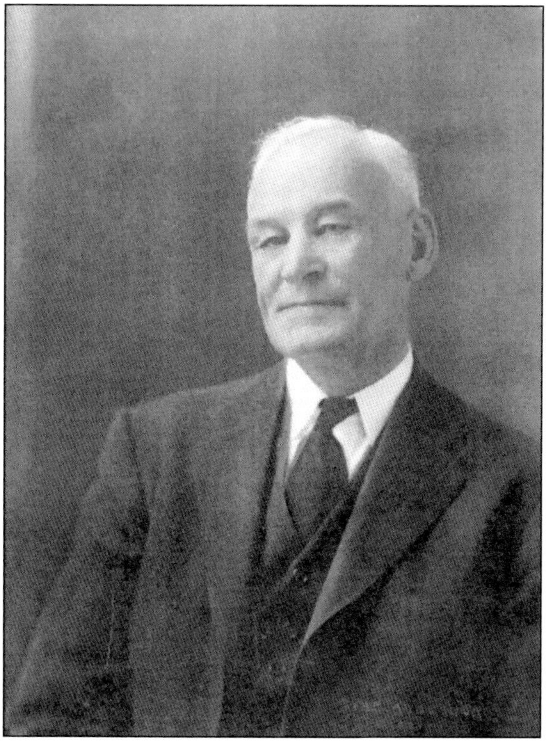

Frederick Smart Parkinson came to Rexburg as a partner with his uncle James Webster Sr. in the Smart and Webster Livestock Company. Later, Parkinson formed a partnership with his brothers Joseph and Ed in the dry farming and sheep business. He owned and operated 4,000 acres of dry farmland on the upper Rexburg bench. He served as mayor of Rexburg in 1915. (Courtesy of Ross Parkinson Jr.)

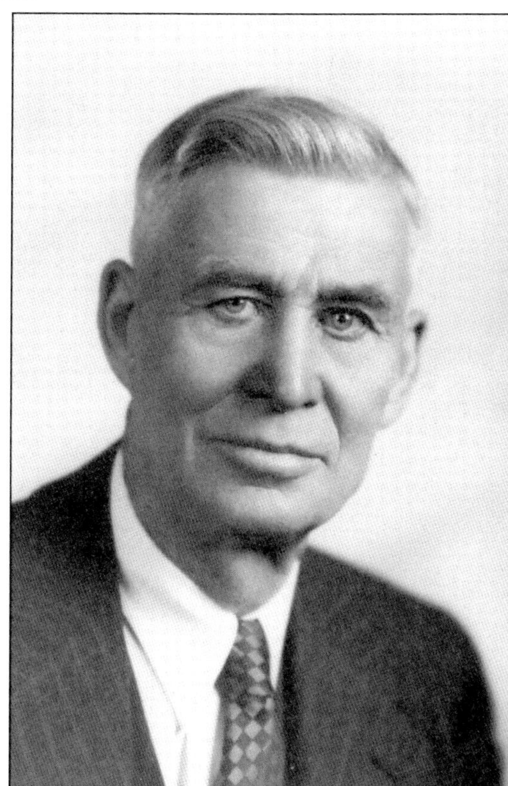

Joseph Smart "Joe" Parkinson, the sheep baron of the Parkinson Brothers Livestock Company, came to Rexburg in 1911. At that time, his brother Fred left on a mission for the Mormon Church, and Joe took over the business. His reputation spread, and he became known as the most prominent sheep raiser in the Northwest. At one time, he and his brother had over 9,500 ewes.

James Whaley Webster Sr. was born in the oldest town in Idaho, Franklin, in 1862. He came to Rexburg on August 8, 1895, and brought three bands of sheep with him. He was associated with his brother-in-law Mr. Smart. He served two terms in the Idaho Legislature and as mayor of Rexburg. Webster's home was the first home in Rexburg to be wired with electricity.

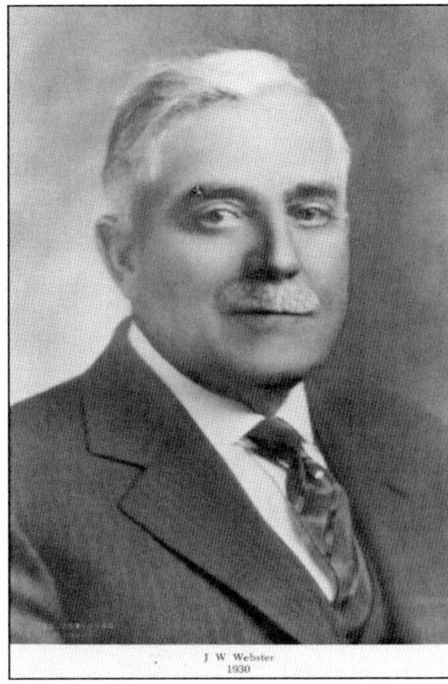

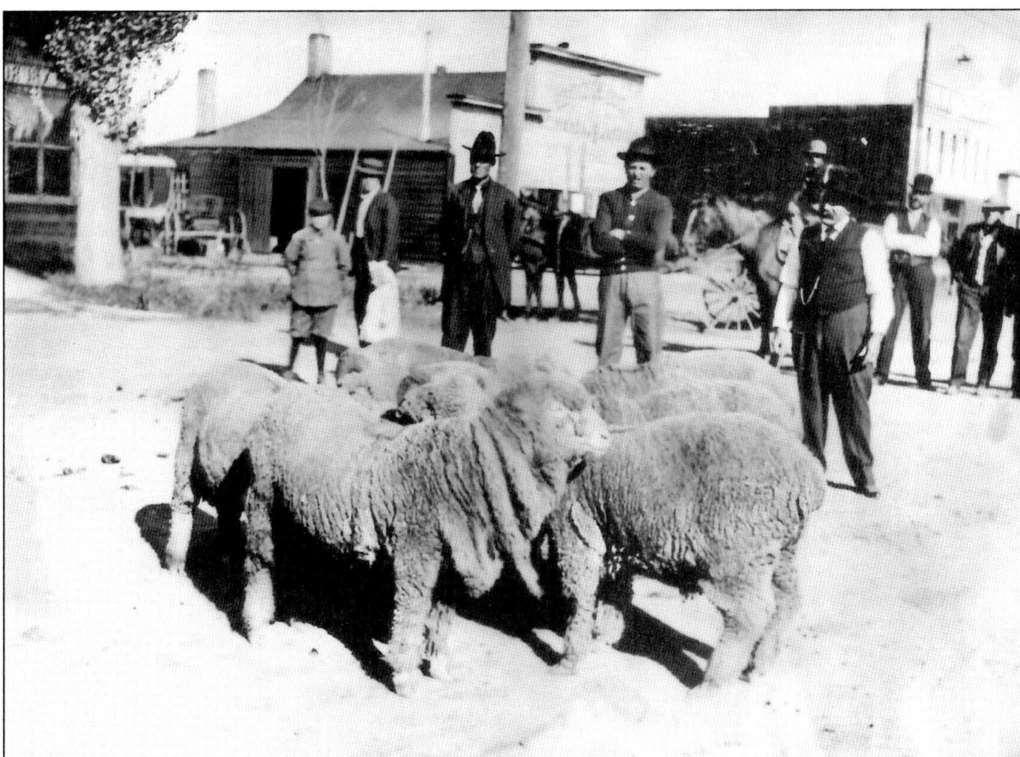

This 1910 picture of Rexburg's Main Street shows merino sheep owned by James W. Webster Sr. The merino sheep were originally from Turkey and are highly valued for their soft wool. Webster is forefront in the picture, and the man standing behind him wearing the vest and derby is James Gillespie, manager of Flamm's Department Store and the first city manager of Rexburg in 1903.

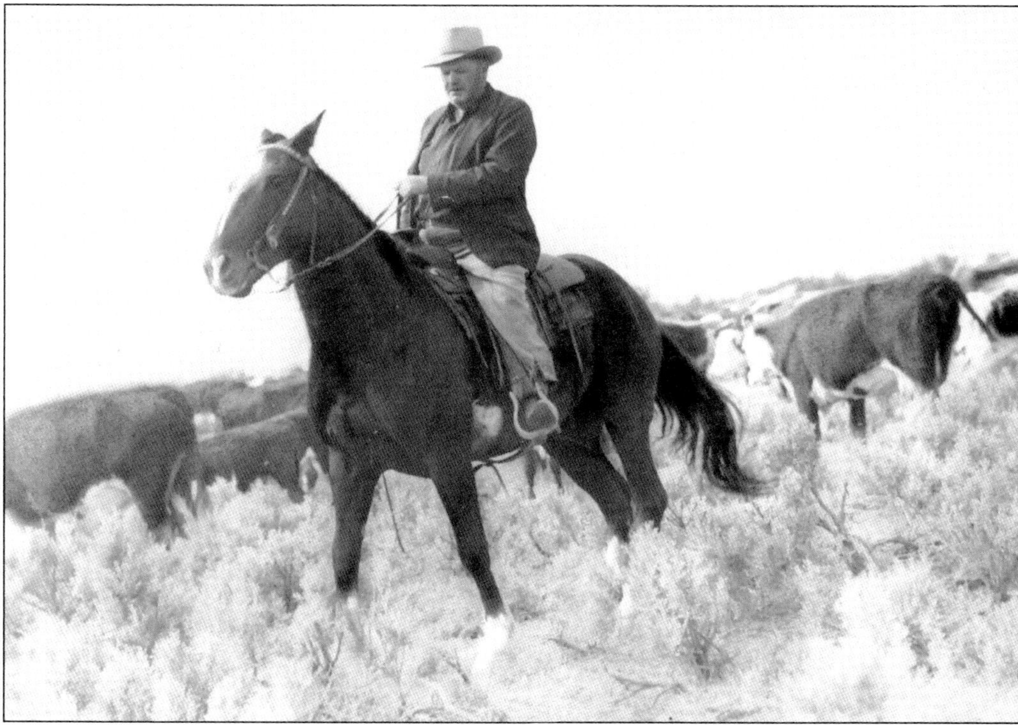

Levi J. and Louise Cartier, French Canadians living in Butte, Montana, were cattle barons and owned mines in several states. The Cartiers were looking for a place near a river where they could run their cattle enterprise during the summer months. They came upon the location west of Rexburg that would become the Cartier Ranch. In 1899, they purchased 2,000 acres of deeded land along the Snake River with over 22,000 acres of state-leased land and Bureau of Land Management grazing land. Royal Justice (pictured above) and Ruth Price Sorenson purchased the Cartier Ranch, the largest ranch in Madison County, on June 28, 1929. The home was destroyed by the raging waters of the Teton Dam flood in 1976. A portion of the land is currently the Cartier wetland and wildlife reserve.

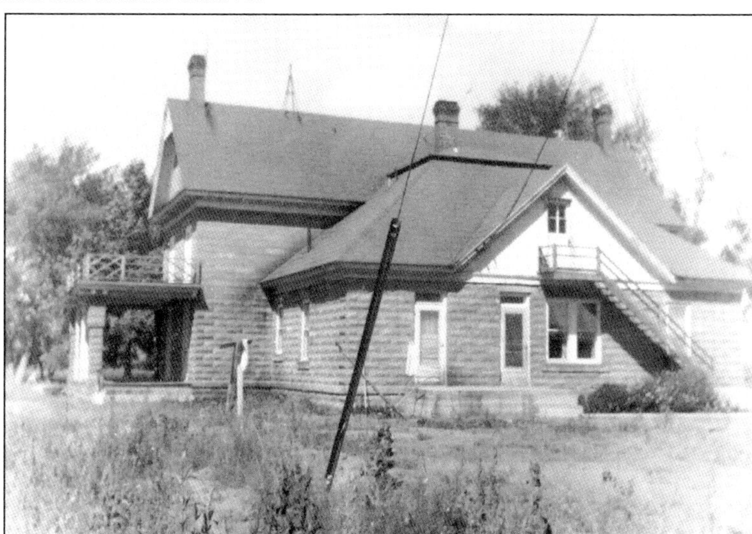

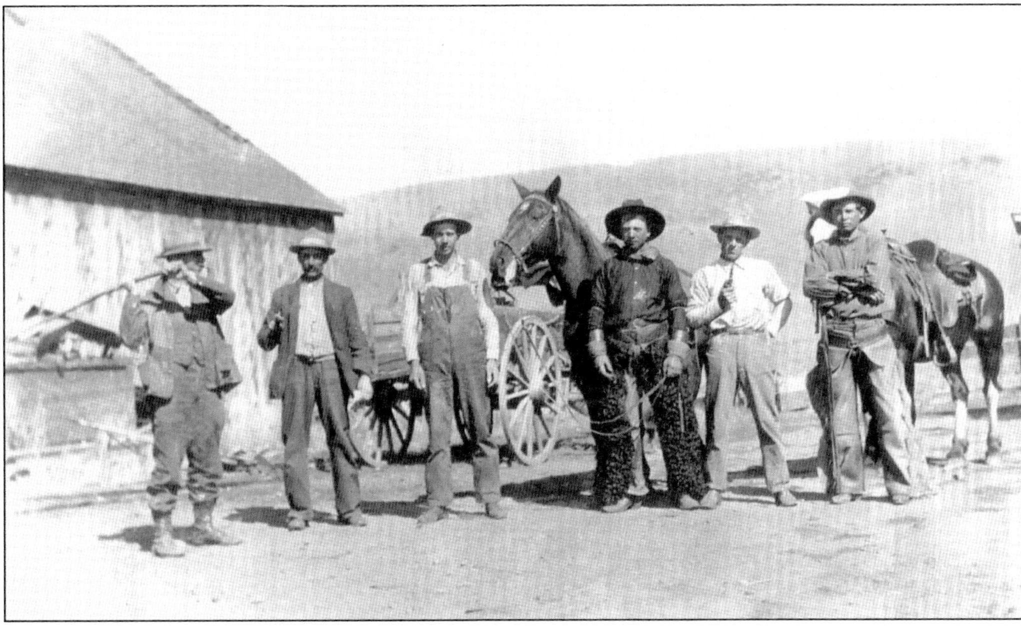

The photograph above shows Rexburg and Egin cowboys who were hired on in 1916 to work at the Wood Livestock Company in Spencer, Idaho. The company, which specialized in cattle and sheep, was the largest livestock venture in the state of Idaho. It offered year-round employment to young teenage boys who worked for one dollar a day. Standing from left to right are Sid Close, Charles Wood, Harry Dunn, Bill Hjort, Melvin Casper, and Dent Rich. Reed Saurey is shown at right branding a horse. The practice of marking cattle, horses and other livestock with a hot iron was a practice brought from Spain into Idaho in the 1860s. The brand was the signature and stood for the pride of name for ranchers and farmers. It was a mark of ownership and protected property from thieves. (Right, courtesy of Carolyn Brizzee.)

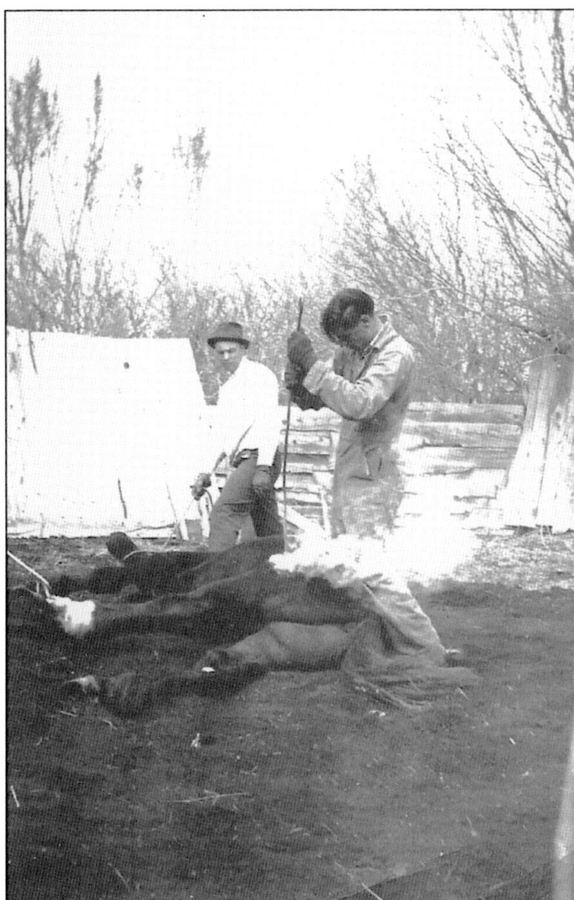

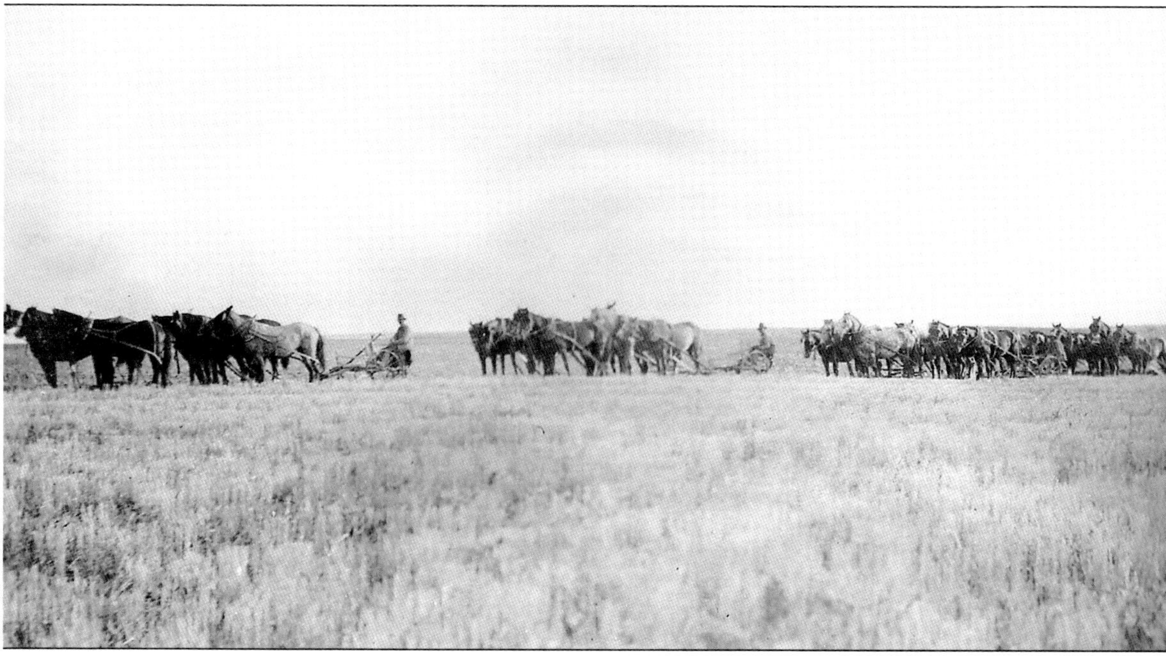

According to Dr. Samuel L. Beal, "The famous Rexburg bench lands were devoted entirely to grazing purposes until the turn of the century when dry farming was introduced. The first dry farm wheat was raised at Herbert on the Rexburg Bench by Albert Luthy in 1898. He hauled his small crop to Henry Flamm's threshing machine which was operating near Sugar City. The yield was only thirteen bushels, and when Luthy asked what the toll would be, Flamm replied, 'Any man who would raise a crop on the bench, and haul it thirty miles to a thresher, must need the grain. I won't charge you a cent.' Luthy's subsequent efforts attracted attention, and others began dry farming, with rather different results. In 1905 James W. Webster and Charles H. Woodmansee, Inc., began operations on a big scale. They introduced modern machinery and scientific technique, which placed dry farming upon a permanent basis." The image shows Fred Parkinson Sr. cutting wheat with horse-drawn mowers in preparation for bundling and threshing the wheat on the Rexburg bench. (Courtesy of Ross Parkinson Jr.)

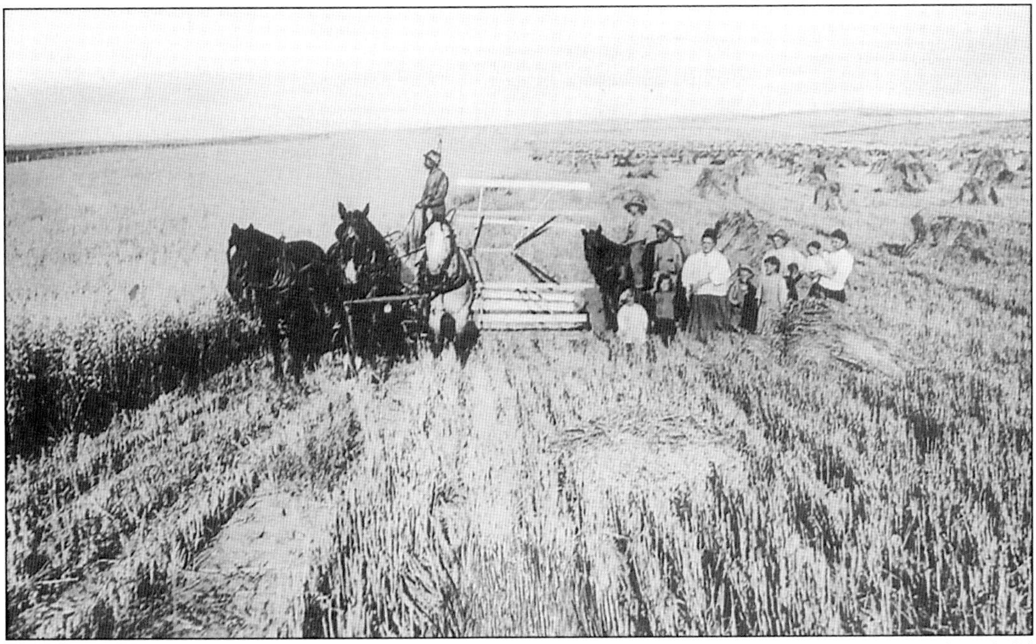

Nicholas Newby's dry farm on the Rexburg bench in this 1900s photograph shows a standing field of wheat that has been cut with a horse-drawn mower. After cutting, a horse-drawn threshing machine lifts the wheat onto a conveyer belt and bundles it. Men then tie the bundles with twine, and the bundles are put on a wagon with a bundling fork and taken to the mill. (Courtesy of Dean Rasmussen.)

On August 3, 1884, Thomas E. Ricks said Rexburg was in need of a flour mill because there was too much wheat grown that year. Four months later, the mill was built, but it burned down in 1889. This photograph is of the second mill, built in 1890 along the Millhollow Road, which blew up in 1915 from an accumulation of combustible barley dust.

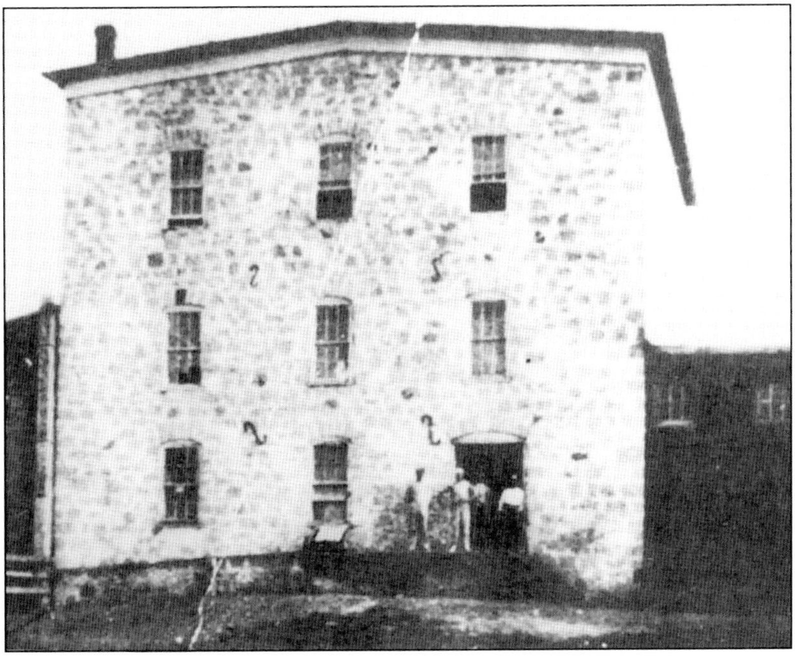

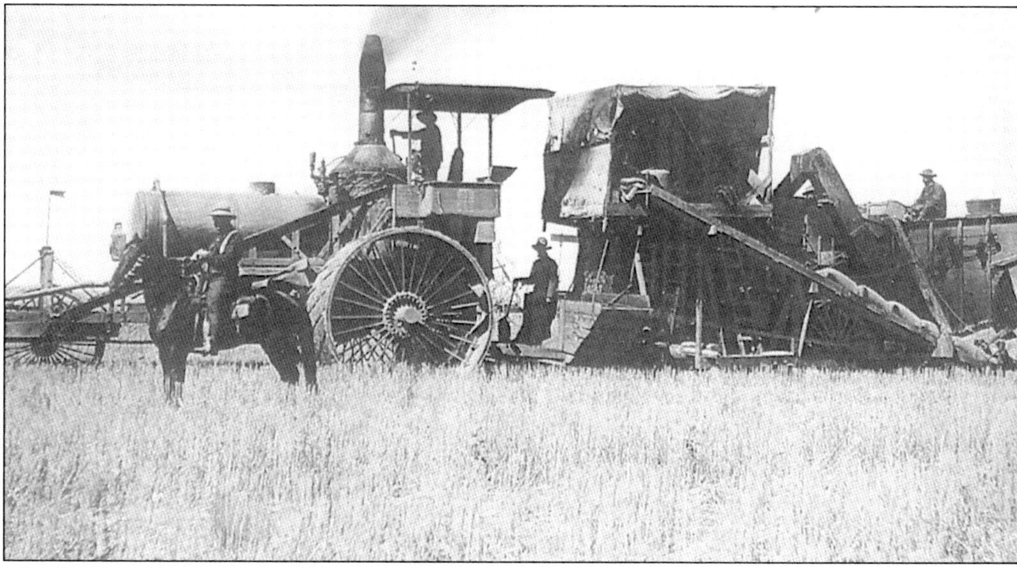

Charles Woodmansee and James W. Webster Sr. were partners in a large dry farm operation. This picture was taken during the grain harvest on their farm. Woodmansee, Webster, and Joseph Jeppesen were the first dry farmers who pioneered the use of steam engine tractors over horse-drawn equipment. These engines were fueled by stoking coal and wood into a furnace that would reach a certain degree and produce steam that made the tractor move. In 1910, Woodmansee was operating this huge steam engine, pulling a combine like the one in the picture, when a spark from the engine ignited the grain field on fire. Woodmansee was surrounded by fire and smoke, and the flames caught the wooden cab of his tractor on fire. He was burned and died five days later. (Above, courtesy of Dean Rasmussen.)

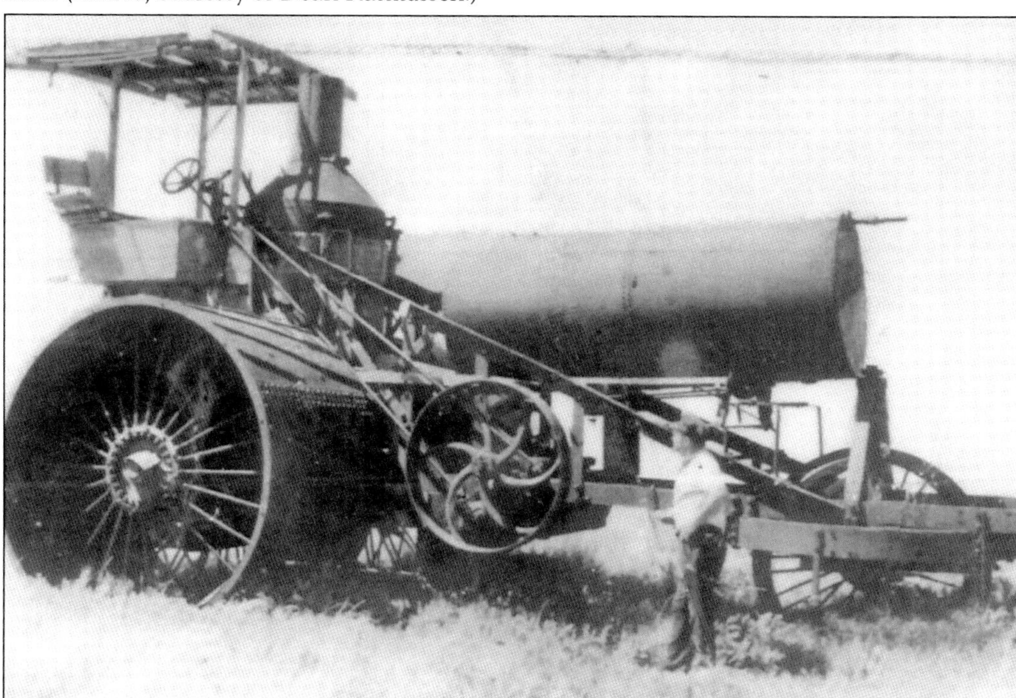

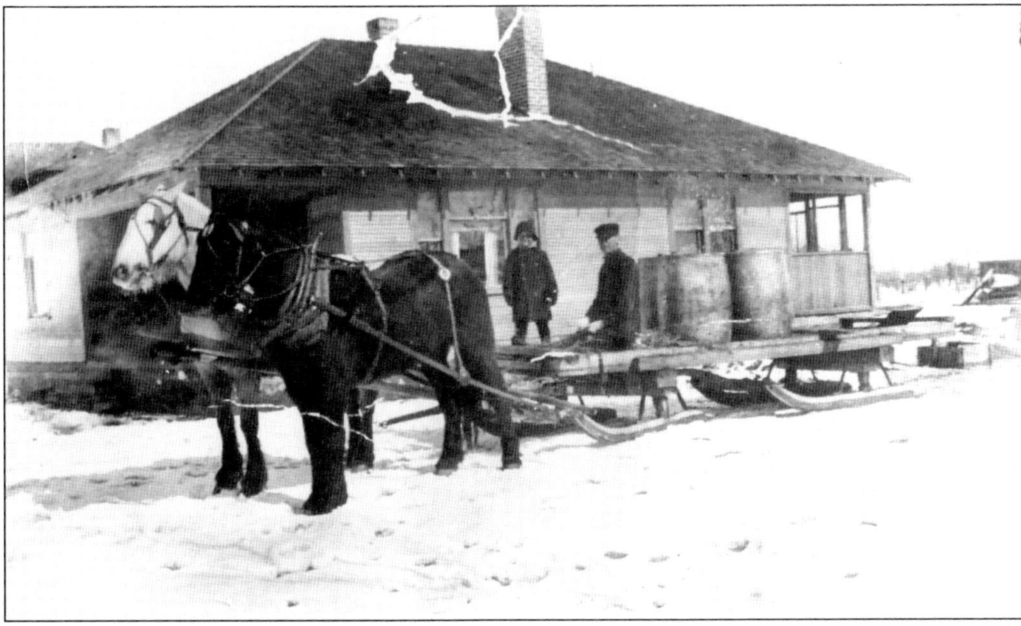

In this February 1918 photograph is Henry Greer Parkinson with his eight-year-old son John D. on his flatbed sleigh loaded with four 55-gallon barrels of oil. Henry was the co-owner of Parkinson Brothers Conoco Oil Company in Rexburg. These oil companies would deliver oil and gas to the fields of the farmers, and the practice continues to this day.

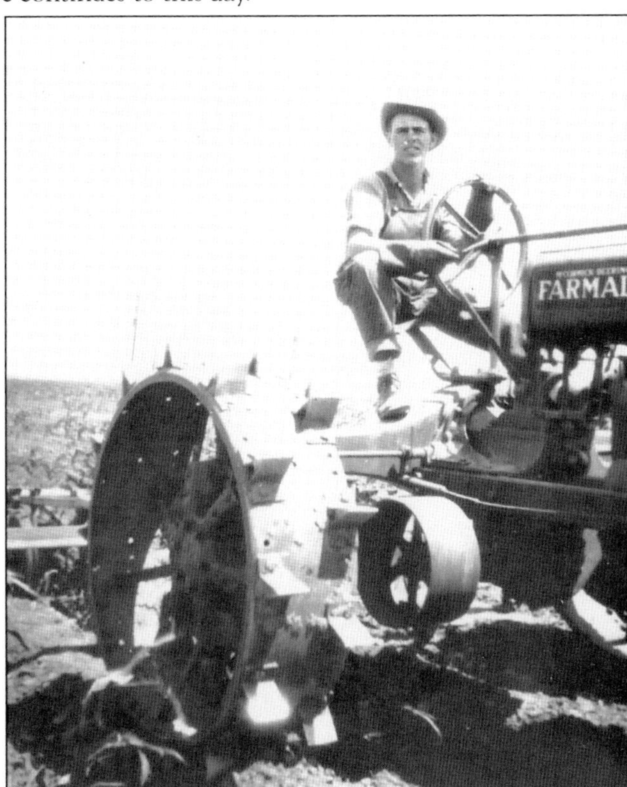

Sixteen-year-old John D. Parkinson is pictured driving a McCormick-Deering Farmall tractor. This tractor was the first gas tractor coming after the steam engine tractor, and it was a forerunner to the present-day Caterpillar diesel-powered crawler tractors. This was the first tractor made by McCormick-Deering, and the serial number was 01. The Parkinson family worked for International McCormick-Deering Manufacturing.

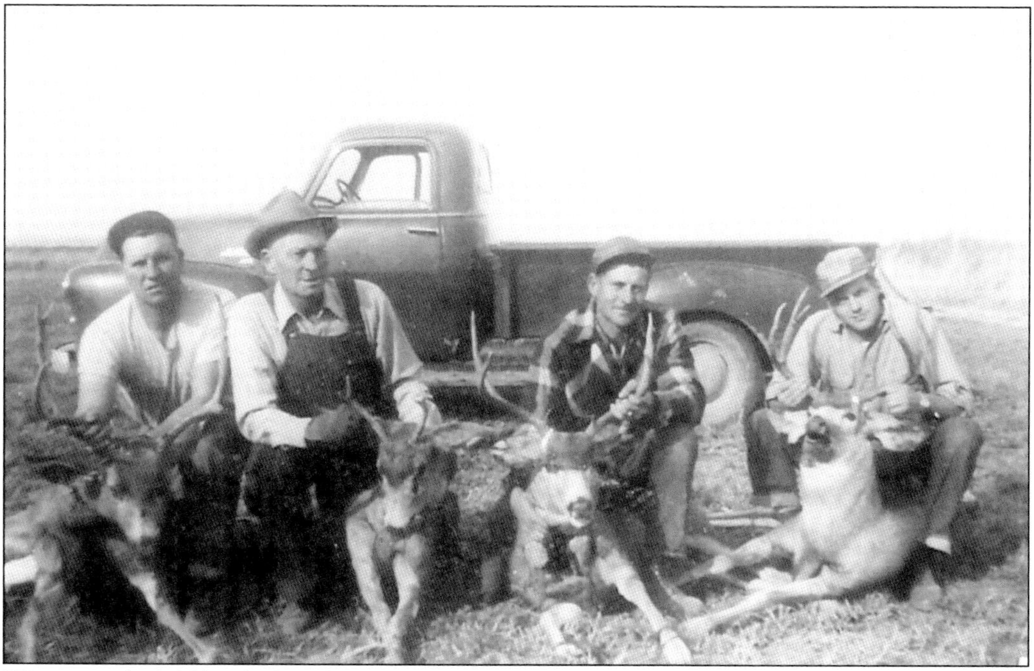

Water was the lifeblood of Rexburg, and canals crisscrossed the county to bring water to the land. Harvey Summers was born and raised in Rexburg, and he and his sons were the first dry farmers on the Rexburg bench to drill an irrigation well and the first to plant potatoes. Their pioneering ingenuity changed the path of agriculture in Eastern Idaho. Pictured above in front of their truck from left to right are Frank, Harvey, Roy, and Bert Summers. The photograph below shows three generations of the George Wyatt Wood family, who were pioneers in dry farming and, later, irrigated potato farming. Pictured from left to right are Bill Wood, Joe Brown, George Brown, Seth Wood, Ken Wood, Jack Randall, Harley Wood, Owen Wood (on tractor), and Ray Pisen Wood (on top of the cab). (Above, courtesy of Gary Summers; below, courtesy of Jamie Wood.)

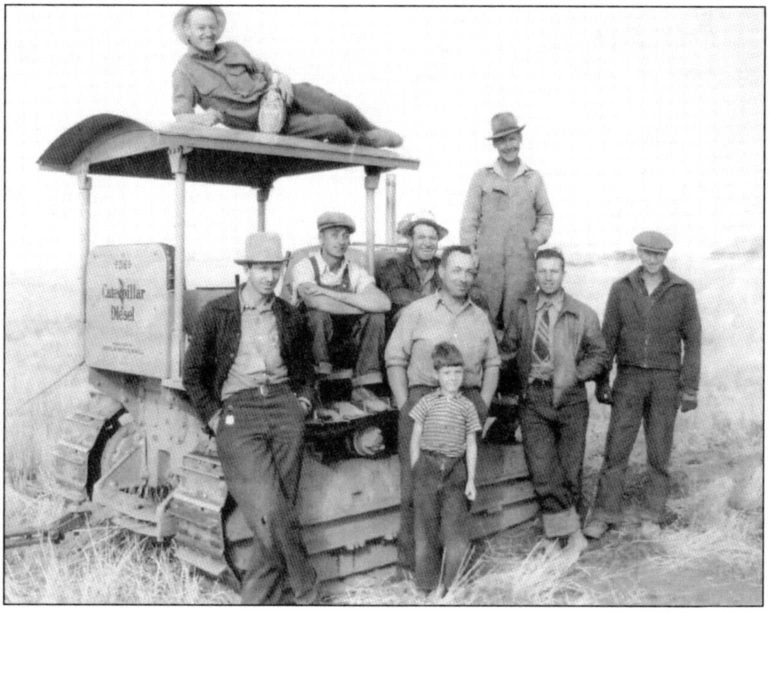

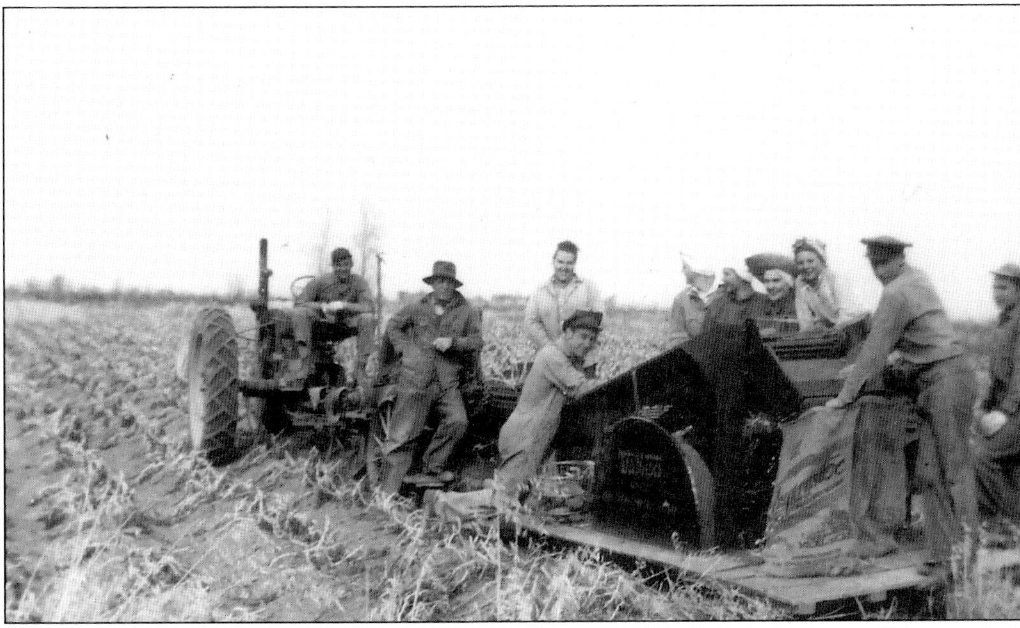

This scene shows men and women during a potato harvest at the Archibald farm in Salem in 1942. Harvesting potatoes was a time-consuming process using machinery and people. The potatoes were dug up, put into bags, driven to the potato cellars, sorted, and stored in preparation to be sold. (Courtesy of Gary Archibald.)

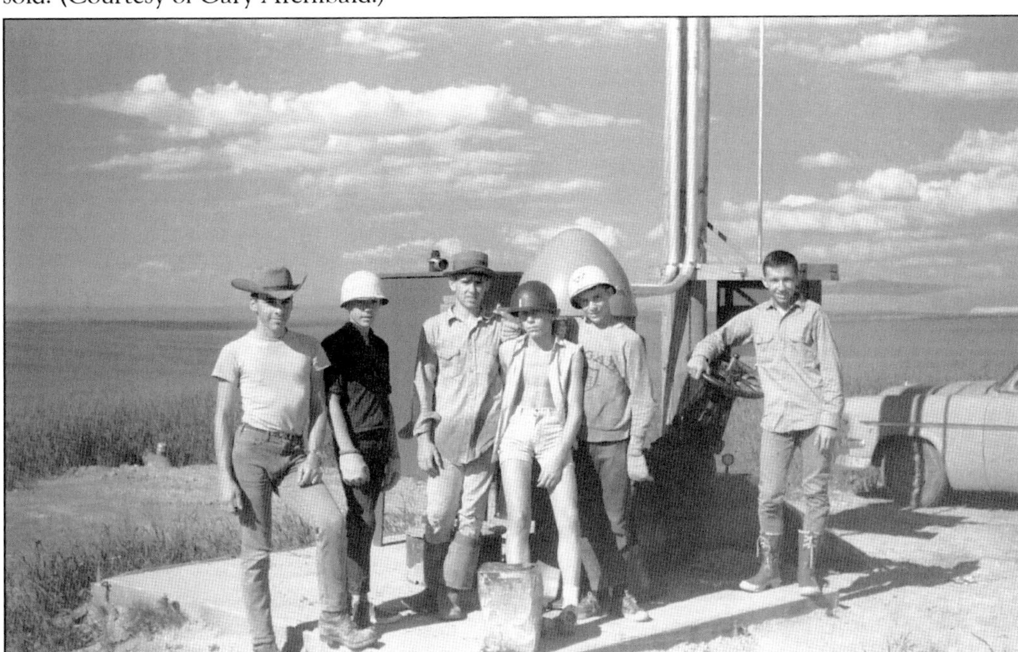

Pipe movers were an important part of the irrigation of crops on the farms. They moved the large metal pipes that brought the water from the wells to the fields. In this 1964 photograph are, from left to right, Bill Cunningham, Jerry Virgin, Glen Cooper, Shane Davis, Jeff Zollinger, and foreman Allan Morton. (Courtesy of Allan Morton.)

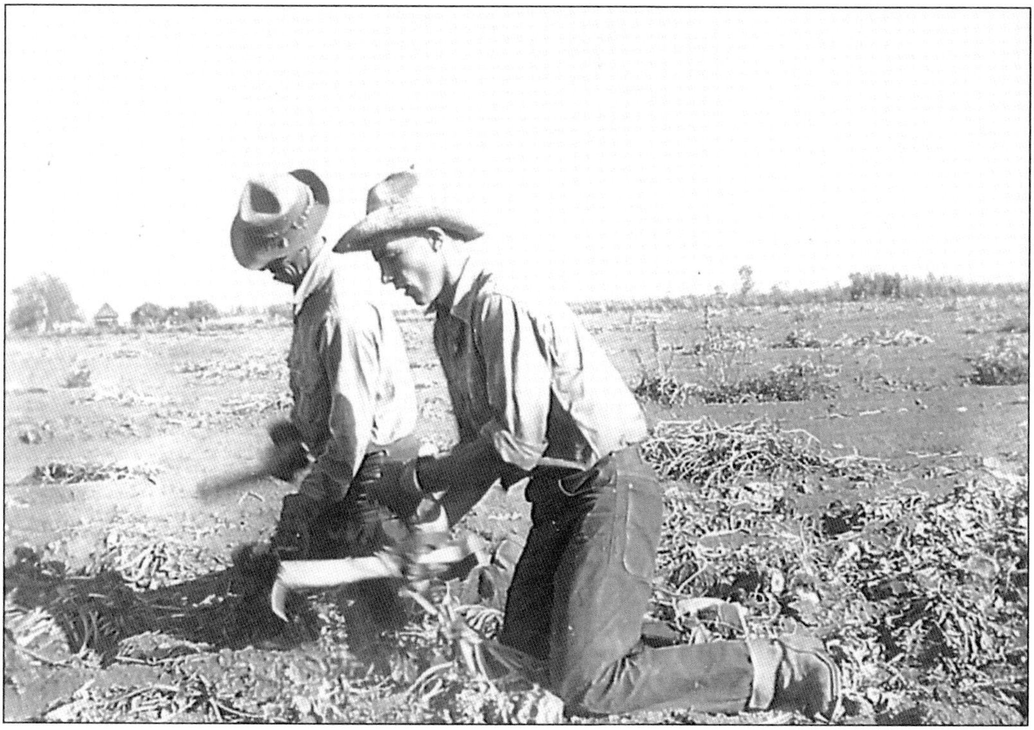

Wendell Oakley (left) and Clair Blaser top beets on the Blaser farm in Plano. Sugar beets were a major farm commodity in the Rexburg agriculture area. (Courtesy of Mildred Blaser Brown.)

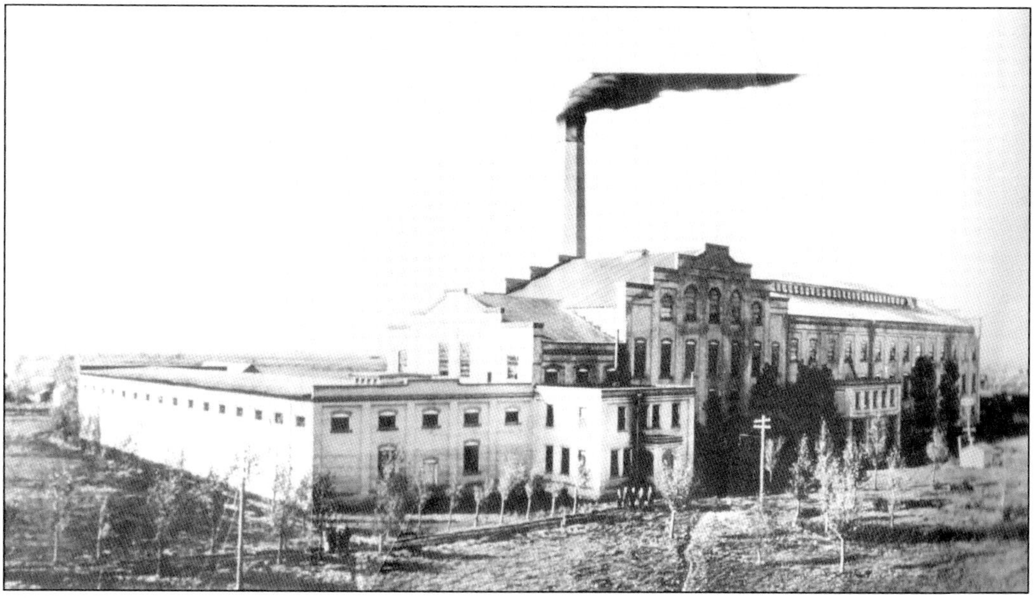

The Fremont Sugar Factory was owned and operated by the Mormon Church. Farmers throughout the valley raised sugar beets and contracted them to the factory. The beets were hauled by wagon to this building for processing. During World War II, portions of the building were used as a German prisoner of war camp, and the prisoners were indentured to the local farmers. (Courtesy of Dean Rasmussen.)

Six

PEOPLE

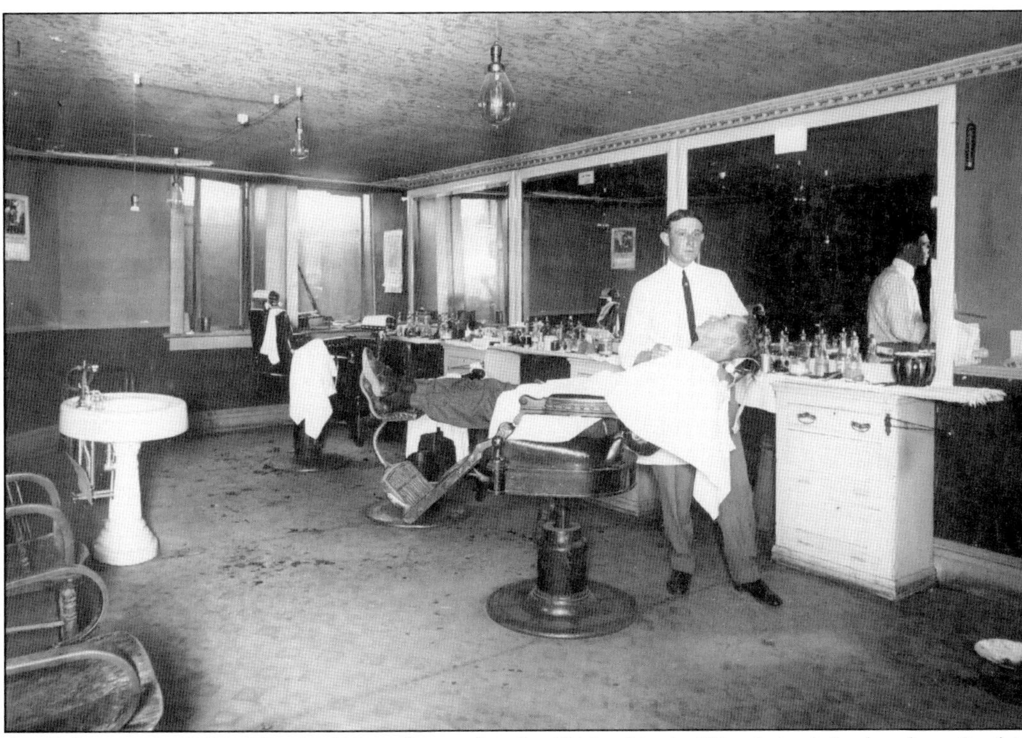

On February 8, 1908, Charles Edward was shot by Eli Larkin in Woodvine's barbershop. Larkin was arrested after he was found hiding in a haystack at the Darby Ranch. He was found innocent by a jury and set free. The defense used was that Larkin had done the community a service by killing Edward, who was a saloon owner of "vicious character." (Courtesy of Dwight Davidson.)

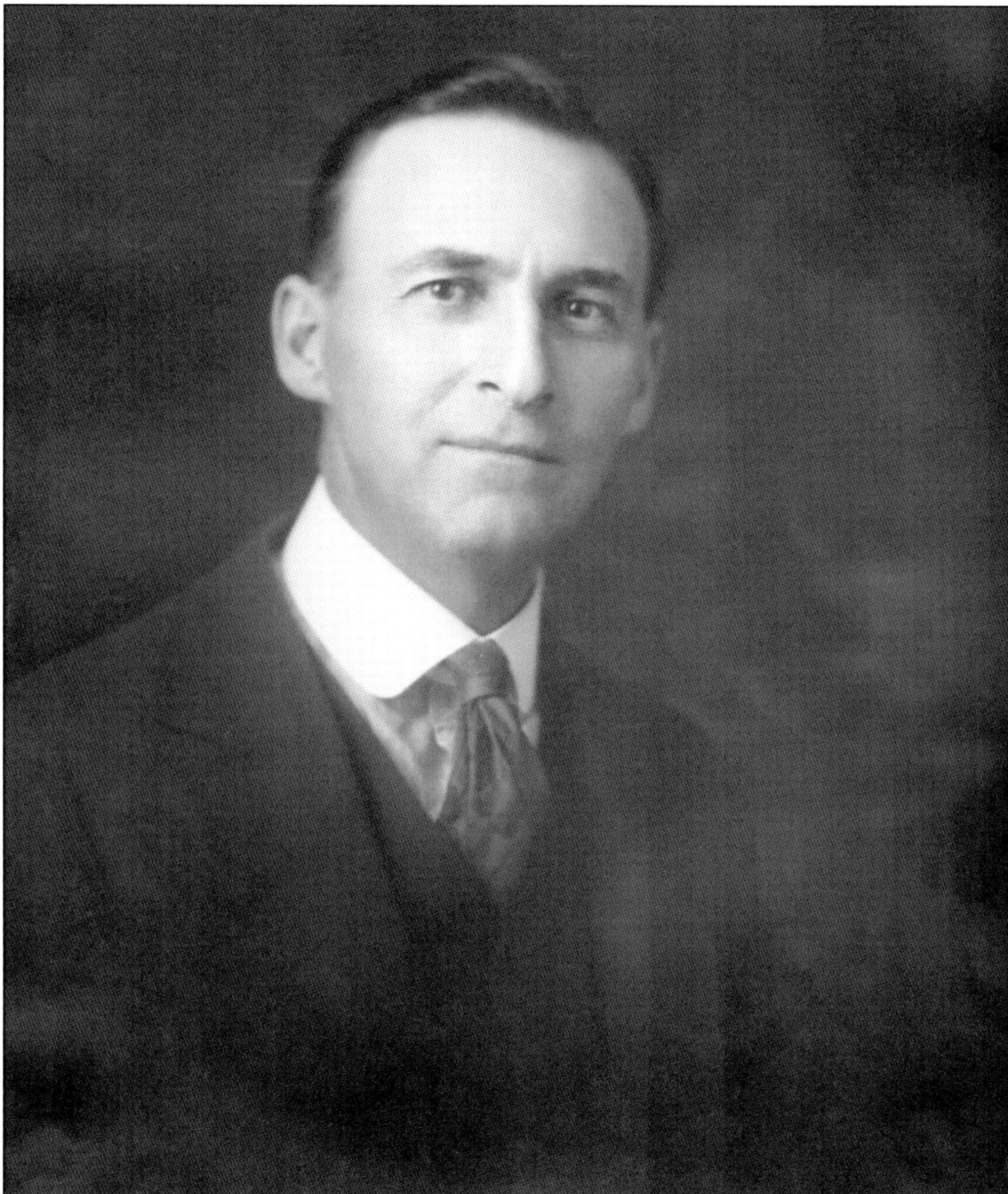

Arthur Porter was born in Auckland, New Zealand, on April 20, 1876. He was called "Artie" by his family. Porter was not quite 10 years old when he came to America on July 16, 1885. In 1902, he accepted a position as a teacher at Ricks Academy in Rexburg, Idaho. He married Nelle Child, a successful voice and piano instructor, on June 24, 1908. Porter was a religious leader serving in many capacities of the Mormon Church. He was a visionary in the development of Rexburg and a champion for the creation of Madison County. Porter was a man of immense integrity and honesty and was a respected citizen of Rexburg. He served as mayor, a city park was named in his honor, and he was a Democratic state representative for Madison County. He owned and operated the *Current-Journal* newspaper, which evolved into the *Rexburg Journal*. He later purchased the *Standard*, which became the *Rexburg Standard Journal*. He owned and operated Porter's Book Store. (Courtesy of Terrell and Margaret Porter Arnold.)

Chief Tendoy, a Native American of the Lemhi Shoshone tribe, looks regal in his native dress in this 1903 photograph. He was visiting his friend Dr. A.W. Nichols, a Rexburg veterinarian. (Courtesy of Dr. Parley Nelson.)

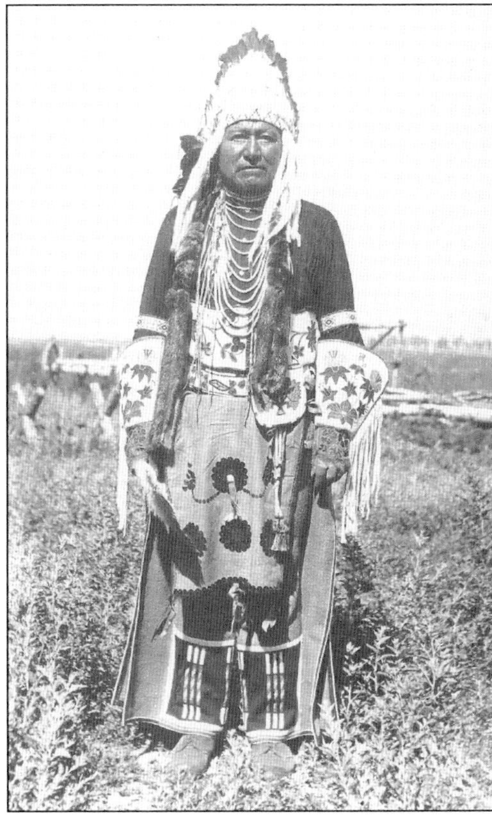

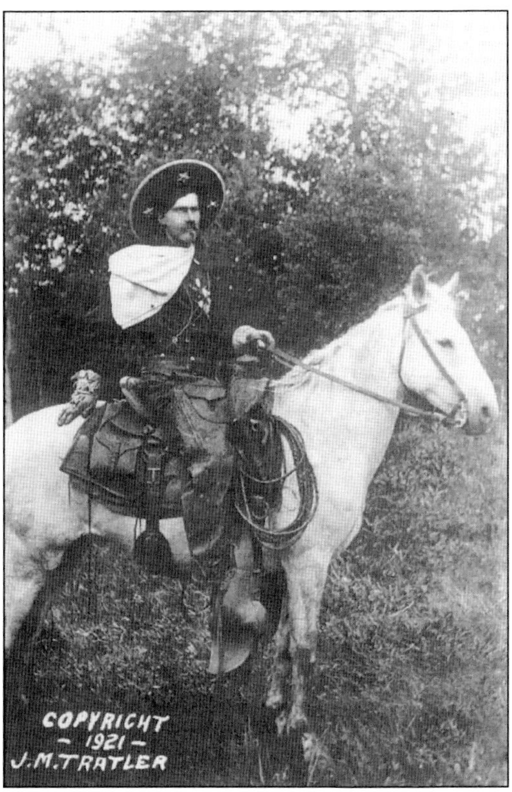

This 1890s cowboy, trick rider, rodeo entertainer, Indian scout, and guide, Richard "Rocky Mountain Dick" Rock, was the second white man to live in Island Park. He performed at rodeos and parades and owned a large ranch on the Idaho-Montana state border where he raised exotic animals. Sadly, in 1902, he was gored by his pet buffalo and died shortly afterwards. (Courtesy of the Library of Congress.)

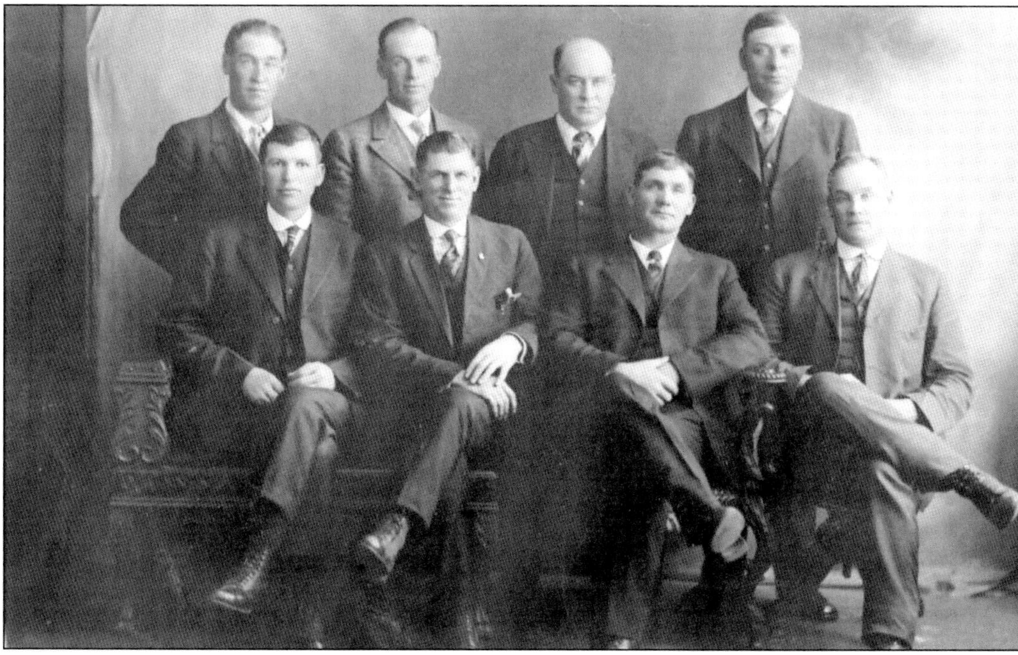

In 1918, these Rexburg businessmen were enticed to buy land in Southern California, but they felt the land was nothing they wanted to invest in. Years later, it became the exclusive area of Beverly Hills. It was a missed opportunity. From left to right are (first row) unidentified, John Greer Parkinson, William Fogg, and John Wood; (second row) Henry Wood, George Wood, James Winmill, and Edmond Parkinson.

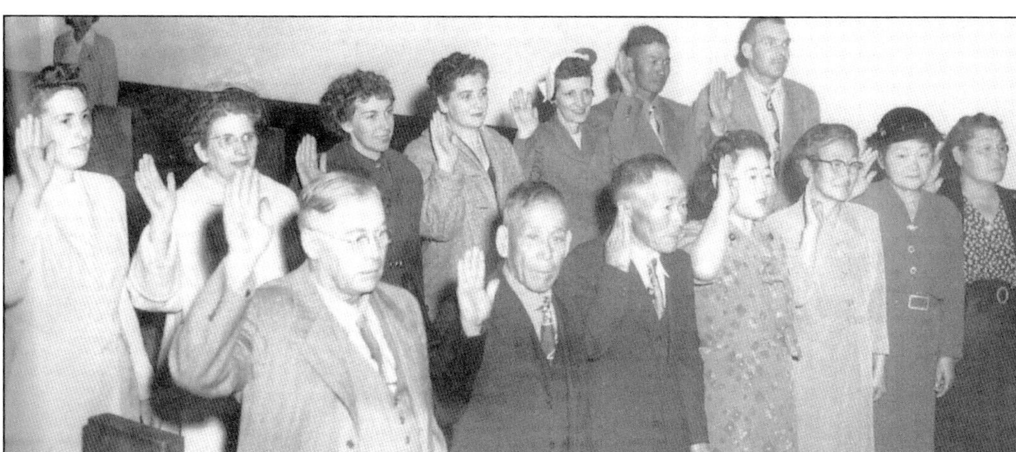

These Rexburg residents met in 1956 at the Madison County Courthouse to take the oath of citizenship to become legalized Americans. From left to right are (first row) unidentified, Mr. Hikida, Kisaburo Sakota, unidentified, Wasuyo Yamasaki, Mrs. Kura Sakota, and Mrs. Fuku Abe; (second row) four unidentified people, Irene Hochstein, Mataki Fujimoto, and George Lewis. (Courtesy of Spence and Dwight Hochstein.)

Morris and Jo Madsen pose with young nephew Howard Ericson. Morris was always in demand because of his quality of work in building houses, remodeling homes, and constructing aluminum windows. Jo was a nurse for Dr. Harlo Rigby in his hospital and then in his office for over 27 years. (Courtesy of Morris Madsen.)

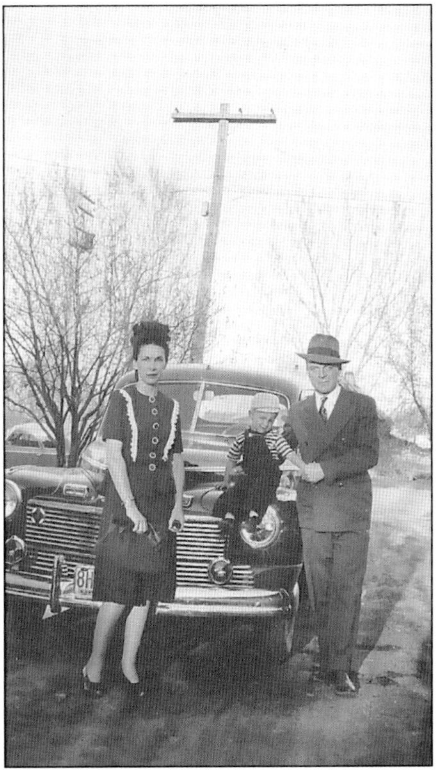

Rexburg physician Dr. Murland F. Rigby (left) and Rexburg businessman and owner of Porter's Book Store Warren Childs Porter debate each other at a Rexburg Kiwanis Club event. (Courtesy of Terrell and Margaret Porter Arnold.)

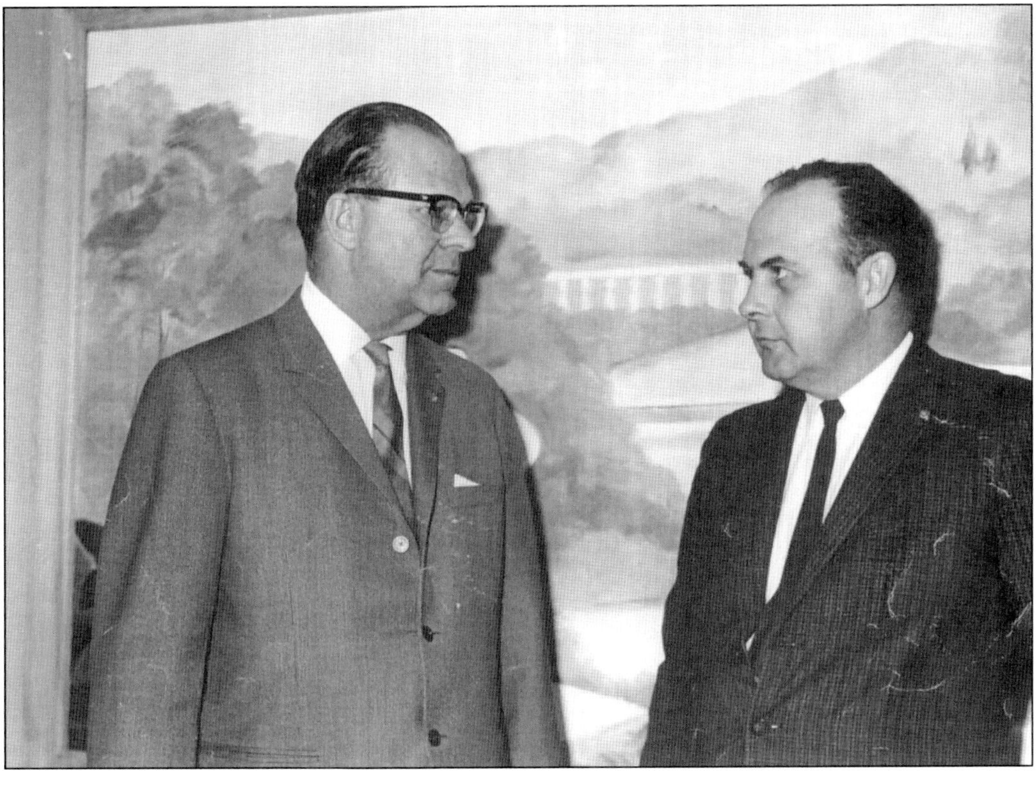

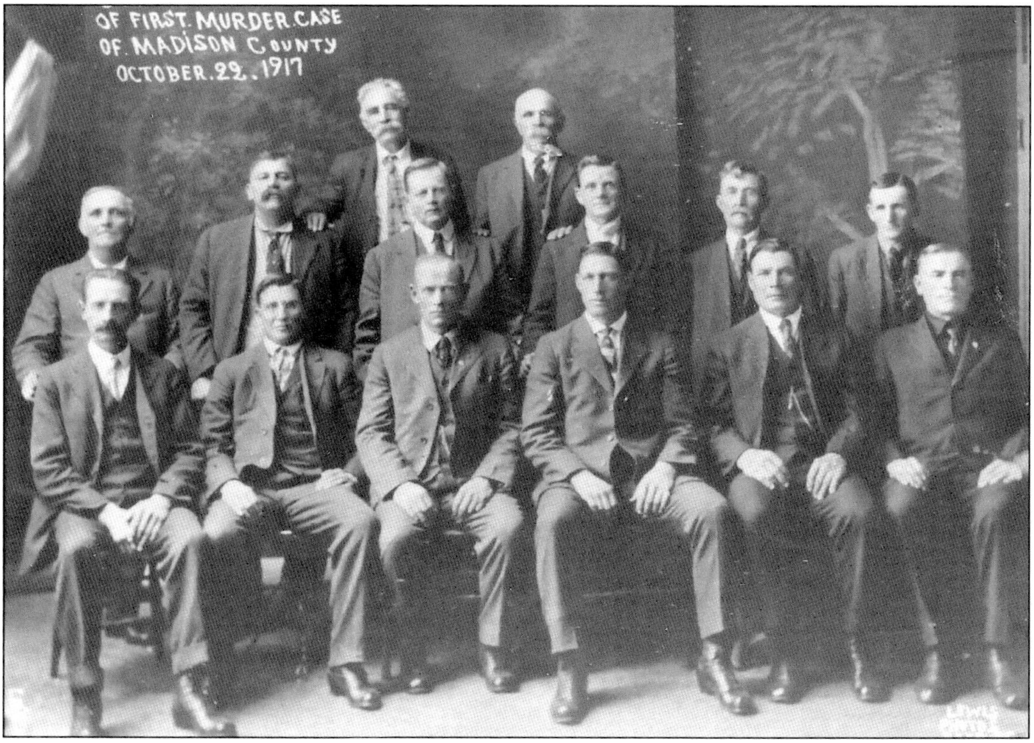

Rexburg's first murder trial was held on October 29, 1917. Pictured from left to right are (first row) jurors Schuyler Clay, Lyman Garner, Frank Spaulding, Joseph Peterson, James Hendricks, and Albert Luthy; (second row) bailiff Martin Nave and jurors George Gunnell, Nephi Johnson, Alfred Young, Christian Fransen, and Albert Zollinger; (third row) foreman Thomas White and bailiff Roman Siepert. The judge presiding over this case was Judge Gunn.

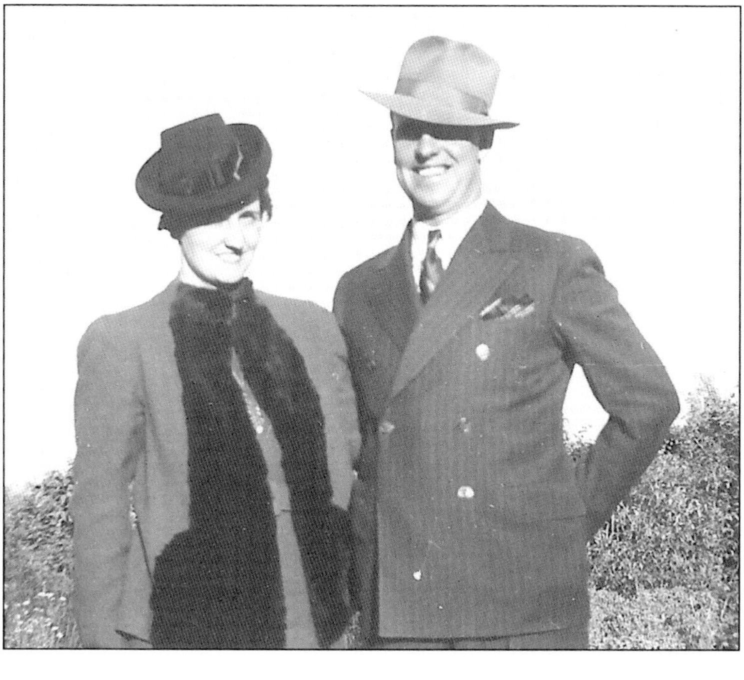

This is a 1938 photograph of Verla J. and John D. Parkinson. Verla came to Rexburg in March 1911 and lived to be 101. She obtained her teaching certificate and later worked as a product training coordinator for Mountain States Telephone. John was born at Moody in 1910. He was a fifth-generation Rexburgite. He owned and operated a 2,200-acre dry farm and served two terms as county commissioner.

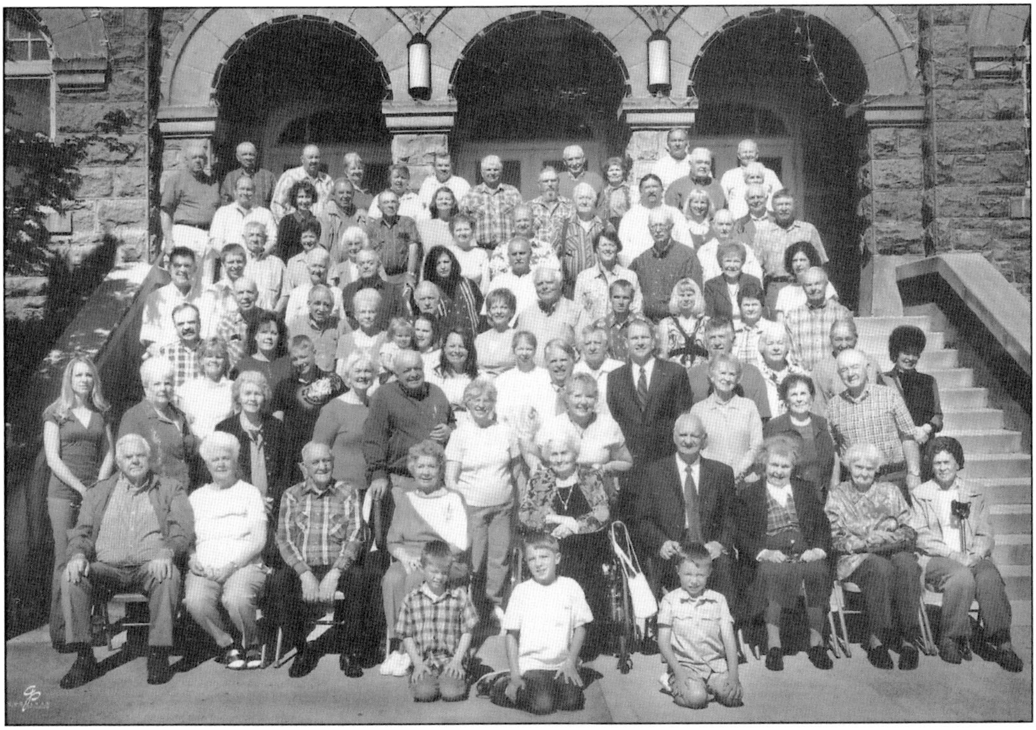

This Parkinson pioneer heritage portrait shows descendants of the first pioneers to migrate to Rexburg between 1883 and 1913. This picture was taken on the steps of the 1911 Fremont Stake Tabernacle on June 14, 2008. (Courtesy of Travis Gugelman studio.)

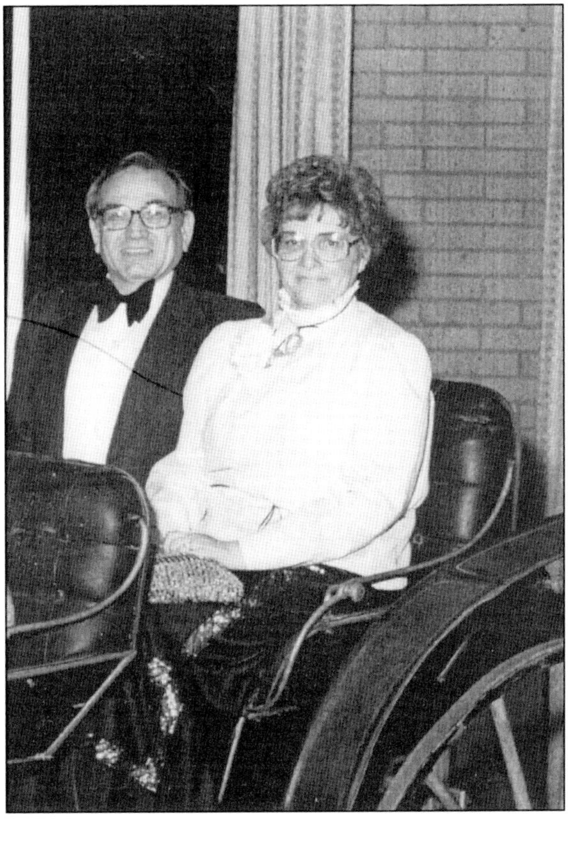

Terrell and Margaret Porter Arnold sit in a buggy at the Rexburg Centennial Ball on March 10, 1983. Terrell and Margaret, Cleo Johnson, Louis Clements, and Lowell Parkinson are considered the resident historians of Rexburg, Idaho. (Courtesy of Terrell and Margaret Porter Arnold.)

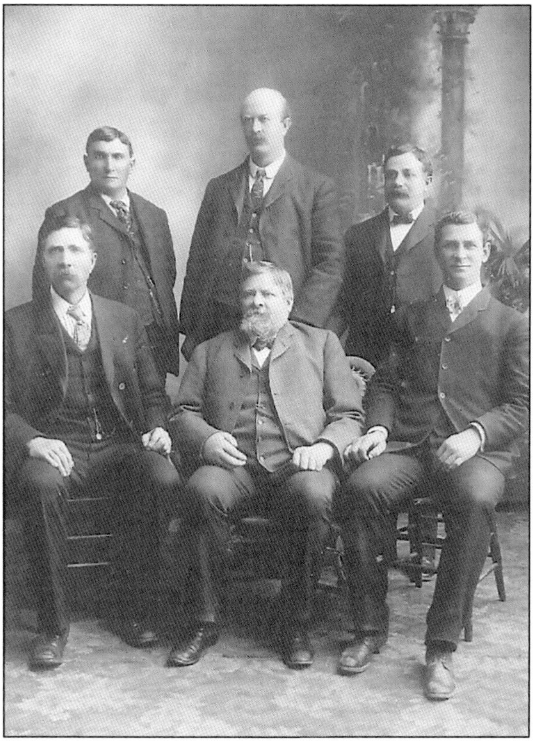

The Mormon Church divides its membership into stakes and wards according to the population of members. Pictured is the Rexburg First Ward Building Committee in 1900. They are, from left to right, (first row) Nathan Ricks, Thomas E. Ricks Jr., and Henry Flamm Jr.; (second row) John Jacobs, Eli McEntire, and James Webster Sr. (Courtesy of Upper Snake River Valley Historical Society.)

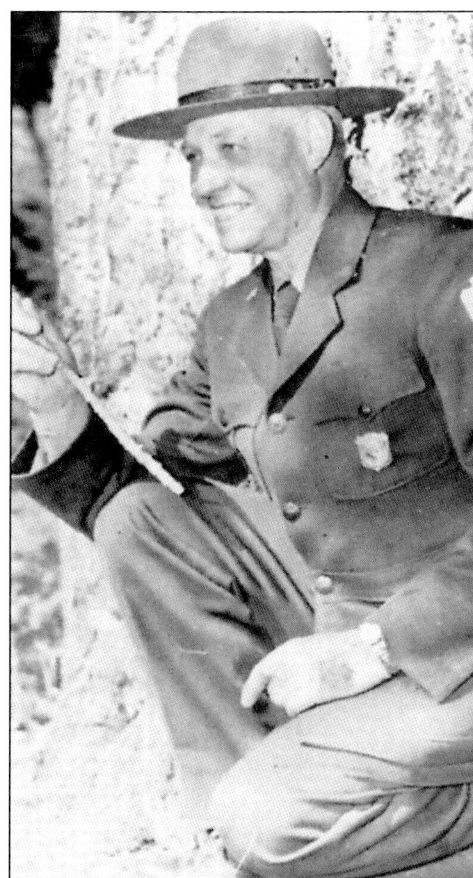

Samuel Merrill Beal came to Eastern Idaho in the early 1920s to teach history and math. He became interested in the local history of the fur traders and was instrumental in finding the exact location of Fort Henry. He interviewed the remaining first settlers that came to Rexburg with Thomas E. Ricks, personally interviewed the daughters of Beaver Dick, and acquired many rare photographs.

Seven

Politics

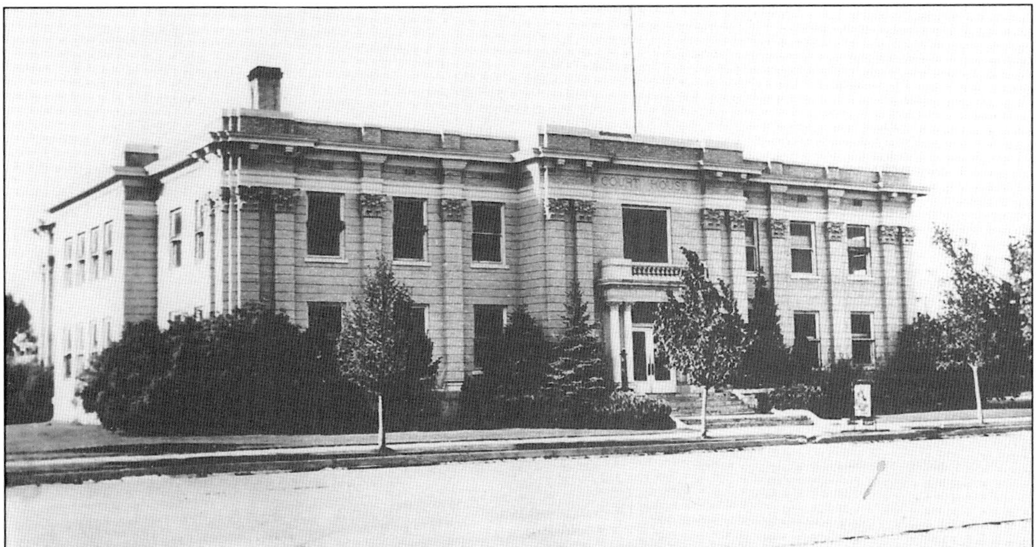

By the stoke of a pen on February 18, 1913, Idaho governor David Haines signed Bill No. 173, thus creating Madison as Idaho's 33rd county. In 1914, the new county needed a courthouse, and so it occupied the second floor of the Winter-Webster Building in Rexburg. In 1919, county commissioner chairman Royal Garn obtained grant money, and in the spring of 1920, this building became Madison County's courthouse.

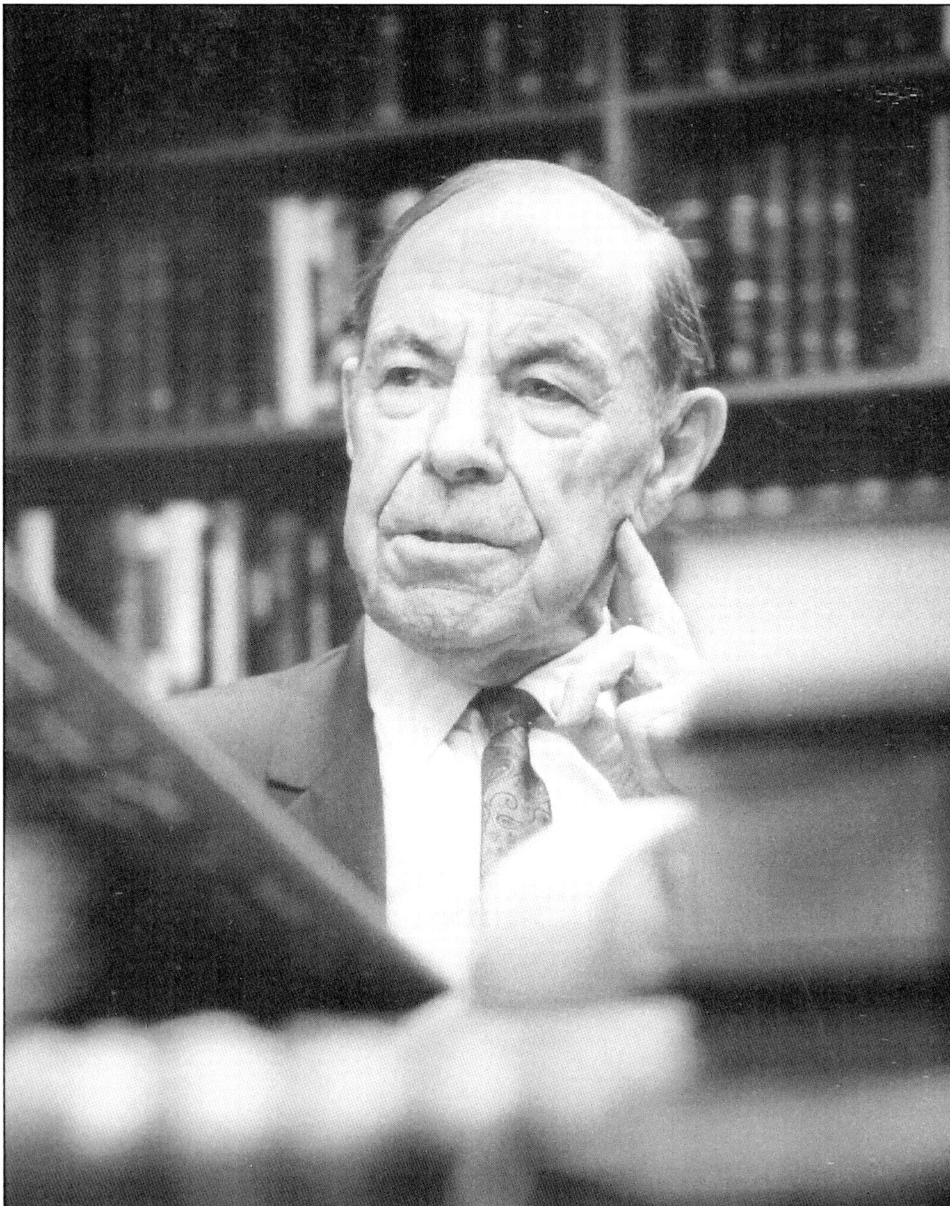

On February 18, 2013, the Madison County Centennial Committee honored William Lloyd Adams as the "founding father of Madison County." In 1909, he moved to Rexburg, married Belva Bird, and took over the operation of his father's *Rexburg Standard* newspaper. He later purchased that paper and operated it for 29 years. In 1933, without attending college, he took the Idaho State Bar Exam and passed it with a 98 percent score. He opened up a law office in 1935 and practiced until his death on August 16, 1969. He selected Mary Smith Oldham as his junior partner. Adams was responsible for writing Bill No. 173 and handing that bill to state representative Steve Hunt, who pushed the bill through the House, and it passed, establishing Madison County. Adams also served as state senator, cast the deciding vote granting women in Idaho the right to vote, established Ricks College as an accredited school, was known as "Mr. Republican" of Idaho, and was honored as number one in the *Idaho 100* book of Idaho's most influential people.

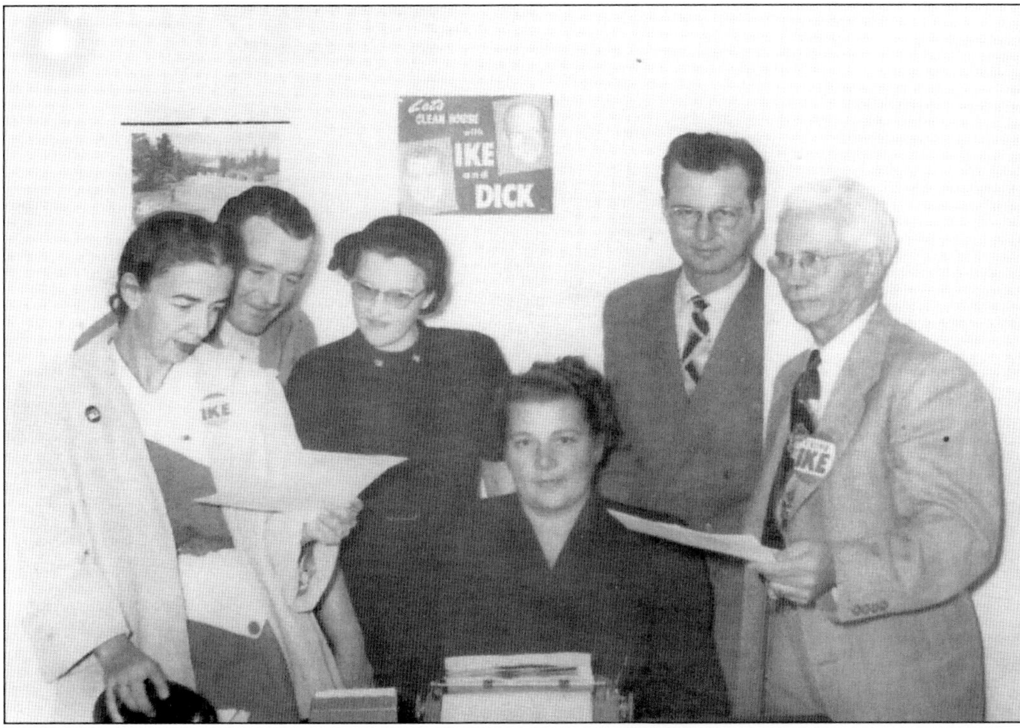

In this photograph, the Madison County Republican Election Committee counts ballots for the 1952 presidential election of Dwight D. Eisenhower. From left to right are Barbara Smith, Johnny Skelton, Jane Poole, Verla Chapman, Bill Kennedy, and Dr. Charles England. (Courtesy of Sherry Bean Thomas.)

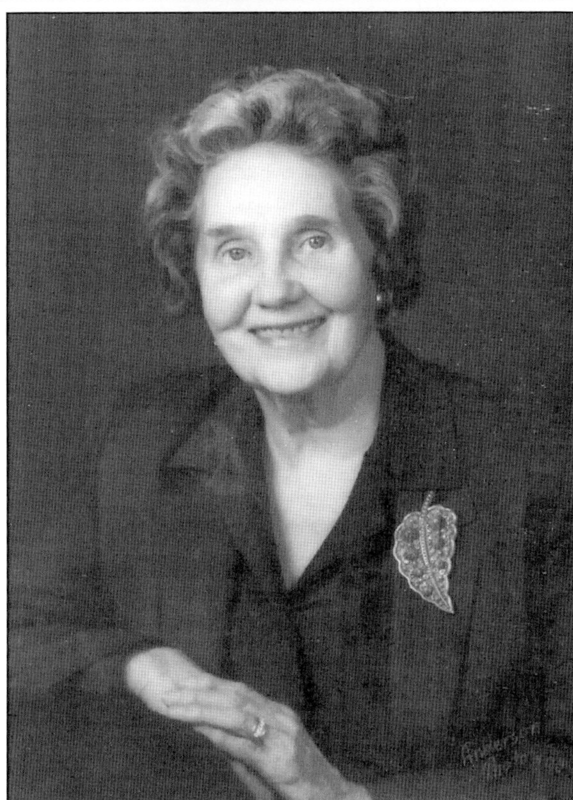

Mary Smith Oldham was Idaho's "first lady of the law." She graduated from the University of Idaho Law School at age 21 and, a month later, was standing before the Idaho State Supreme Court arguing a case. She was a popular political speaker and served as Rexburg's first woman justice of the peace as well as Rexburg and Sugar City's first woman city attorney. (Courtesy of Rhea Schroeder.)

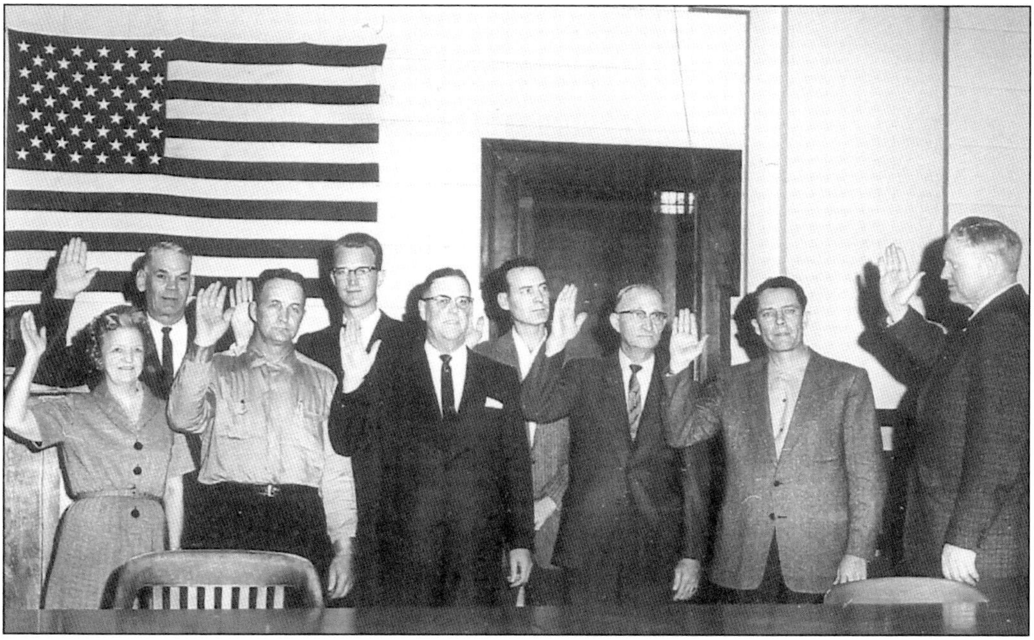

The elected officials of Madison County are being sworn in by Commissioner Ferrel Rock in 1964. Standing from left to right are Agnes Bird (treasurer), Marion Hacking (judge), Ray Pocock (county commissioner), Kent Jolley (county prosecuting attorney), John Parkinson (county commissioner), Edward Richardson (county coroner), Ben Summers (county assessor), and Ford Smith (sheriff). (Courtesy of Terrell and Margaret Porter Arnold.)

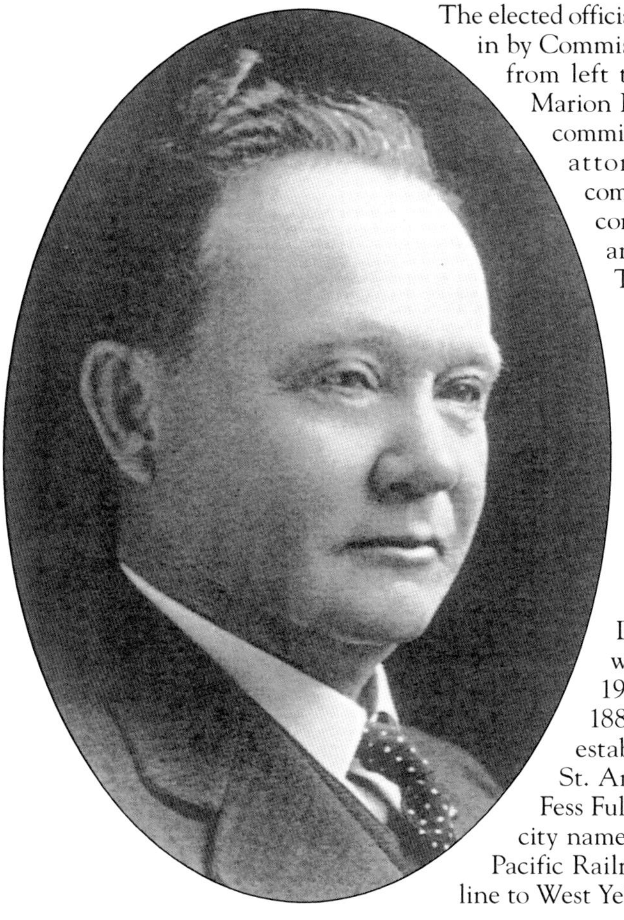

Democrat Charles Calvin Moore was the 13th governor of Idaho from 1922 to 1924. He moved to Idaho in 1889 and taught school in Hibbard. He established the Idaho Reform School in St. Anthony in 1903. In 1906, Moore and Fess Fuller purchased land and platted a new city named Ashton, which enabled the Union Pacific Railroad to create a depot and extend its line to West Yellowstone.

Urshel Henry Bigler, the third elected sheriff in 1932, had settled in Rexburg with his family in 1897. They purchased a large tract of land on the northwest edge of Rexburg, and in 1910, they sold that land to the City of Rexburg to be used as the Rexburg Fair Grounds. The family specialized in raising purebred sulky racehorses. Bigler's word was stronger than a written contract.

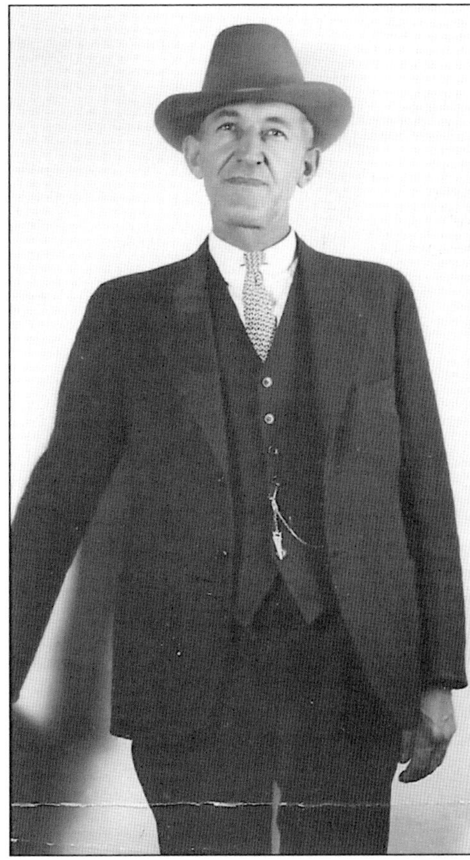

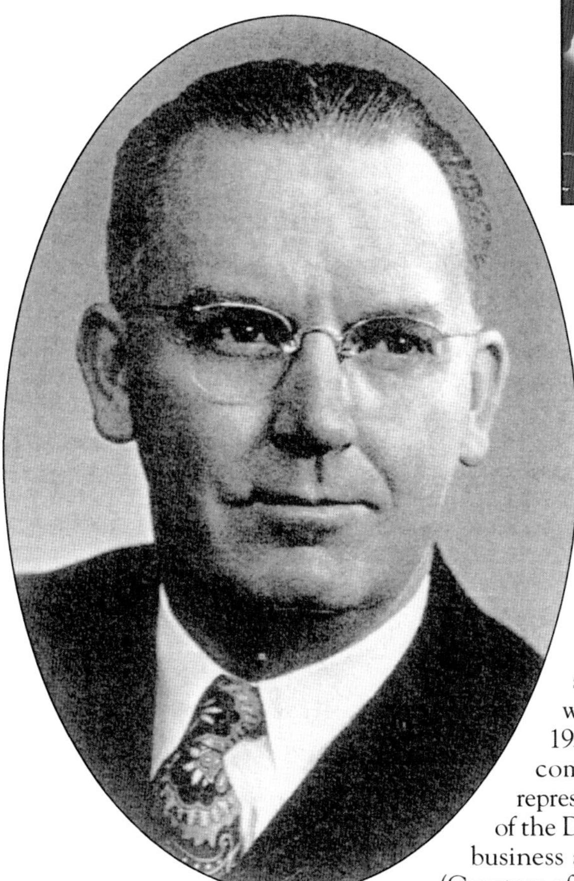

The first Mormon to hold the three highest elected positions in Idaho—secretary of state, lieutenant governor, and governor—was Arnold Williams. He began his career in 1932, serving two terms as Madison County commissioner, as a Madison County state representative in 1936, and as majority floor leader of the Democrats in 1941. He owned a dry-cleaning business and was Rexburg's horseshoe champion. (Courtesy of Norman Ricks.)

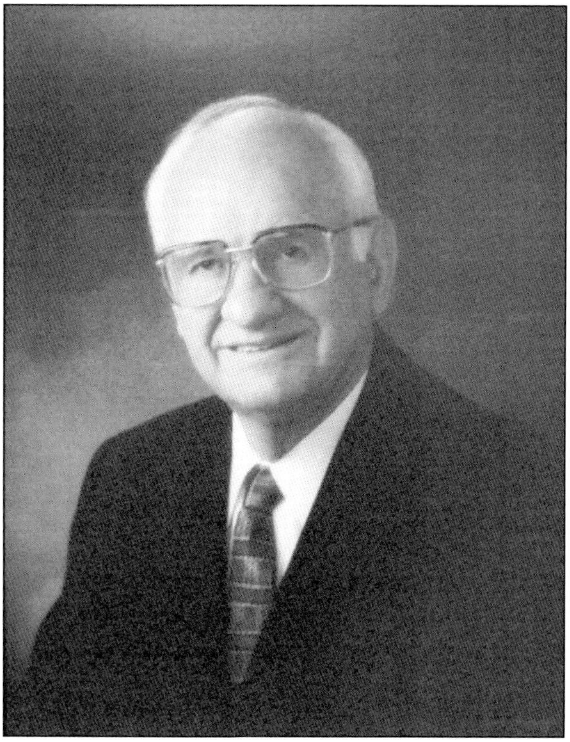

Rexburg-born Mark Ricks is a descendant of Rexburg's founder, Thomas E. Ricks. Mark, a prominent potato farmer, served as a state senator from Madison County in 1994. In 2006, he was appointed lieutenant governor of Idaho. He was the Mormon Church regional representative when the Teton Dam flood occurred in 1976. He was responsible for bringing immediate assistance to all flood victims. (Courtesy of Mark Ricks.)

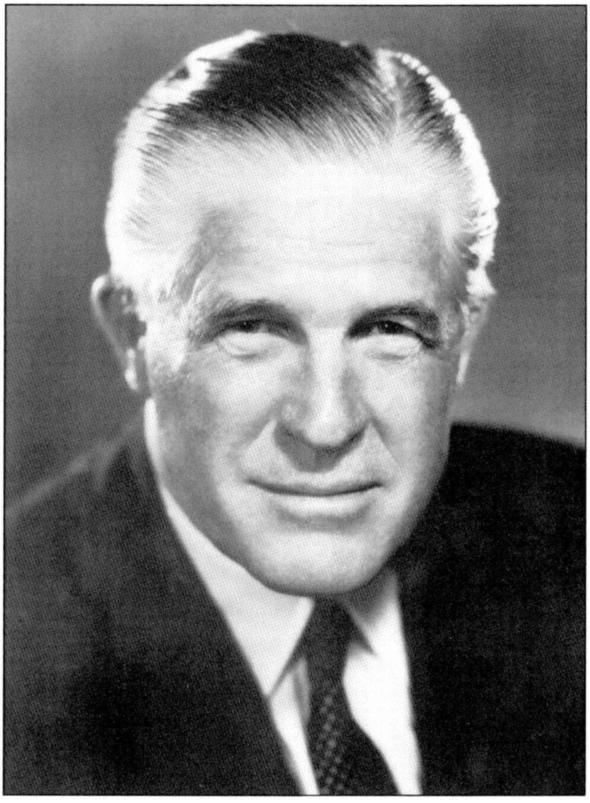

George Wicken Romney moved with his family from Colonia Juarez, Mexico, to Rexburg in 1917. His father was a building contractor and his uncle George was the president of the Ricks Normal School. He later on became chief executive officer of American Motors, was elected governor of Michigan, and in 1968, ran as a Republican presidential candidate. He served under Richard Nixon as secretary of the US Department of Housing and Urban Development.

This is a 1966 photograph of the ribbon cutting after the completion of the Twin Bridges farm-to-market road between Rexburg and Ririe. From left to right are Elmer Moss (Jefferson County commissioner), Lalovi Rigby (former Madison County commissioner), John Parkinson (Madison County commissioner), and Clifford Bright (Jefferson County commissioner). Parkinson, the inspiration behind the building of the bridge, lobbied to acquire grant money to build the Twin Bridges Sportsman Park.

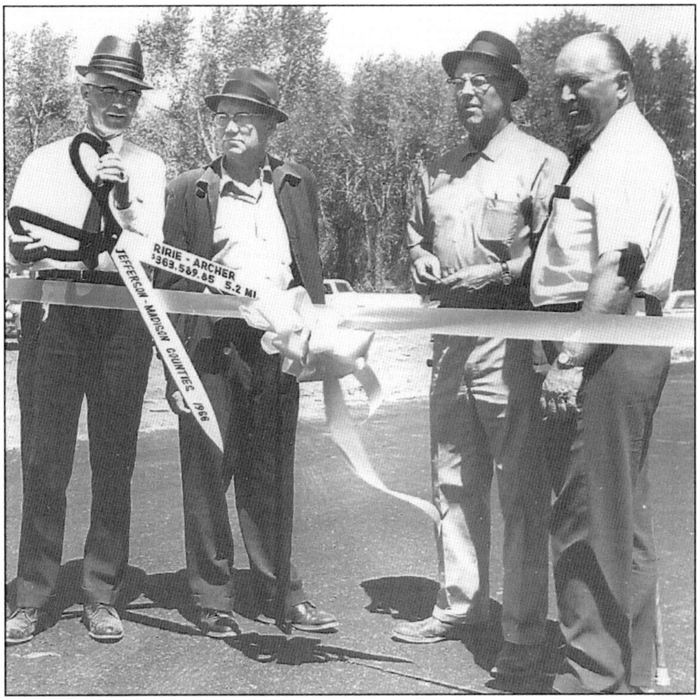

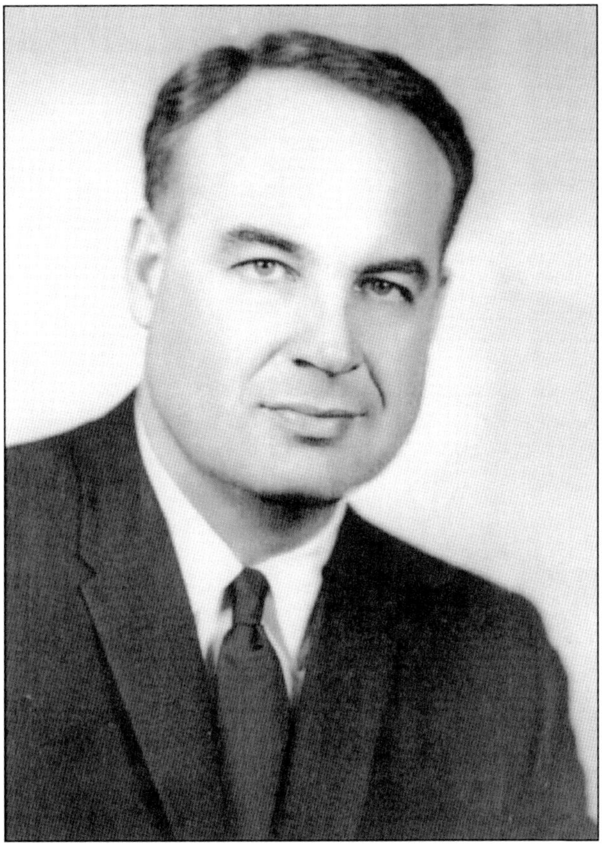

Sherman P. Lloyd was born in St. Anthony and grew up in Rexburg. He attended Washington and Adams Elementary Schools and graduated from Madison High School and Ricks Normal School. He moved to Utah, where he was elected as Republican state senator from Utah County and was later elected to six terms as a US congressman for Utah.

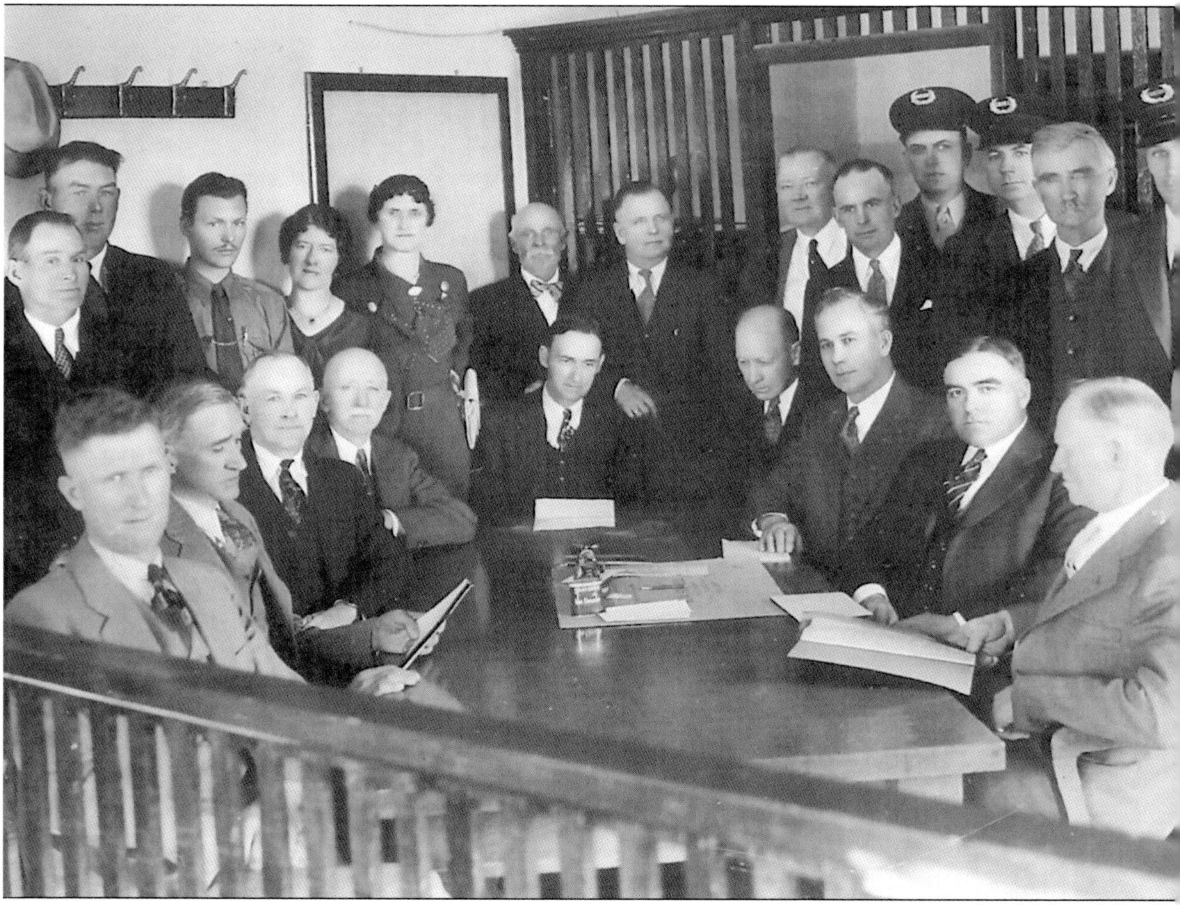

In 1903, the population of Rexburg had obtained a large enough citizenry that the area was allowed to graduate from a village to a city. Jacob Flamm was the mayor at that time. As the community grew, so did the positions that were needed on the city council to operate city business. This photograph is of the Rexburg City Council in 1932; from left to right are (first row) Lester Petersen, Fred Shirley, David Stowell, James Blake, Arthur Porter (mayor), Charlie Poole (city attorney), Frank Kelly, James W. Webster, and Hugh Wright; (second row) Rex Leatham, Roy Sutton, Raymond Z. Hill, Jesse Atkinson, Sarah Barnes, Elijah Cable, Tom Richman, Dr. Parley Nelson, Glenn Herdti, Raymond McEntire, John Clark, Joseph Jolly, and LeRoy "Bud" Armstrong. (Courtesy of the Upper Snake River Valley Historical Society.)

Eight

Religion

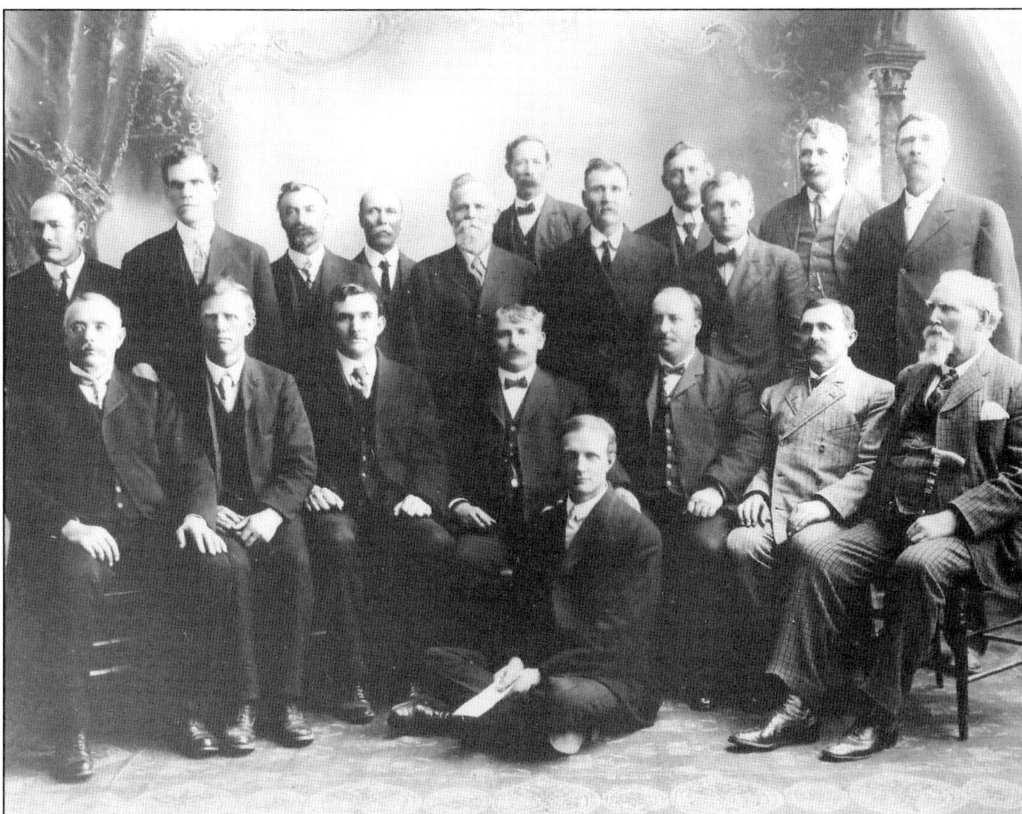

This photograph of the Rexburg Mormon Stake High Council was taken around 1900. They are, from left to right (seated on floor) William Gee; (first row) Pete Hanson, Charles Thomason, Mark Austin, Thomas Bassett, Albert Heath, Jacob Brenner, and David Osborn; (second row) Eugene Belnap, Ezra Dalby, Mr. Robison, William Cloward, unidentified, John Garner Sr., Jess Lloyd, unidentified, Victor Hegsted, Timothy Winter, and Nathan Ricks.

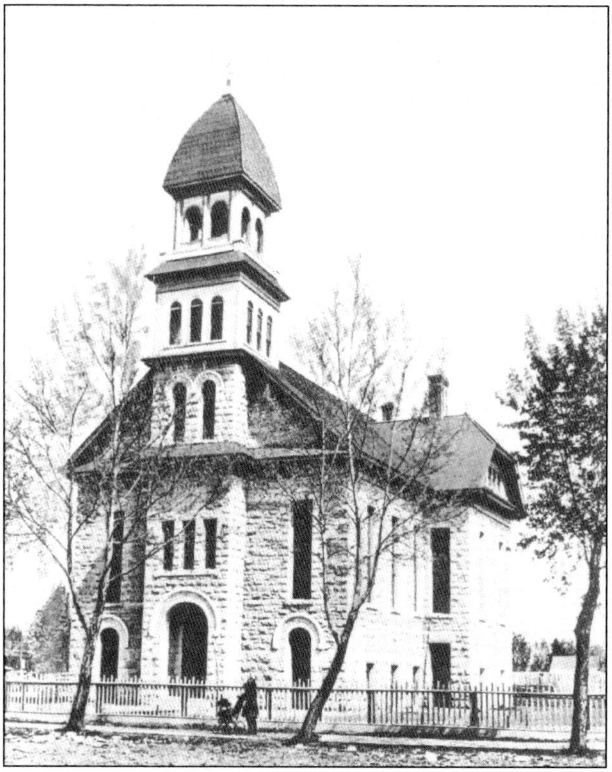

Rexburg First Ward was the oldest ward in the Snake River Valley. It was organized on April 1, 1884, with Thomas E. Ricks Jr. as bishop and John L. Roberts and Andrew S. Anderson serving as counselors. This building was used as a house of worship from 1907 until June 5, 1976, when it was destroyed by the raging waters of the Teton Dam flood. (Courtesy of Cleo Johnson.)

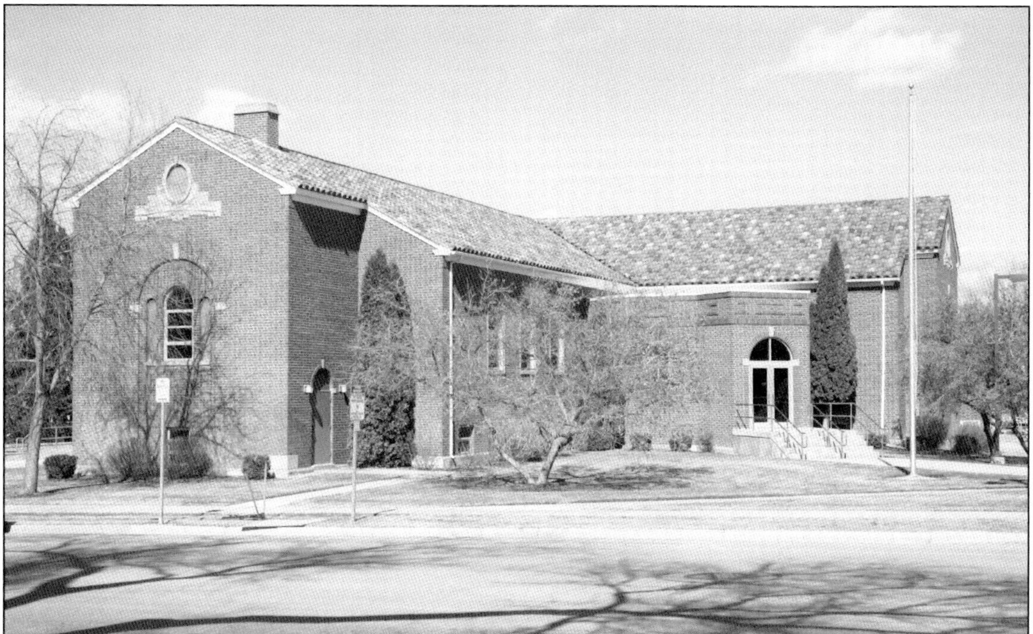

The Rexburg Fourth and Sixth Ward Mormon Chapel, built in 1930, is located on the corner of South First East and East First South in this 1935 photograph. This is the oldest chapel still in use in the Upper Snake River Valley. Henry Blunck served as the first bishop, with Fred Schwendiman and David Dole as counselors. (Courtesy of Allan Morton.)

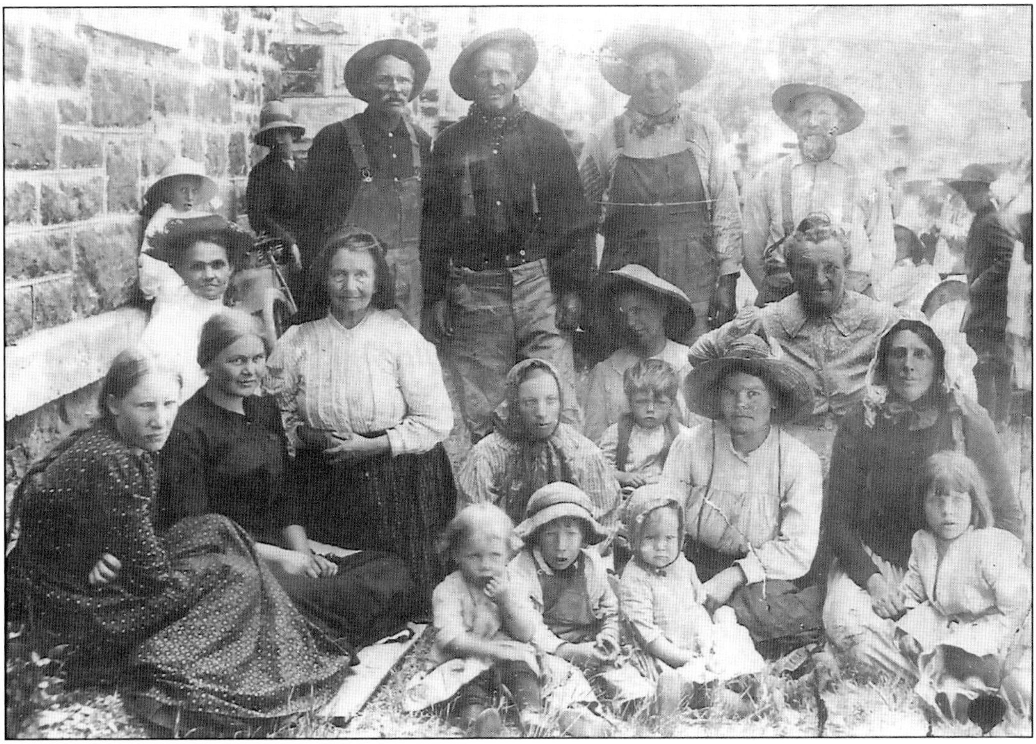

This photograph was taken during the Burton Ward Pioneer Celebration on July 24, 1912. Pictured are, from left to right, (first row) Verla Jensen, Anderson boy, Mary Jensen, and Mary Farnsworth; (second row) Miss Stewart, Carolyn Jensen, Bertha Humphrey, Lizzie Jensen, and Ethel Farnsworth; (third row) Eva Jensen, Elizabeth Jensen, Mrs. Alfred Anderson and her small son, and Mrs. Sorenson; (fourth row) Bud Johnson, Mr. Stoddard, Alonza Farnsworth, and Mr. Sorenson. (Courtesy of Fredonia Jensen Swenson.)

The Rexburg Mormon First Ward Church women's organization washboard band is seen in this 1932 photograph. From left to right are (first row) Mable Brown, Luella Smith, Elizabeth Smith, and Arvilla Allen Smith; (second row) Leota Bollingbrooke, Nellie Roylance, Martha Evans, Arzetta Parkinson, Myrtle Garner, Olive Anderson Webster, and Harriett Anderson.

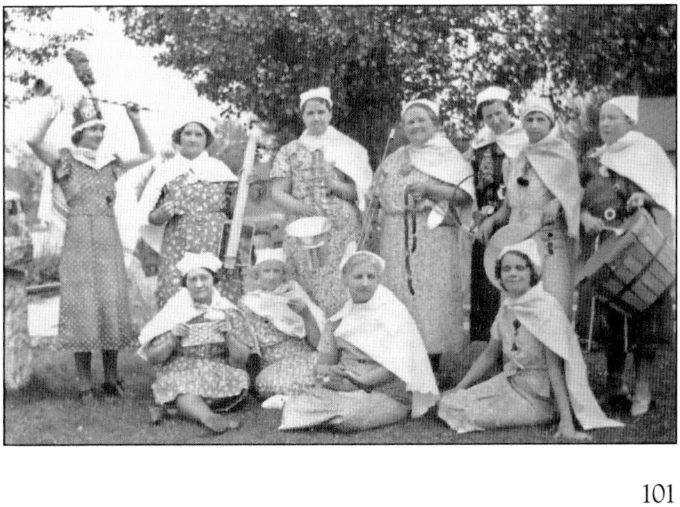

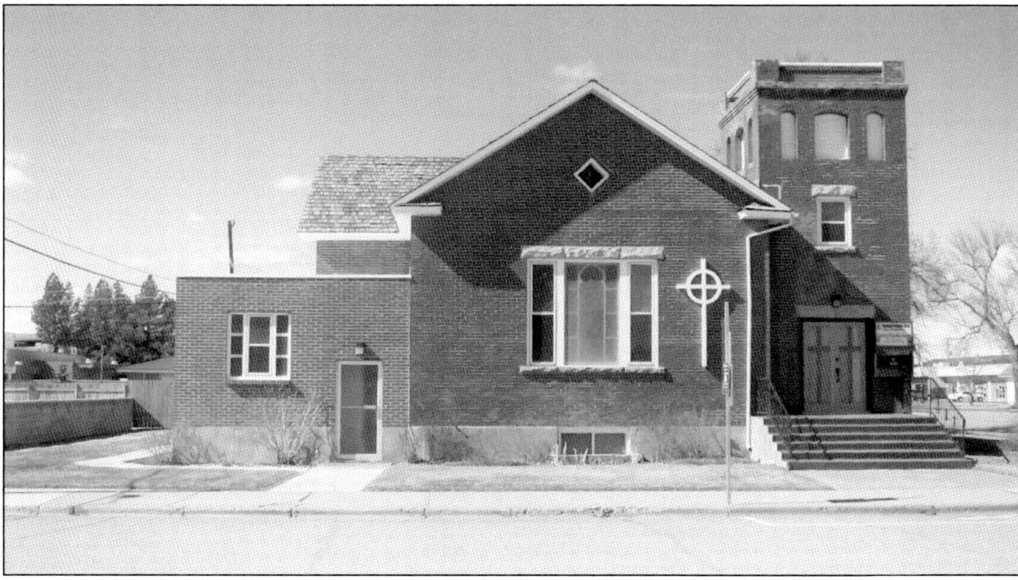

Construction of the Presbyterian Community Church began late in the fall of 1916. The building was completed and dedicated on March 17, 1918. The first pastor was J.H. Baird. The Presbyterian church, the oldest church building standing in Rexburg, is located on the corner of College Avenue and East First South. (Courtesy of the Upper Snake River Valley Historical Society.)

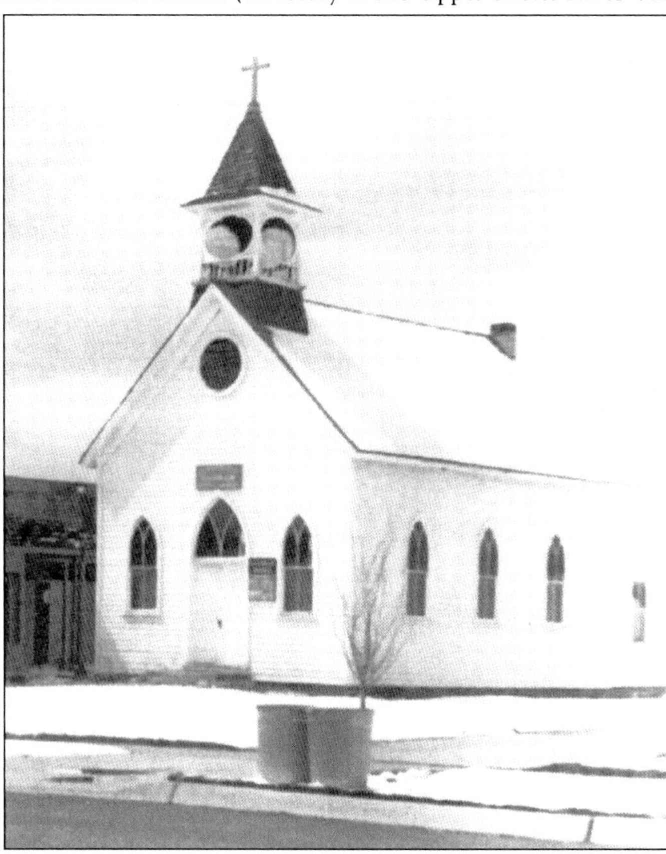

St. Patrick's Catholic Church was built in 1903 and accommodated the Catholic community from Rexburg to Rigby. Sadly, this historic building was torn down in 1963, and a new church building was erected to the south of the old church. (Courtesy of Terrell and Margaret Porter Arnold.)

Nine

Parks, Recreation, and Parades

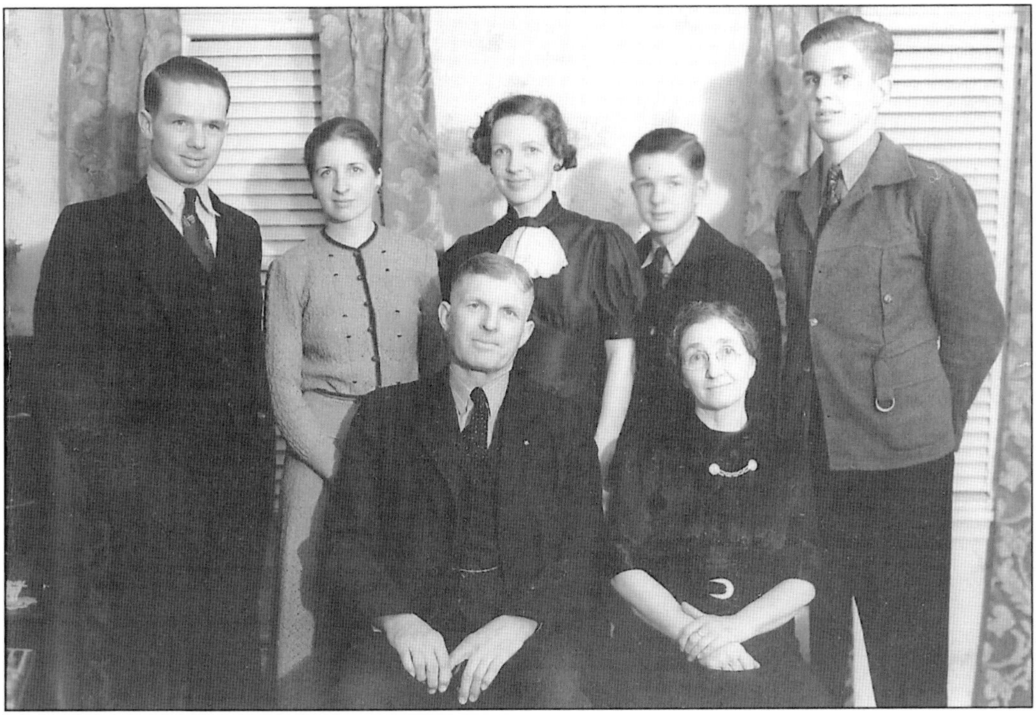

Joseph Fred and his wife, Josephine Huskinson Smith, are pictured with their children standing behind them: from left to right, Ross, Lucille, Marie, John, and Eldon "Dick" Smith. Fred, mayor of Rexburg from 1953 to 1958, was successful in negotiating a lease with the Mormon Church to use a block of land the church owned, known as the missionary farm, to create a park that was named Smith Park in his honor. (Courtesy of Richard Smith.)

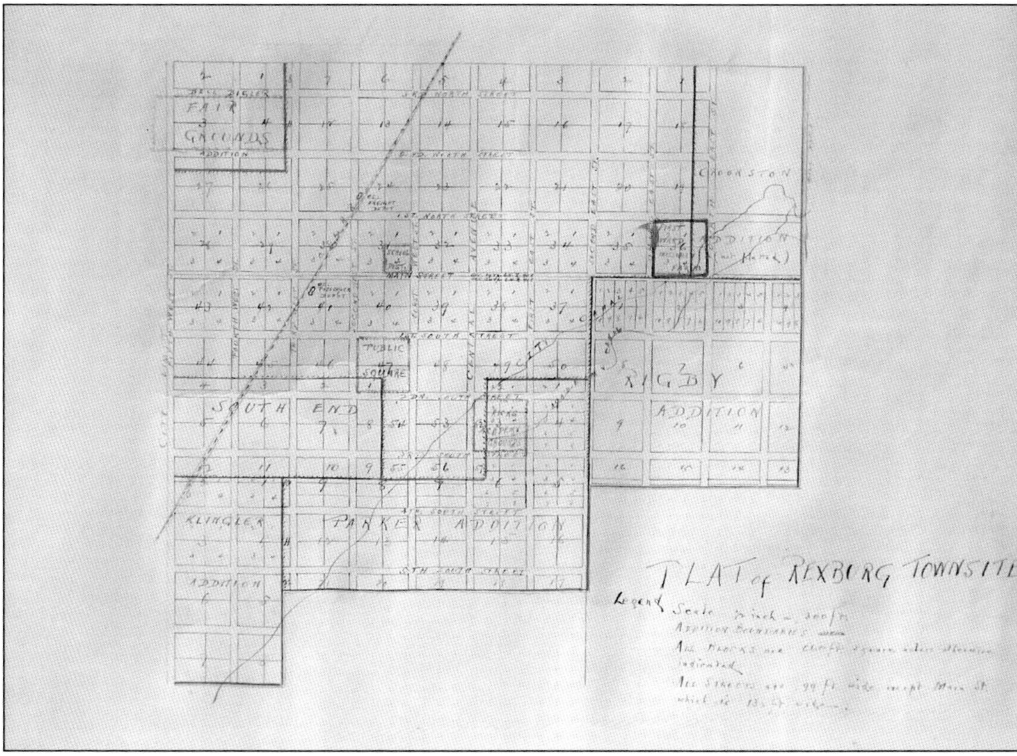

The outlined area above near the upper right-hand corner of this 1903 plat of Rexburg in Fremont County is the missionary farm. The missionary farm was used by local Mormon families, and each family was allocated a small portion of ground to grow their vegetables. A canal ran past the property, offering surface irrigation to the crops. In the 1880s, this land was set aside and dedicated for the site of a future Mormon temple; however, that never came to fruition. The 1960 photograph of Smith Park below, looking northeast toward the baseball diamond, shows a rock home in the distance. The home belonged to James Gillespie, who drafted the plat map of 1903. Located in the southwest corner of the park sits the 1910 Webster-Woodmansee steam engine tractor. (Below, courtesy of Dorothy Kennedy.)

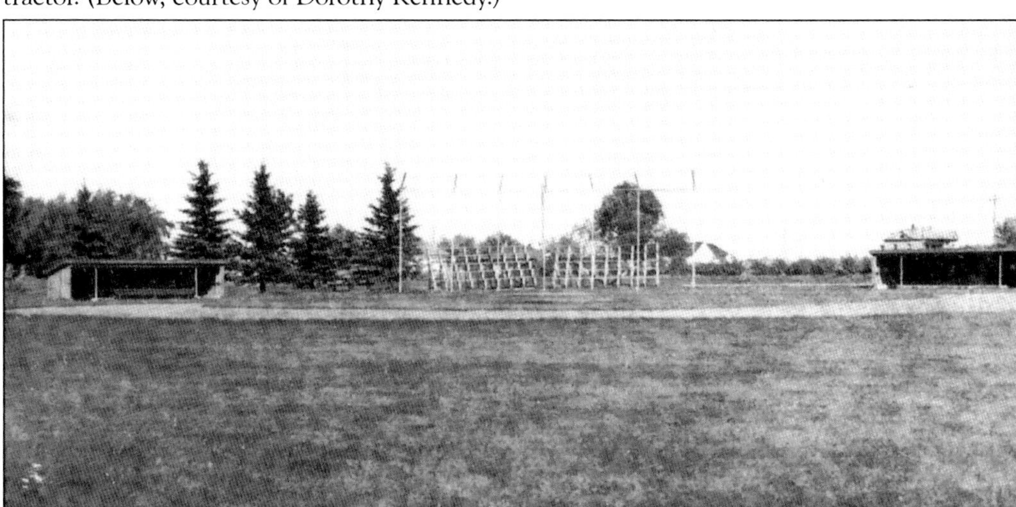

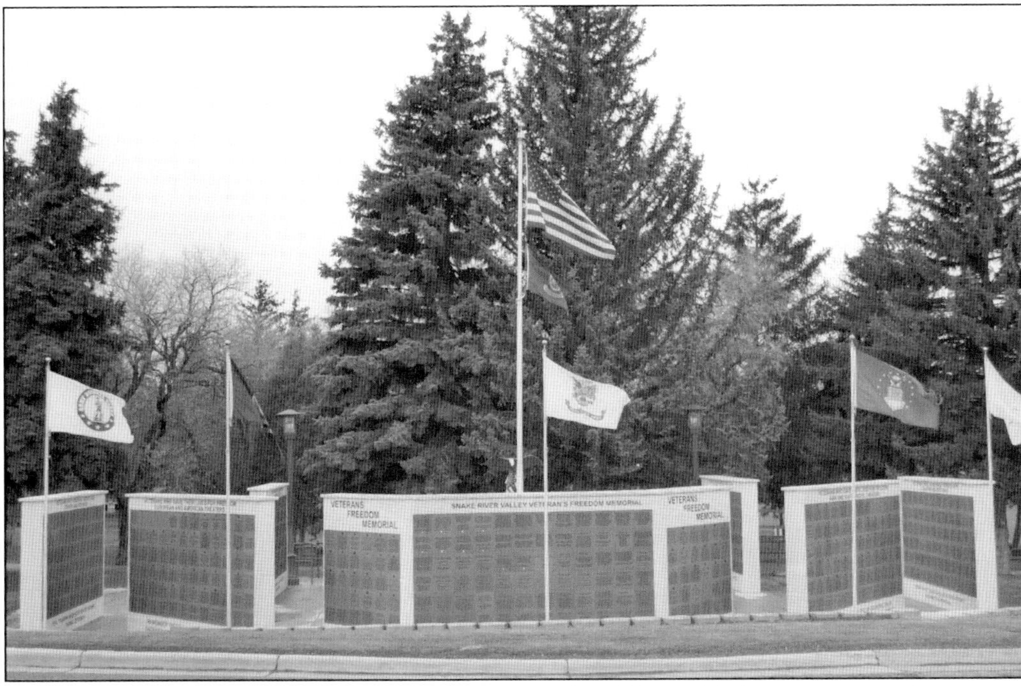

Veteran's Freedom Memorial, located at the east side of Smith Park, is shown in this picture. This memorial honors all military personnel in wars, beginning with the Nez Percé War of 1877 to the present day. This beautiful memorial was the creation and inspiration of brothers Lynn and Gary Archibald.

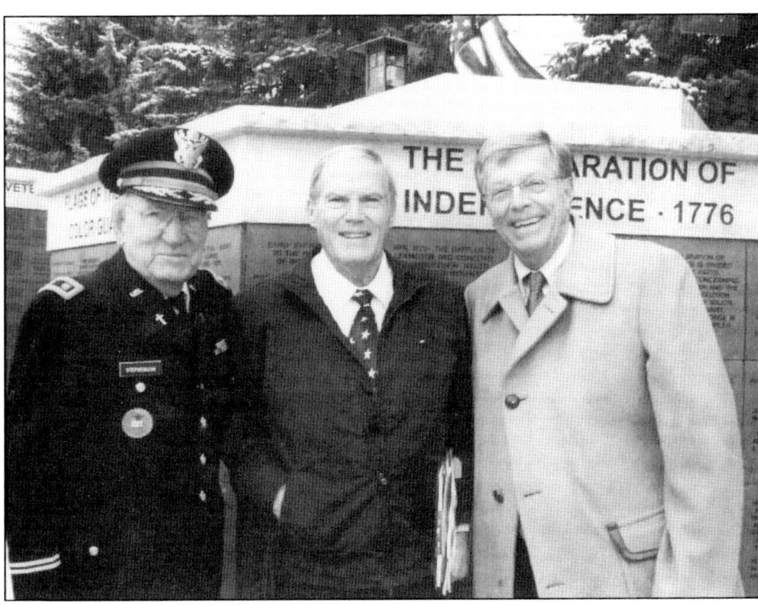

This photograph was taken on Veteran's Day 2010 at the dedication of the Veteran's Freedom Memorial. Standing from left to right in front of the memorial are World War II veteran Eldred Stephenson (97 years old, wearing his original uniform) with Lynn Archibald and Gary Archibald. (Courtesy of Eldred Stephenson.)

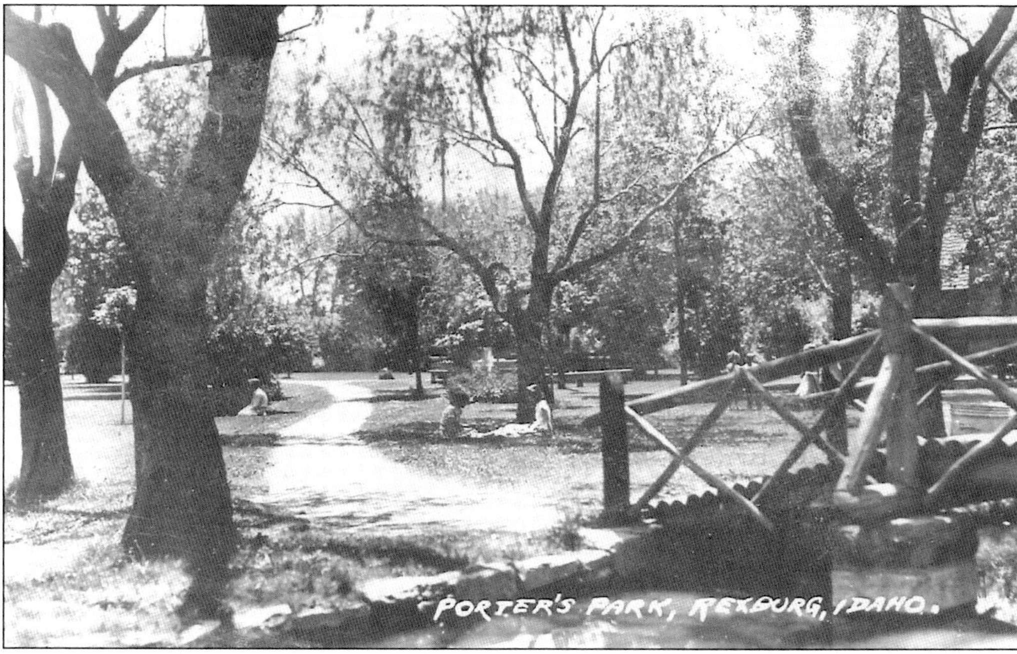

The land where the present Porter Park now stands was originally given to the city of Rexburg by its founder, Thomas E. Ricks. Seen in this 1935 photograph are an attractive wading pool, tennis court, lily pond, rustic bridge, public restroom, and baseball diamond. In May 1952, the park was named Porter Park after Arthur Porter for his role as founder, instigator, and guiding force.

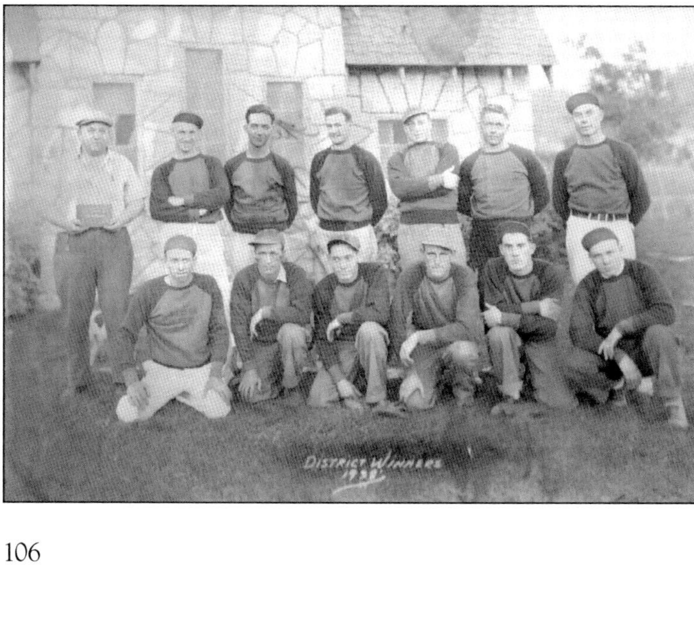

In this 1938 photograph, the Taylor Chevrolet Championship baseball team stands in front of a rock building erected by the Civil Works Administration in 1935 at Porter Park. From left to right are (first row) Ray Siglin, Volney Oldham, Ted Ellis, Carl Anderson, Rollie Smart, and John Porter; (second row) Bob Archer, Glen Peterson, Harold Blackburn, Tom Hemming, Ed Levine, Roy Cole, and Ralph Peterson.

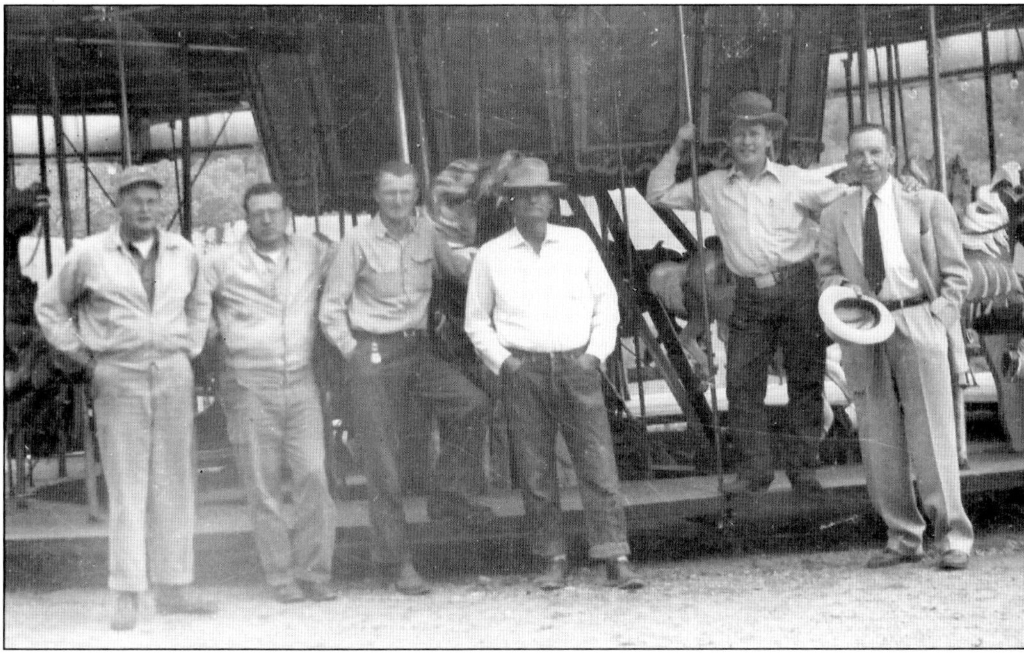

The merry-go-round in Porter Park cost $5,000, and Jess Welker and Dar Mickelsen furnished the truck to haul it from Ogden Canyon to Rexburg. Standing from left to right in this 1952 photograph are Gerald Holley, Terrell Arnold, Gordon Smith, Claude Christensen, John Atkinson, and Harmon Perry. In 1976, this merry-go-round was honored as the Idaho Centennial Carousel, celebrating 100 years of Idaho statehood. (Courtesy of Terrell and Margaret Porter Arnold.)

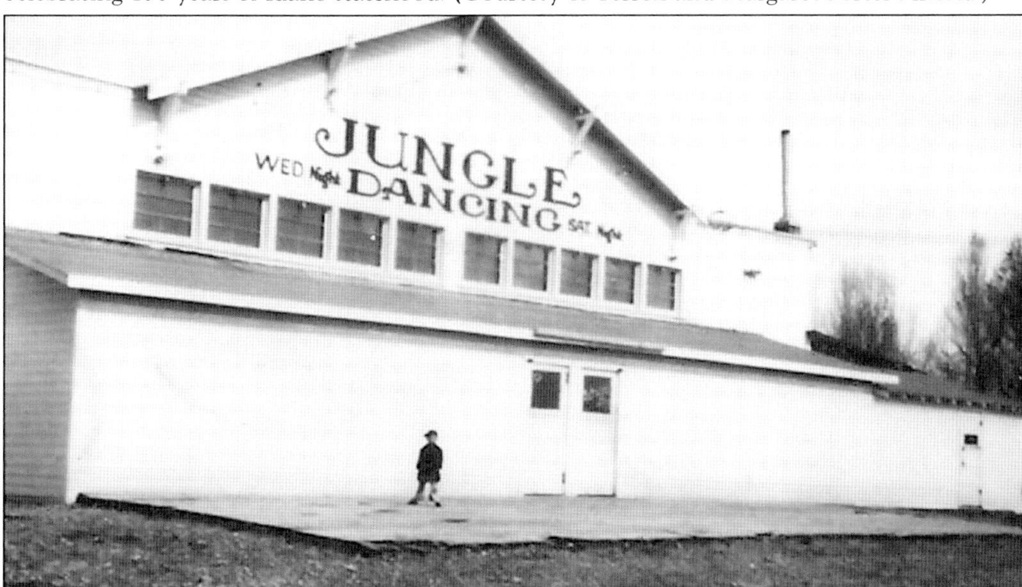

From the 1920s to the 1940s, dance halls provided popular entertainment for people in the Rexburg area. Two of the dance halls in Rexburg were speakeasies: Cahoon Park, surrounded by a lake, and the Jungle Dance Hall. Other dance halls in the area were the Burton Hall, Playmore Hall (located on the second floor of the Woodman of the World building), Green Canyon, and Archer Hall.

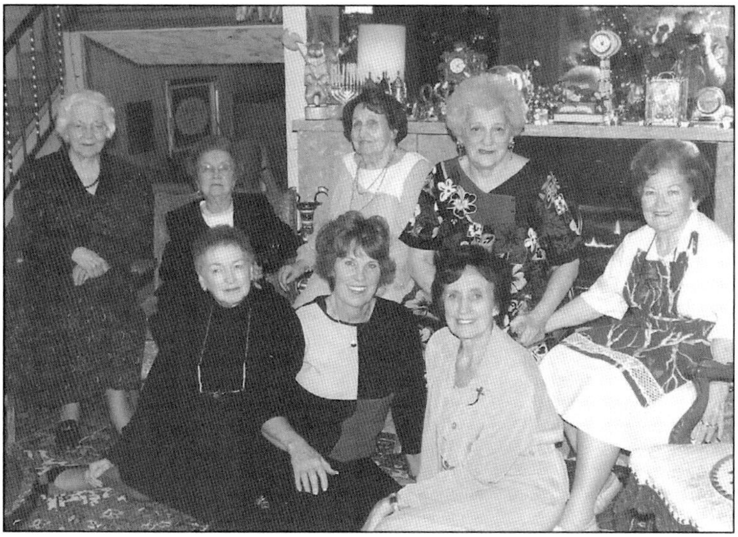

The Book Lore Club was organized during the Depression by eight women who hungered for an outlet to socialize with other ladies and have the opportunity to read good books. The club lasted from 1933 to 2004. From left to right are (first row) Joan Haeberle, Elaine Holloway, and Phyllis Bond; (second row) Edna Taylor, Marguerite Hill, Verla Parkinson, LaRue Clarke, and Dr. Mary Hess.

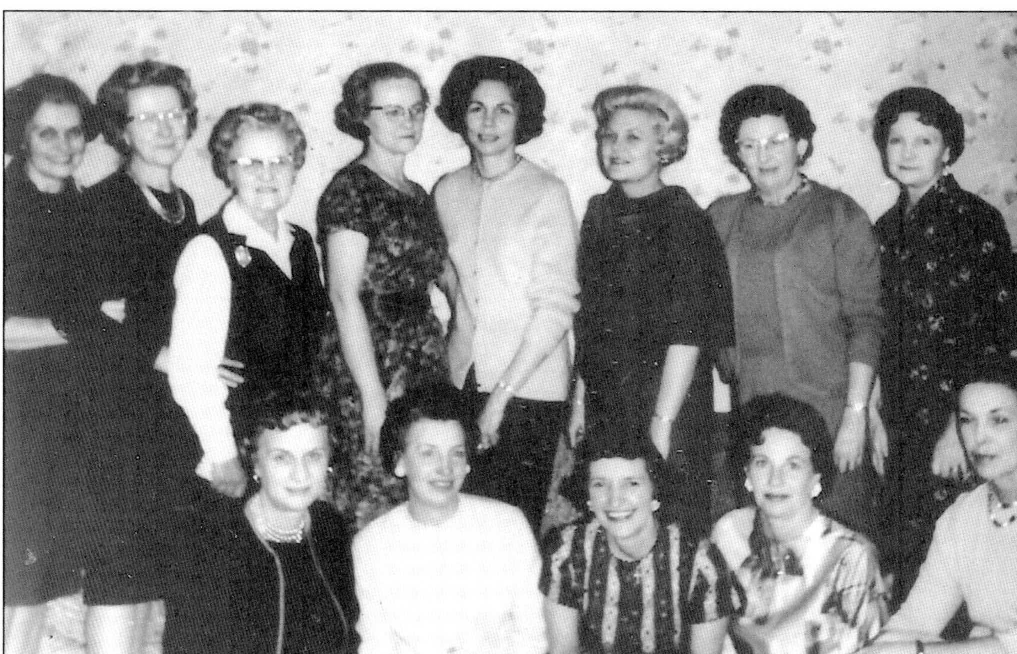

Club 13 was a bridge club that met monthly with one member hosting and preparing a meal prior to playing bridge. Members pictured are, from left to right, (first row) Lavinna Stoddard, Marjorie Lovgren, Irene Hochstein, Grace Wood, and Jo Madsen; (second row) Marie Cunningham, Elva Purrington, Golda Woodmansee, Yordis Wilding, Norma Frew, Becky Bott, Alta Christensen, and Vera Wilding. (Courtesy of Irene Hochstein.)

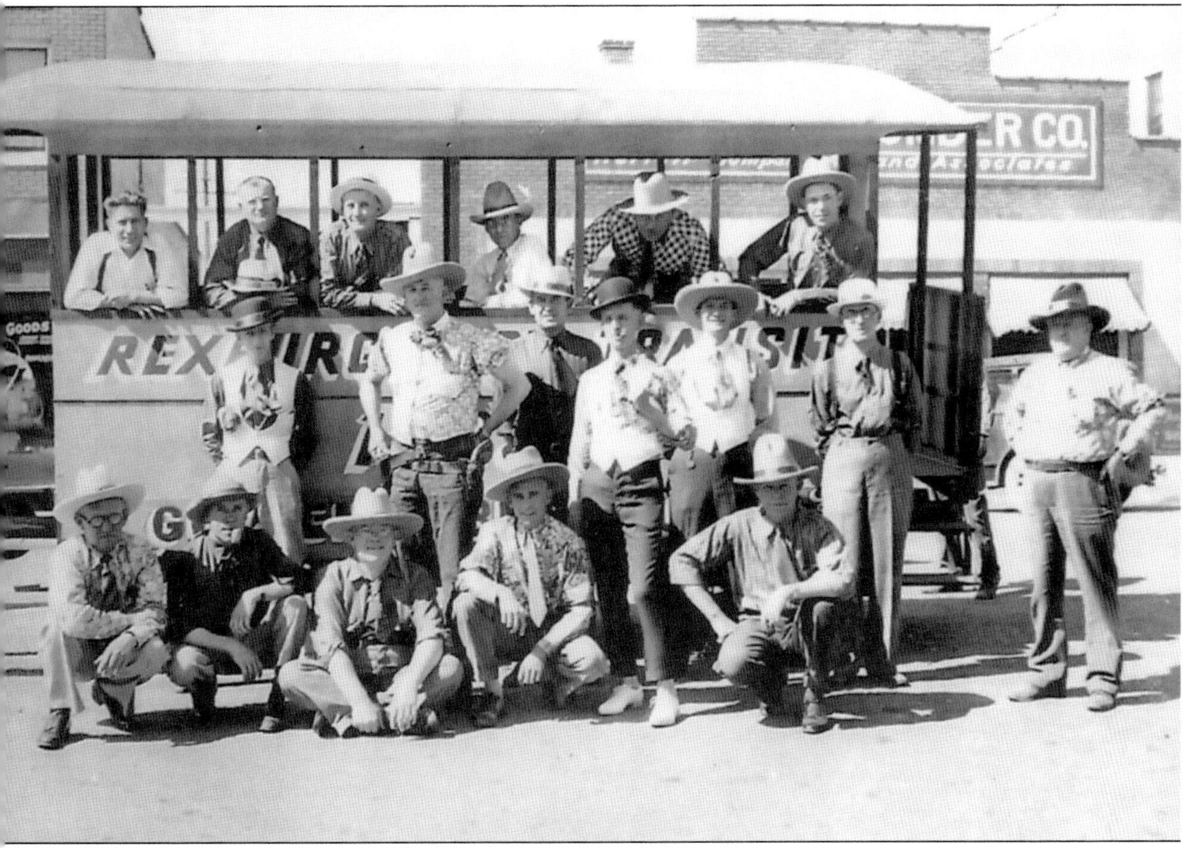

Pictured is the Golden Jubilee committee for the Whoopee Days parade, which took place on July 4, 1933. Pictured are, from left to right, (first row) Dr. William Sumner, Mel Ward, Dr. Parley Nelson, Glenn Herdti, and Bill Hansen; (second row) Loren Johnson, Forrest Erdman, Don Wright, Walford Johnson, Ferrel Nelson, Arthur Porter, and Frank Turner; (third row, inside the trolley) Pete Thompson II, Perce Craven, Bill Moore, Howard Gentles, Ed Levine, and William Lloyd Adams. In 1909, a young Lloyd Adams came to Rexburg and took over as publisher of the *Standard* newspaper. He and his fiancée, Belva Bird, were standing on the sidewalk on Main Street waiting for the Fourth of July parade to commence. All of a sudden, riding fast down the street, came six cowboys, dressed in angora chaps, western shirts, and cowboy hats, shooting their pistols in the air and yelling "Whoopee!" *Whoopee* was a word cowhands used to get cattle moving as well as a word used after having a few too many brews at the saloon. Whoopee Days became the name of the yearly Fourth of July celebration for 83 years.

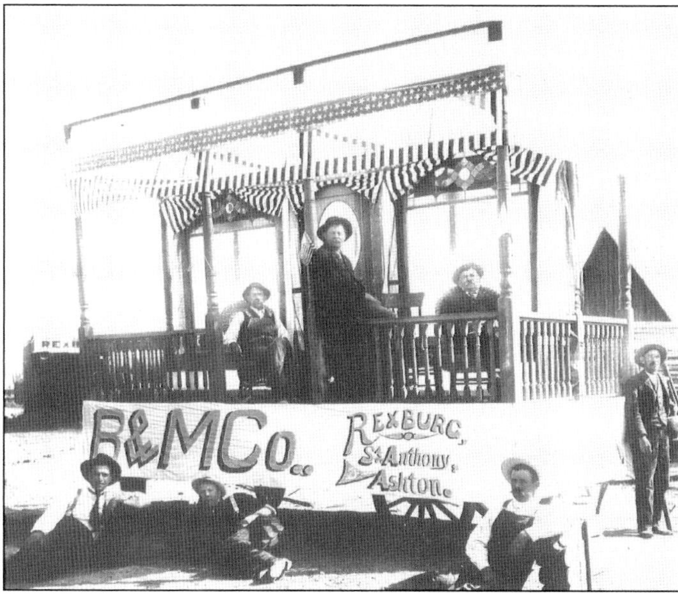

This 1906 photograph shows a horse-drawn float advertising the Building and Manufacturing Company, which later became Mickelsen Lumber. The only man identified sitting on the ground is Peter Mickelsen Sr. (at right in front of the float), who later became mayor of Rexburg; the other three men are unidentified. Sitting on the float from left to right are unidentified, John Nephi Johnson, and George Bickmore Gunnell. (Courtesy of Upper Snake River Valley Historical Society.)

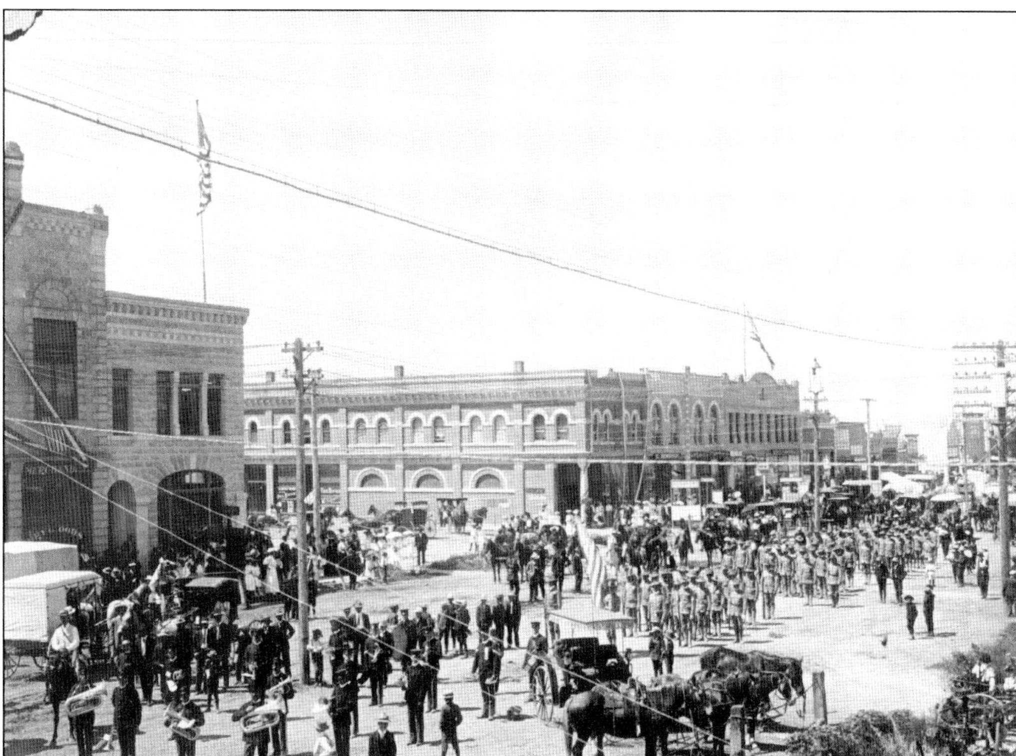

This scene shows a Fourth of July parade in 1913, the first parade celebrating the newly created Madison County, on the corner of East Main Street and South First East. The building on the left was the Waldram's Confectionery, and upstairs was Madison County's first courthouse. (Courtesy of BYU–Idaho Special Collections and Archives.)

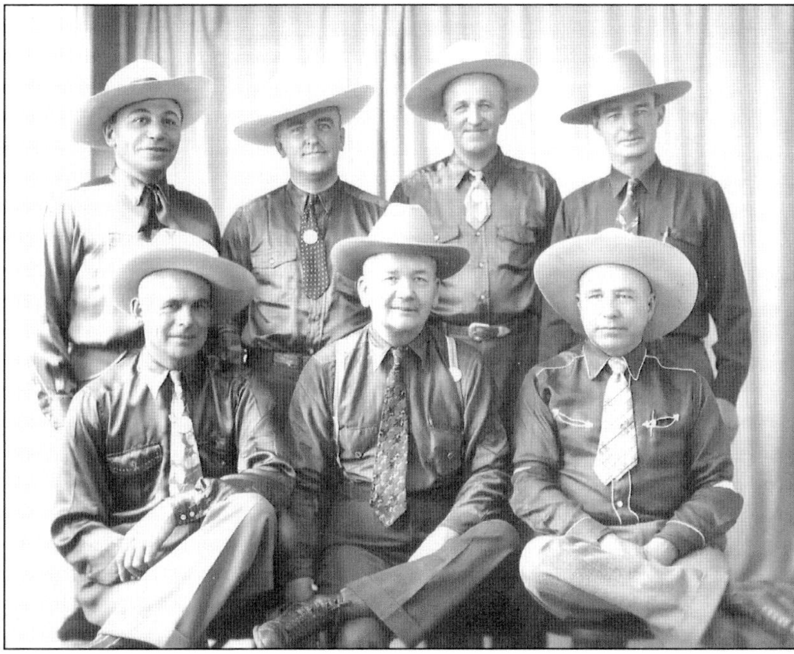

Members of the Rexburg Chamber of Commerce dressed up for the 1933 Golden Jubilee, honoring 50 years of the existence of the city of Rexburg. Pictured from left to right are (first row) Glenn Herdti, Jim Graham, and March Hopkins; (second row) Ed Levine, Gilbert Larsen, Forrest Erdman, and David DaBell. (Courtesy of Steve Herdti.)

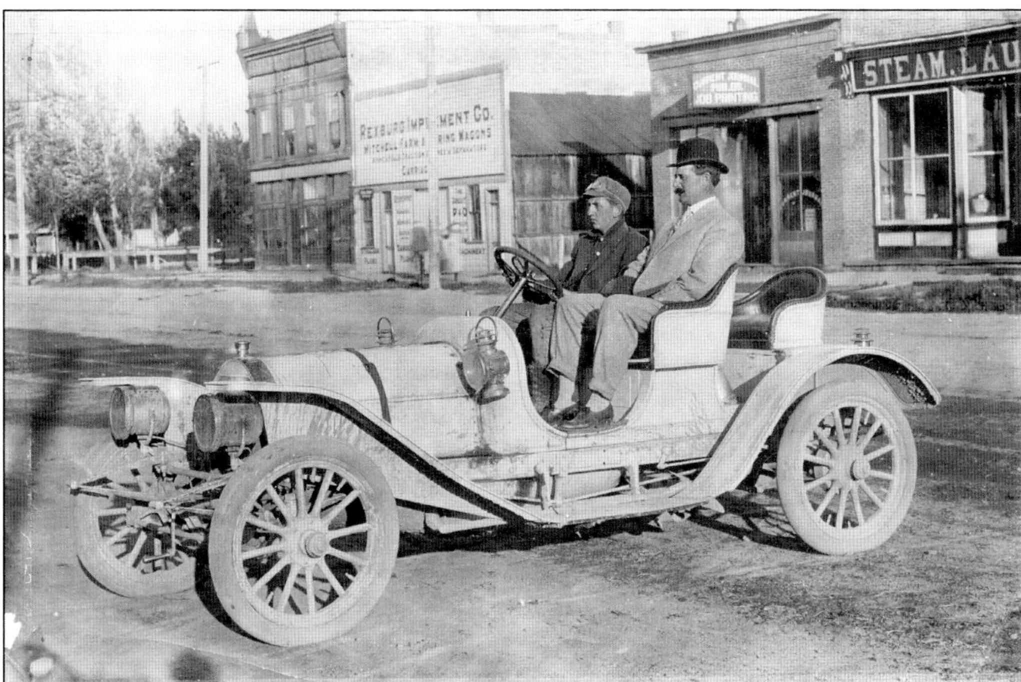

In 1909, cars were a new invention, and TV and radio had not yet been invented. The manufacturers of new cars would organize a car caravan from the East Coast to the West, stopping at small communities and presenting a car parade. This picture shows one of the car parades in Rexburg. Note the *Current Journal* newspaper office. (Courtesy of BYU–Idaho Special Collections and Archives, MSSI 44: Merrill Dee Beal papers.)

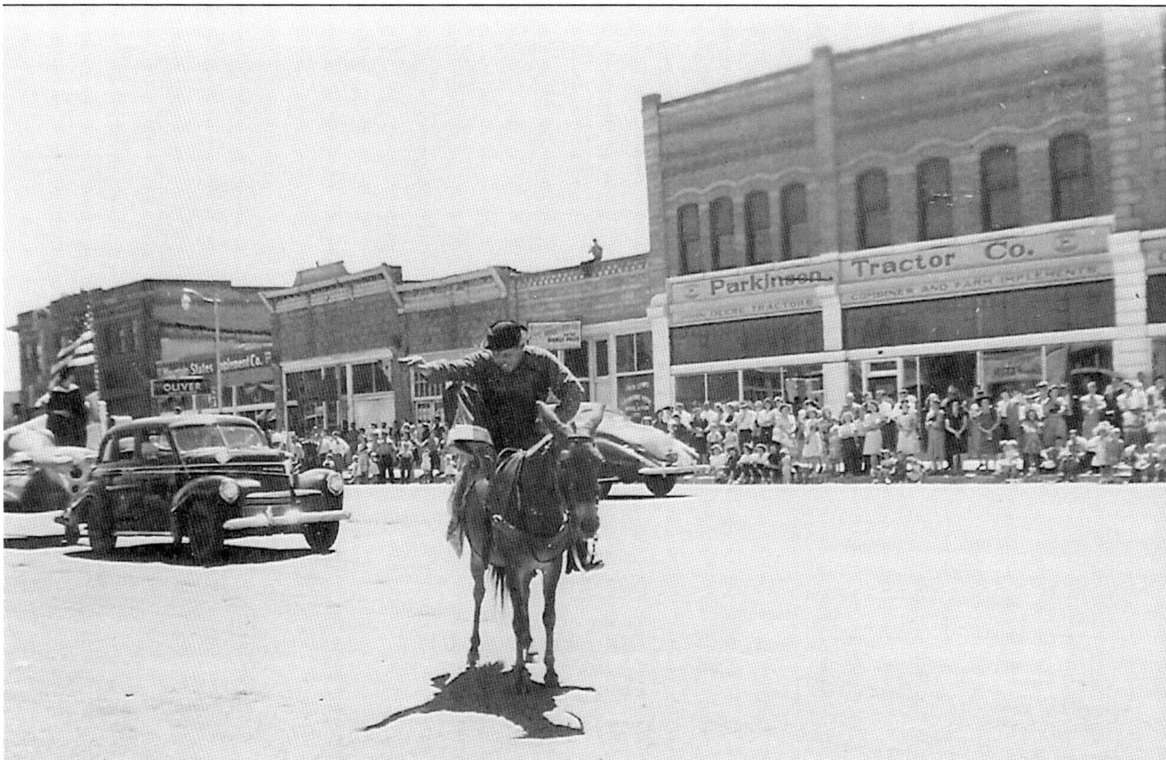

A Whoopee Days parade in 1945 shows the popularity of these parades in the Upper Snake River Valley. People from Idaho Falls to Ashton would come to Rexburg to observe the parades, knowing that they would not disappoint. A group of people is shown in front of the Parkinson Tractor Co., which offered John Deere tractors and Caterpillar equipment.

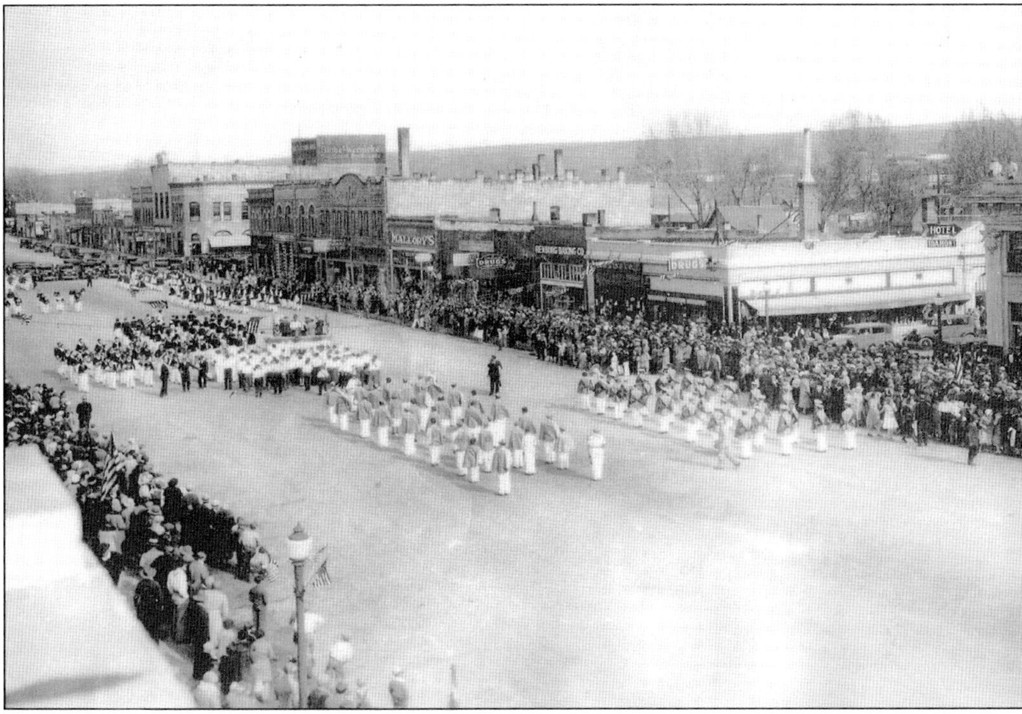

Madison High School's homecoming parade travels down Main Street in this 1933 photograph. There is an abundance of musical talent in the community of Rexburg. Music was an important part of education at the high school as well as the college level.

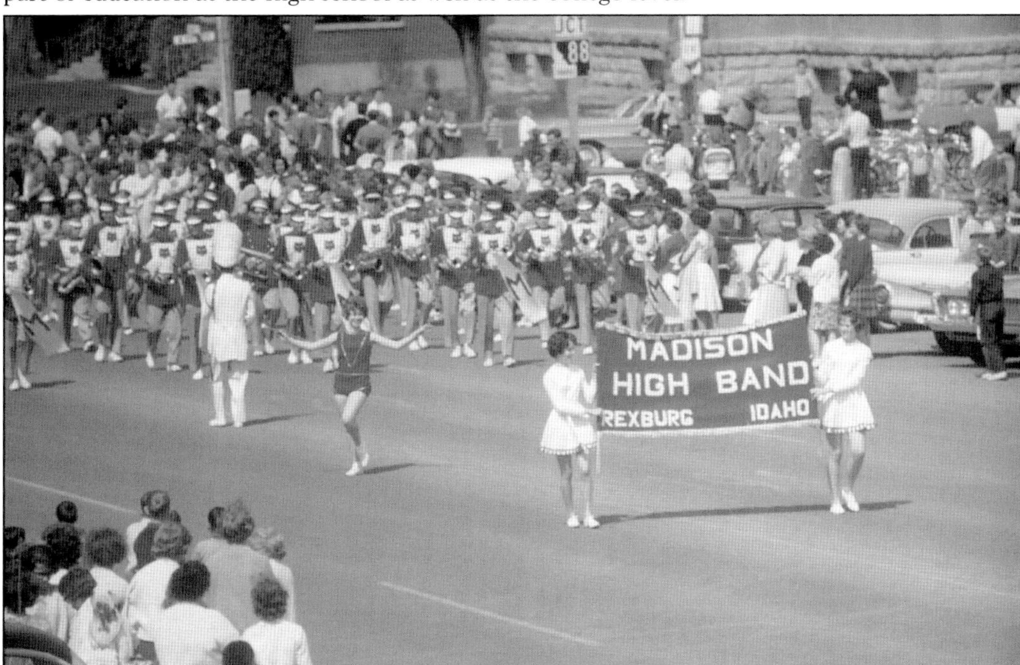

On May 8, 1964, the Madison High School Band celebrates "M" Days in this high school parade. (Courtesy of Allan Morton.)

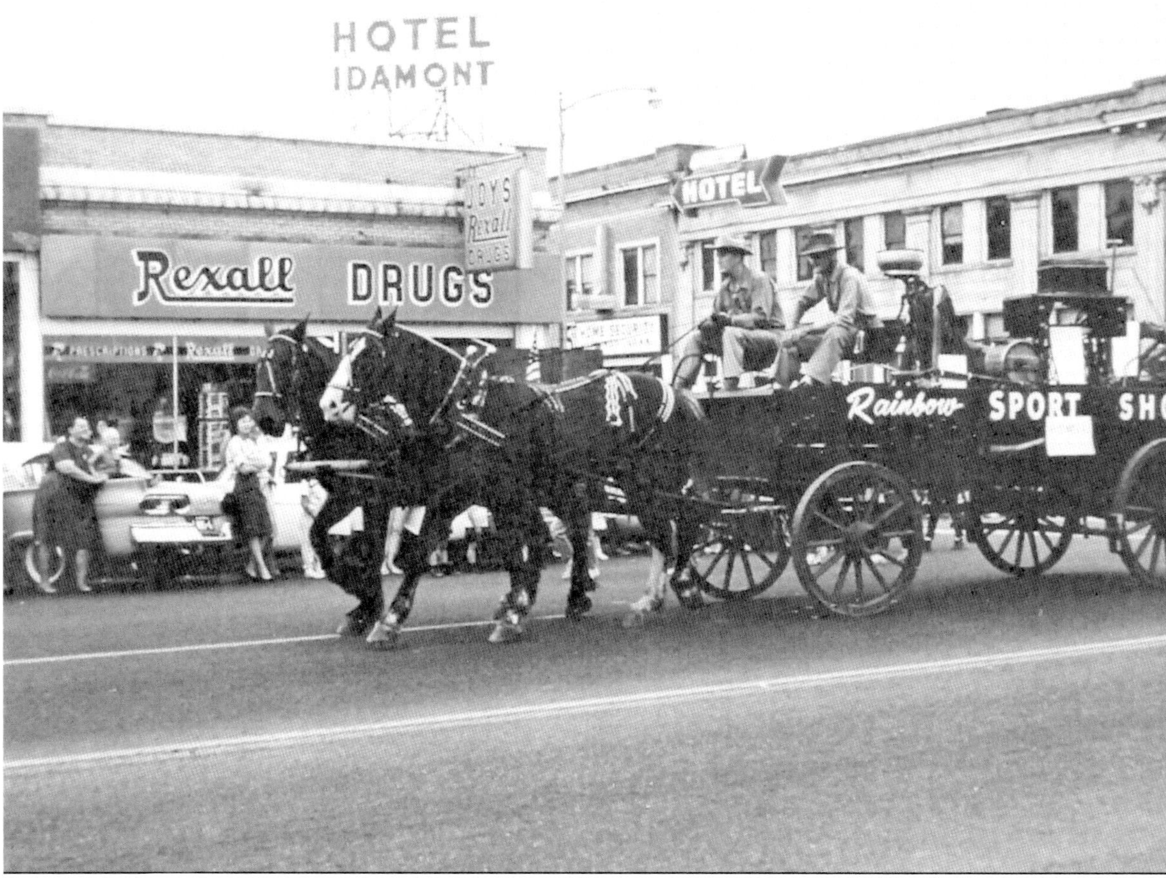

This photograph of the Whoopee Days Fourth of July Parade in 1963 shows DeWayne Wilding (left) and Talmadge "Bill" Hill (right) driving a team of horses pulling a wagon representing the Upper Snake River Valley Historical Society. In the background is Irving Woodmansee's Rexall Drugs on the corner of North College Avenue and Main Street, and the building behind the wagon was the former Dr. William Sutherland Hospital.

Ten

EVENTS

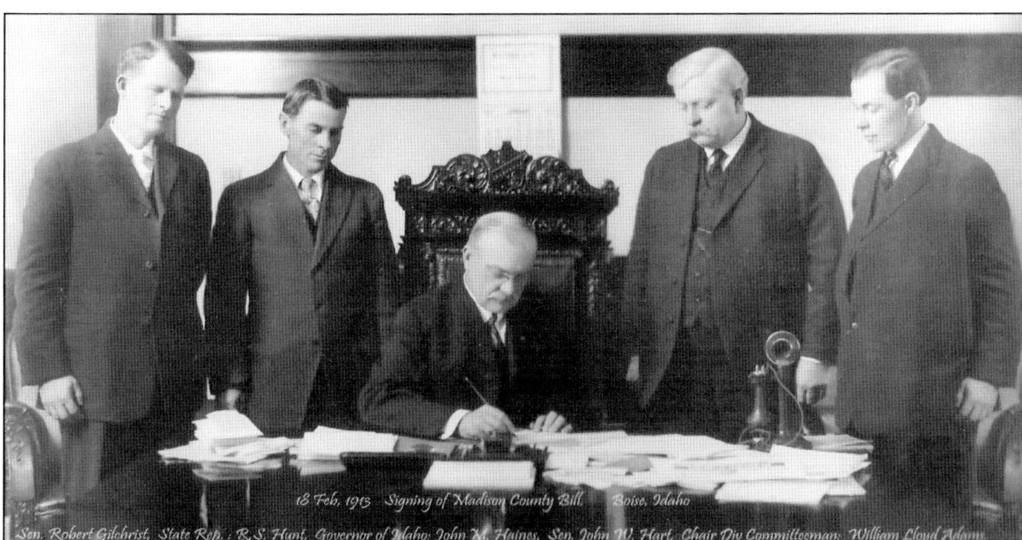

This is an image of the February 18, 1913, signing of Madison County Bill No. 173 at the capitol building in Boise, Idaho. From left to right are state senator Robert Gilcrist, state representative Steve Hunt, governor of Idaho John Haines, state senator John W. Hart, and chair division committeeman William Lloyd Adams. This bill diminished the size of Fremont County, and from the reduction of that landmass, Madison, Jefferson, and Teton Counties were created.

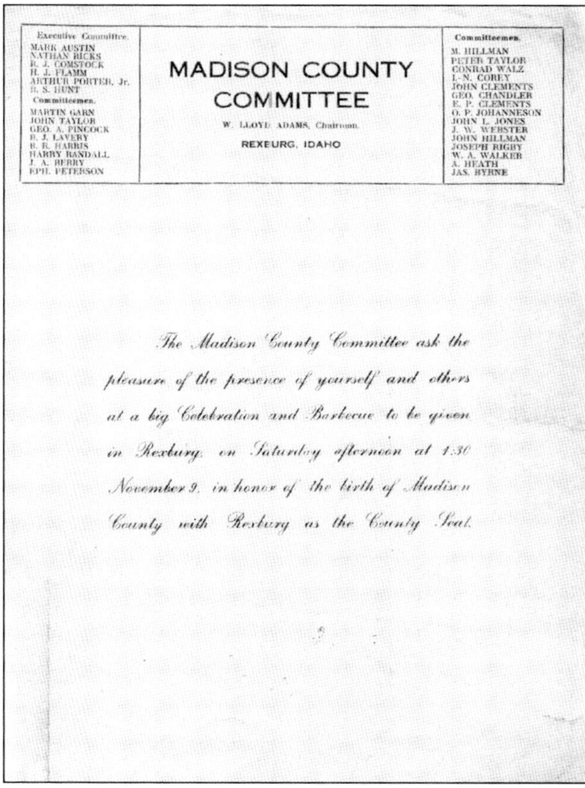
Executive Committee.
MARK AUSTIN
NATHAN RICKS
R. J. COMSTOCK
H. J. FLAMM
ARTHUR PORTER, Jr.
R. S. HUNT
Committeemen.
MARTIN GARN
JOHN TAYLOR
GEO. A. PINCOCK
R. J. LAVERY
R. R. HARRIS
HARRY RANDALL
J. A. BERRY
EPH. PETERSON

MADISON COUNTY
COMMITTEE
W. LLOYD ADAMS, Chairman.
REXBURG, IDAHO

Committeemen.
M. HILLMAN
PETER TAYLOR
CONRAD WALZ
L.-N. COREY
JOHN CLEMENTS
GEO. CHANDLER
E. P. CLEMENTS
O. P. JOHANNESON
JOHN L. JONES
J. W. WEBSTER
JOHN HILLMAN
JOSEPH RIGBY
W. A. WALKER
A. HEATH
JAS. BYRNE

The Madison County Committee ask the pleasure of the presence of yourself and others at a big Celebration and Barbecue to be given in Rexburg, on Saturday afternoon at 1:30 November 9, in honor of the birth of Madison County with Rexburg as the County Seat.

This invitation was sent out on November 9, 1913, and in honor of the birth of Madison County, people were invited to a barbecue and celebration. Lloyd Adams was the committee chairman with the following committee members: Arthur Porter, Mark Austin, Nathan Ricks, R.J. Comstock, H.J. Flamm, R.S. Hunt, Martin Garn, John Taylor, George A. Pincock, R.J. Lavery, R.R. Harris, Harry Randall, J.A. Berry, Ephriam Peterson, M. Hillman, Peter Taylor, Conrad Walz, L.N. Corey, John Clements, George Chandler, E.P. Clements, O.P. Johanneson, John I. Jones, J.W. Webster, John Hillman, Joseph Rigby, W.A. Walker, A. Heath, and James Byrne.

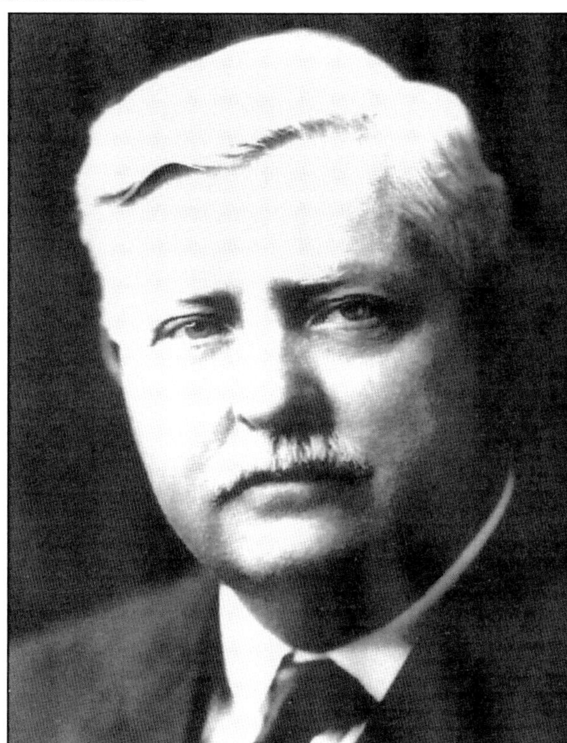

Few men in the state of Idaho contributed more to its growth and development than John W. Hart. He started at the young age of 20 as general superintendent of Wood's Livestock Company, was a member of the board of directors for Ricks College and one of the signers of the Madison County bill, and was confidant to Sen. William Borah and presidents Harding, Coolidge, and Hoover. (Courtesy of Gary Archibald.)

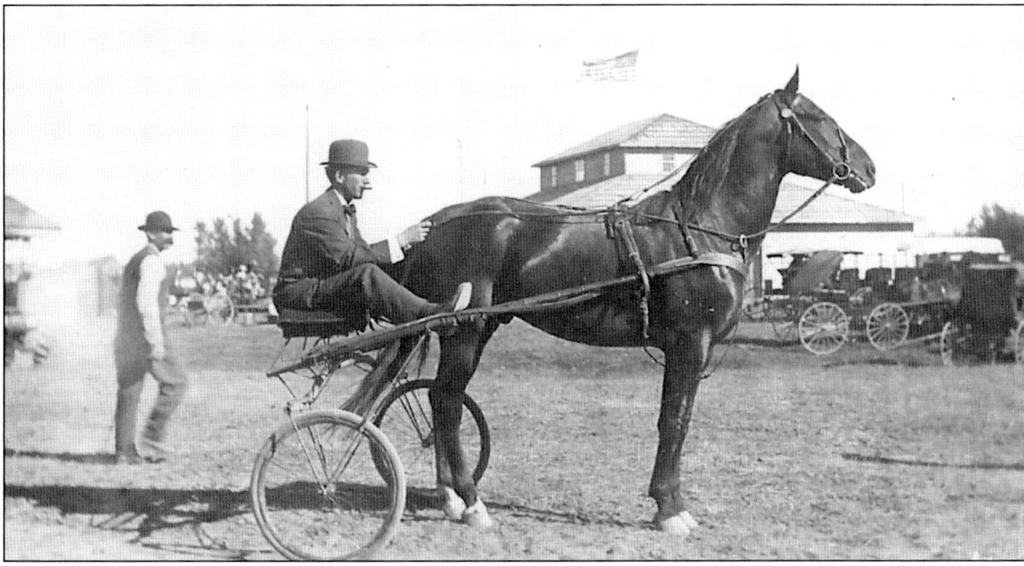

In 1911, there existed a love/hate relationship with horses. On one hand, horses were a necessity for transportation and assisting with farming; on the other hand, everyone loved a good racehorse. Shown above is Urshel Bigler driving a sulky race cart pulled by a purebred sulky racehorse at Rexburg's first fair. The Biglers owned a racetrack and large barns that were used in their racehorse business. They sold their land to the City of Rexburg, but the city was unable to keep up the payments, so the county took over the payments, and the land became the Madison County Fairgrounds. For 103 years, the fairgrounds have provided entertainment for the community such as cutter races, horse racing, fairs, carnivals, and musical concerts. (Above, courtesy of Dona Bigler.)

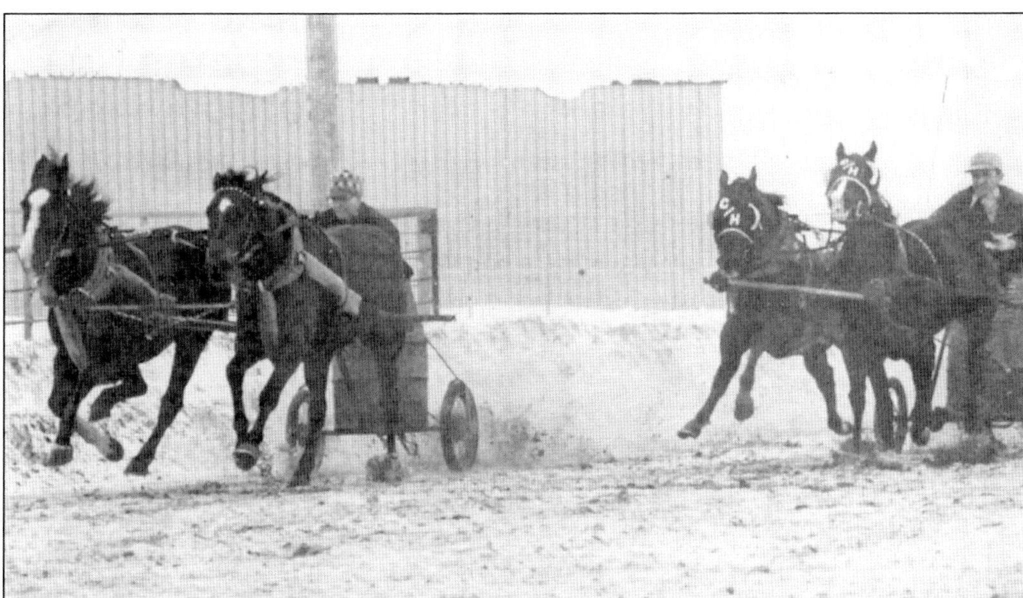

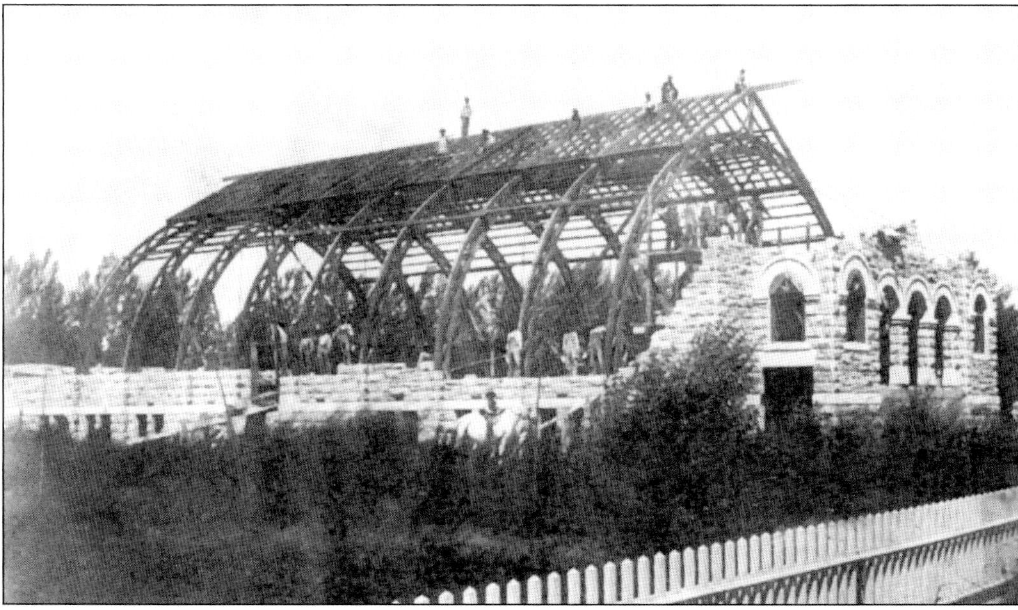

The cornerstone of the Fremont Stake Tabernacle was laid on July 15, 1911. The tabernacle was named in honor of the American pathfinder and frontiersman Capt. John C. Fremont. Religion has always been the cornerstone of the Mormon community, and during its 103 years of existence, the tabernacle served as a Mormon Church meetinghouse with a baptismal font in the basement. This building withstood the Teton Dam flood and stands today as the city's cultural center, the home of the Upper Snake River Valley Historical Society, and the flood museum. (Above, courtesy of Upper Snake River Valley Historical Society.)

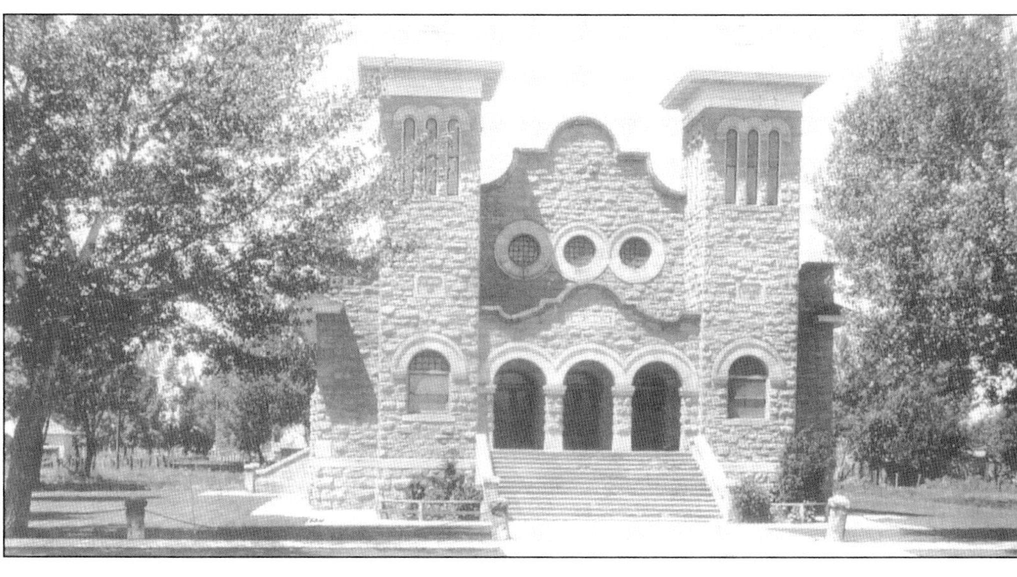

Sgt. Ephriam Harland Davidson was a US 6th Marine Regiment marine gunner and a veteran of six battles during World War I in eastern France. His platoon captured 2,300 German soldiers and liberated a small city in eastern France. He was awarded the French Croix de Guerre and a Purple Heart. He was present in Paris when Woodrow Wilson signed the armistice ending World War I.

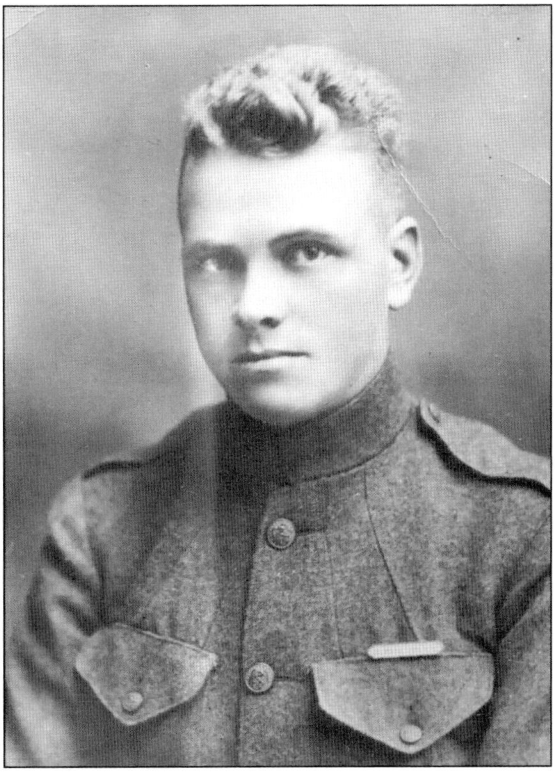

Hyram Peterson sits center on World War I cannon. Hyram was one of over 500 of Rexburg's young men to serve their country in World War I. The immediate trigger for World War I took place on June 28, 1914, with the assassination of Archduke Franz Ferdinand of Austria, heir to the throne of Austria-Hungary. (Courtesy of Dwight Davidson.)

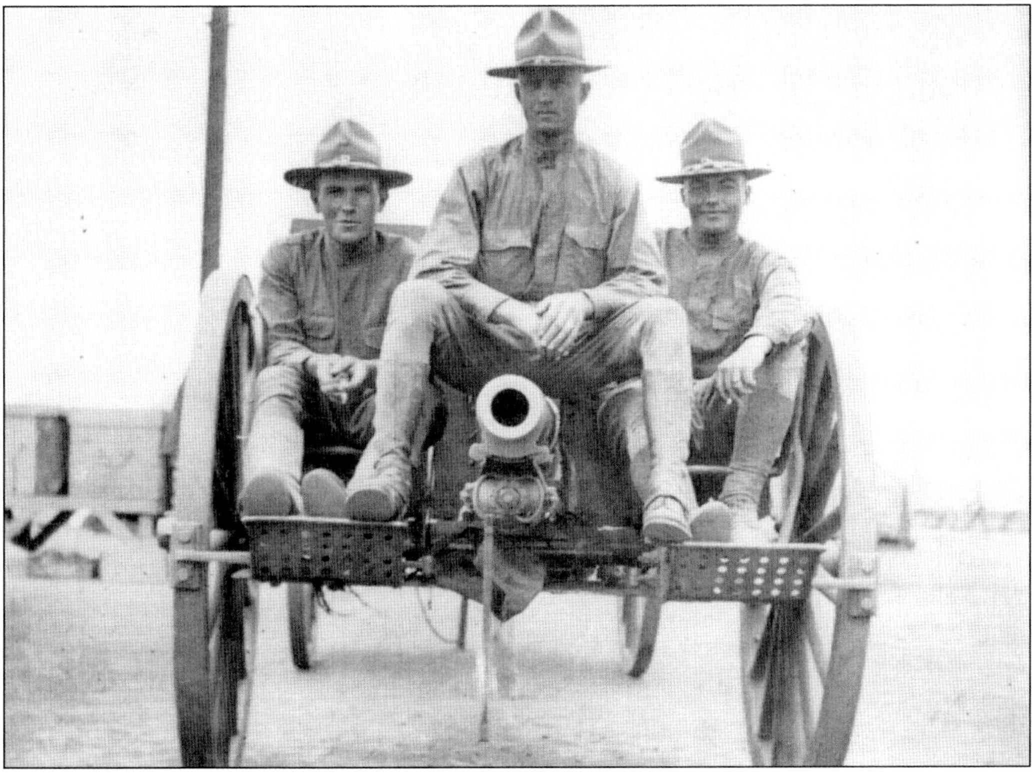

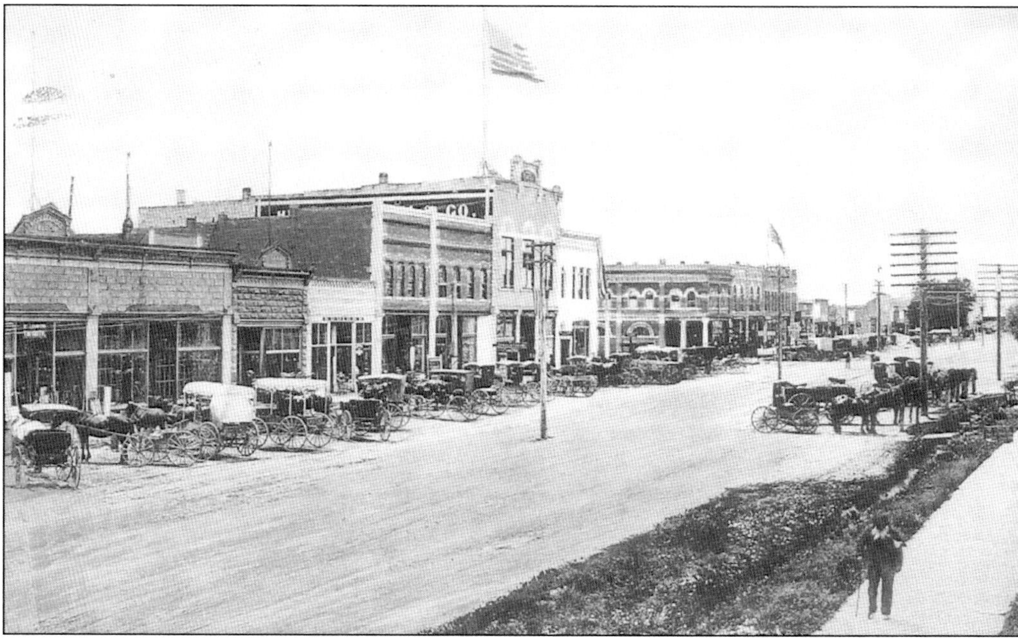

This 1906 photograph looks west down Main Street. The buildings, from left to right, are the Woodmansee building, Curt's Tin Smith, a former First National Bank, Squires Bookstore, Flamm building, the Flamm Opera House, a newly constructed First National Bank, and Waldrum's Store. In 1903, electricity was brought to Rexburg; in 1905, board sidewalks appeared on Main Street; in 1906, a water system was constructed; and by 1919, asphalt was laid down Main Street. (Courtesy of Dean Rasmussen.)

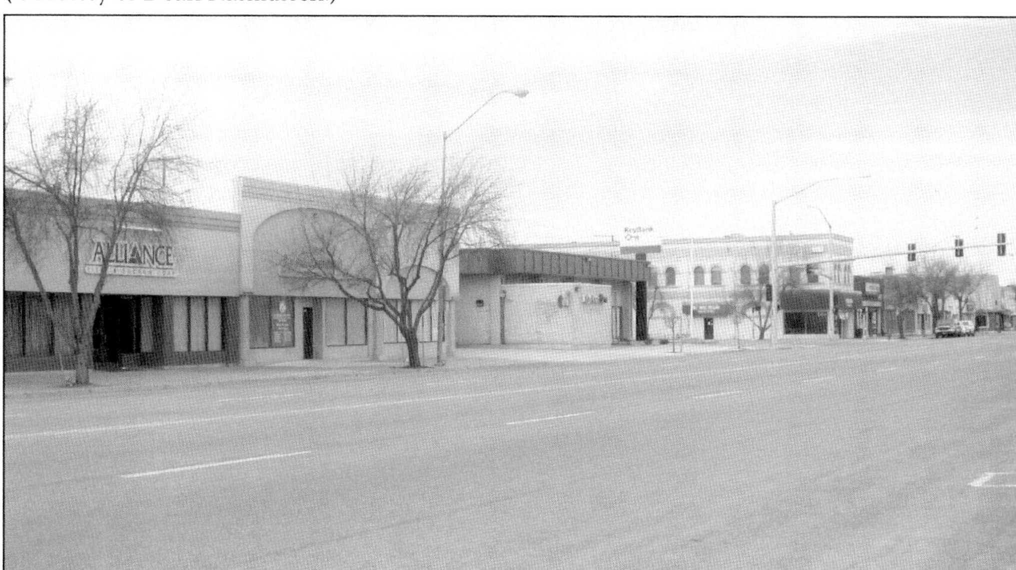

This March 16, 2014, photograph looks west down Main Street from the same perspective as the image on the top of the page. Of the original buildings, the following buildings remain: Alliance Title (formerly the Woodmansee building), Rudd and Company (formerly Curt's Tim Smith), and further down the street, the New York Burrito (formerly Waldrum's Store). All the other buildings were destroyed by the Teton Dam flood.

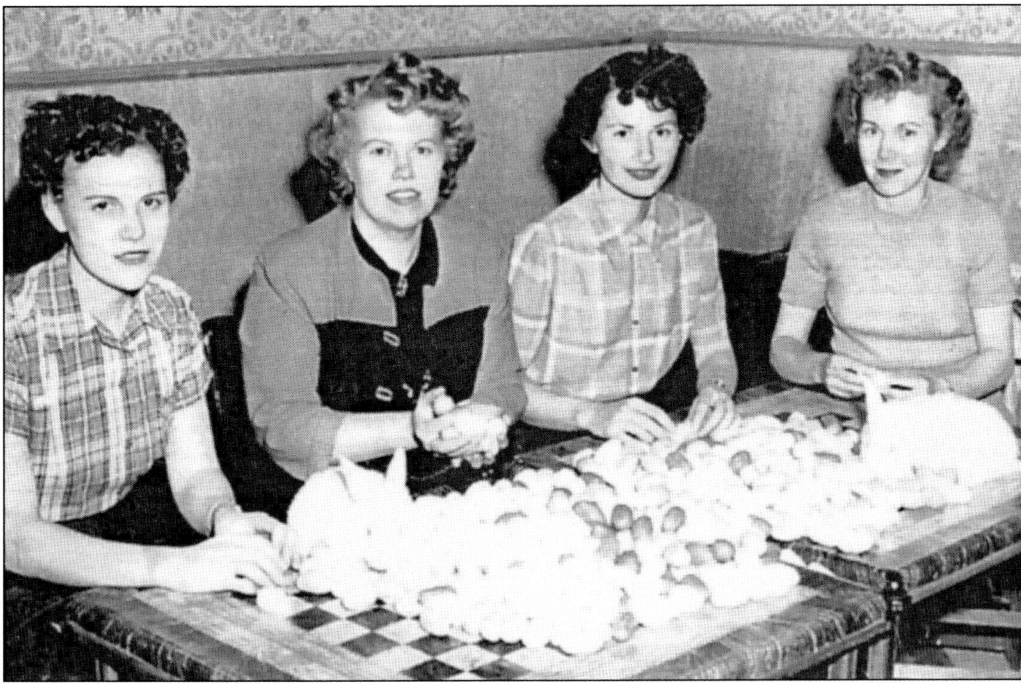

Several clubs in Rexburg provide services for the community, such as the Lion's Club breakfast and the annual Lion's Club Easter egg hunt, as demonstrated in this 1955 photograph of ladies coloring eggs. From left to right are Donna Peacock Meikle, Wilma Sumner Bean, Elaine Lawrence Holley, and Blanche Fitzpatrick. Below, members of the Lion's Club plan the next upcoming event in this 1950 photograph. From left to right are (left side, seated) Glen and Wilma Bean, Ondlyn Wiser, Elaine Anderson, Dr. Eugene Peterson, and Dorothy and Joe Horkley; (left side, standing) Lois and Dr. Olef Hoffman, Roland Wiser, and Dorothy Peterson; (right side, seated) Maughn and Valeria Parkinson, Berkley and Dorothy Parkinson, Lila and Craig Moore, and Seth and Teddie Lou Wood; (right side, standing) Gladys and Jack Randall, Eldred and Peggy Stephenson, and Louise and Henry Deitrich. (Both, courtesy of Sherry Thomas.)

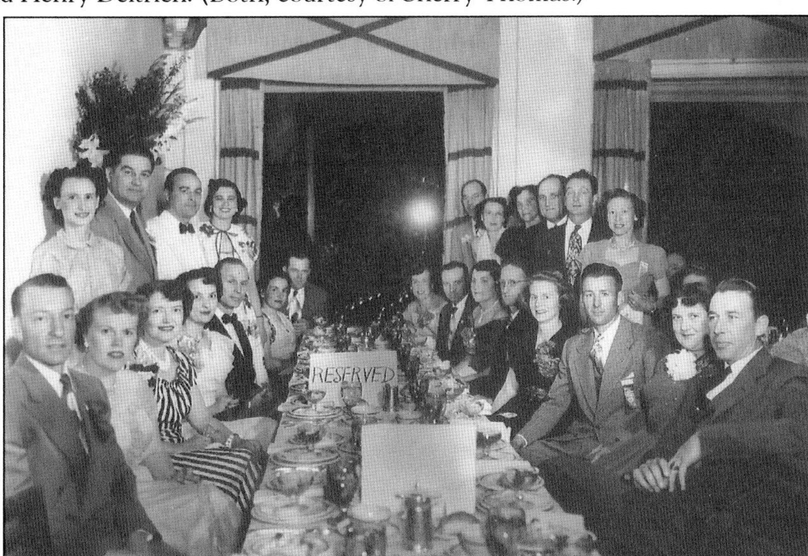

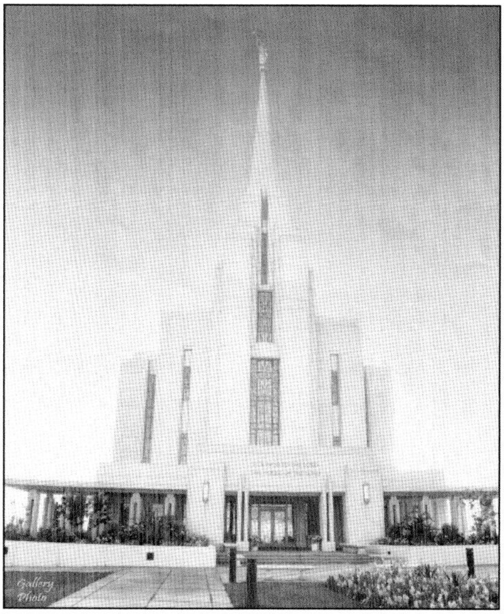

In the Mormon religion, a temple is a building dedicated to be a house of God and is reserved for special forms of worship. A temple differs from a church meetinghouse, which is used for weekly services. The Rexburg temple was dedicated on February 10, 2008, and is the fourth Mormon temple in the state of Idaho. The temple rests atop a shield volcano on the Wasatch Fault, as does much of the city.

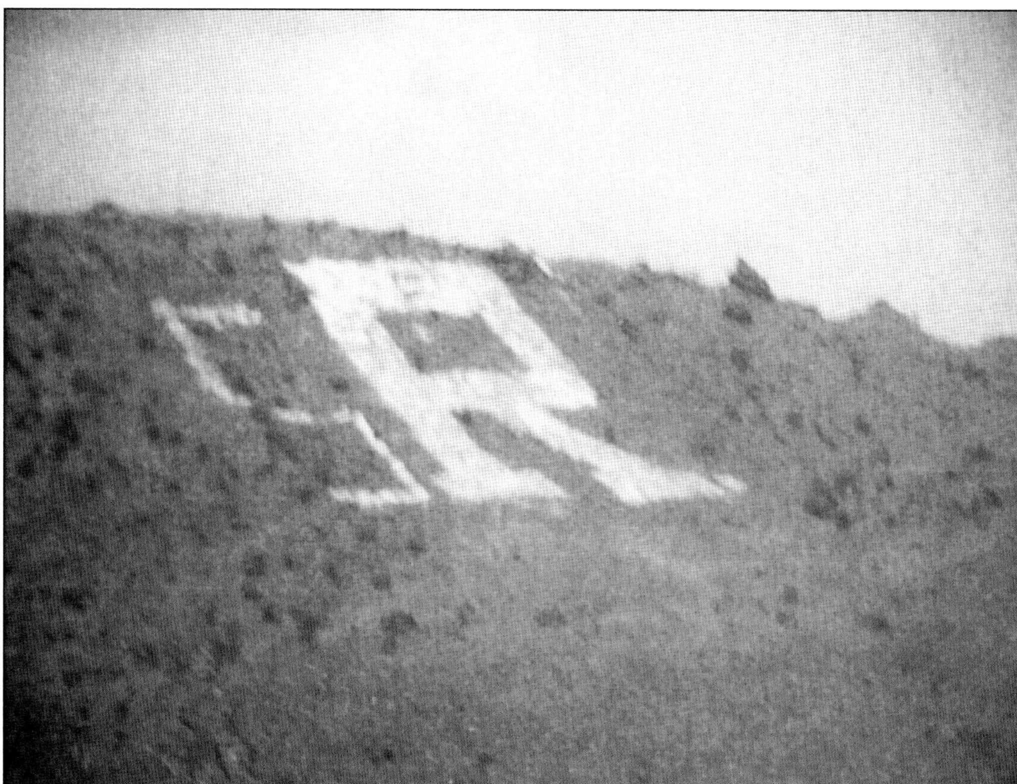

This picture of the "R" on the Menan Butte was taken miles away by Carl Agren. He took his binoculars, focused them on the "R" with his left hand and, with his right hand, placed the lens of his camera against the lens of the binoculars, and snapped this picture. The "S" to the left of the "R" was made of old whitewashed lumber that was hauled up to the butte by Madison High School students from the class of 1965. The number "65" was to be placed on the right side but was never completed.

Pictured are some of the Madison High School students of the class of 1965; from left to right are Doug Ladle, Gerry Daniel, Cathy Hanks, Kareen Raybould, Val Clark, Bruce Pond, Donna Lewis, Norman Hanson, and Brent Lawyer. (Courtesy of Carl Agren.)

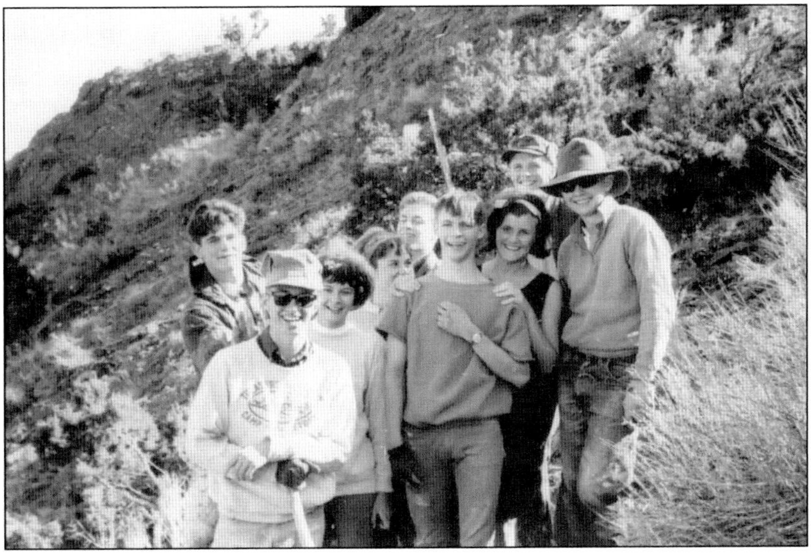

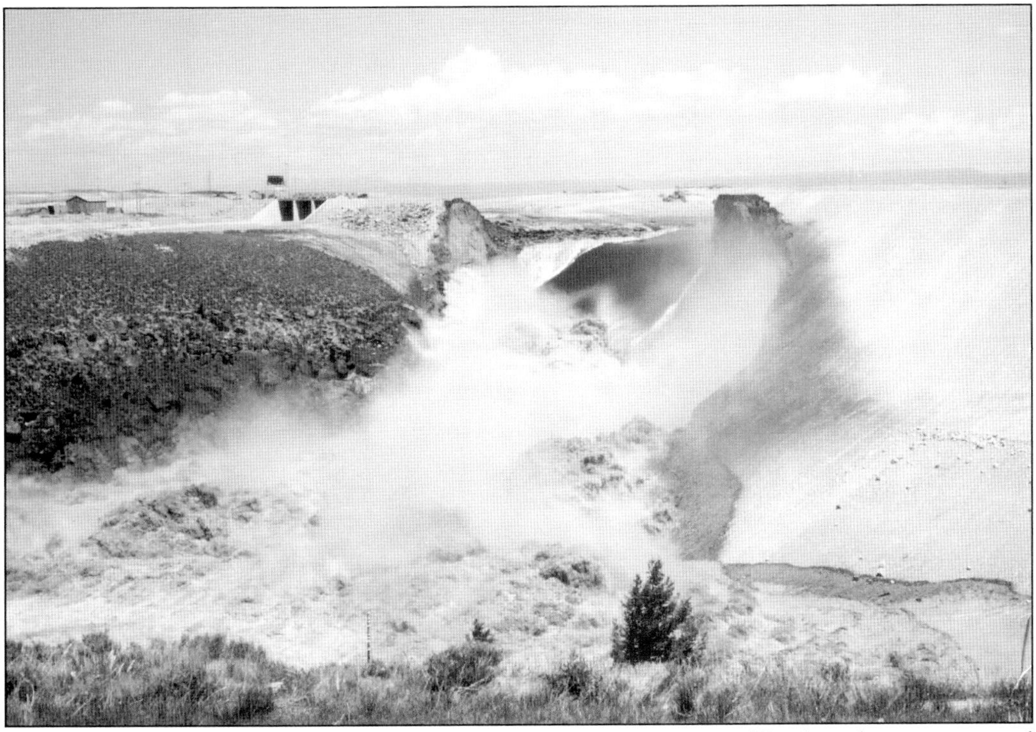

The single most life-changing event to ever occur in the 131 years of Rexburg history occurred on Saturday, June 5, 1976, when the earthen Teton Dam in the Teton Canyon burst, sending millions of gallons of water racing into the Upper Snake River Valley and down the streets of Rexburg. (Courtesy of the *Rexburg Standard Journal*.)

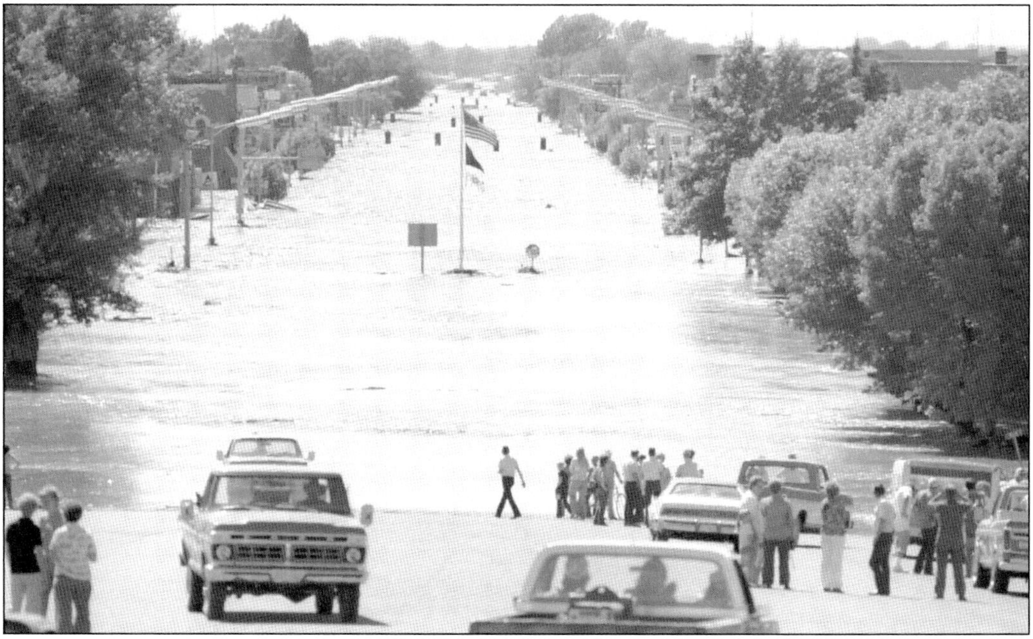

This view looks from the steps of Madison Memorial Hospital west down Main Street as the waters fill the streets, destroying everything in their path. The flood destroyed a third of the city and eradicated not only five generations of history but also the spirit of many people who lost everything. With pioneer determination and the help of family and volunteers, the city of Rexburg rose up from the mud and became a community again. (Courtesy of Dwight Davidson.)

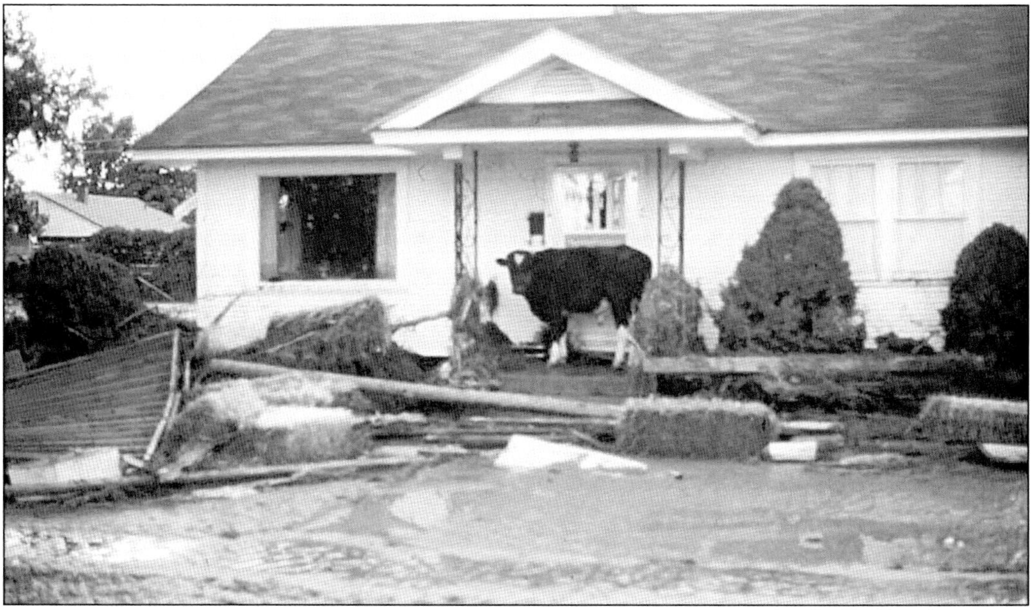

After the Teton Dam flood, some animals were able to float on top of the floodwaters and were then dropped off miles away as the waters receded, while others were not so fortunate. Many homes had the same fate as the livestock, as some stayed on their foundations but were damaged beyond repair, and some bobbed along with the flow of the water. (Courtesy of the *Rexburg Standard Journal.*)

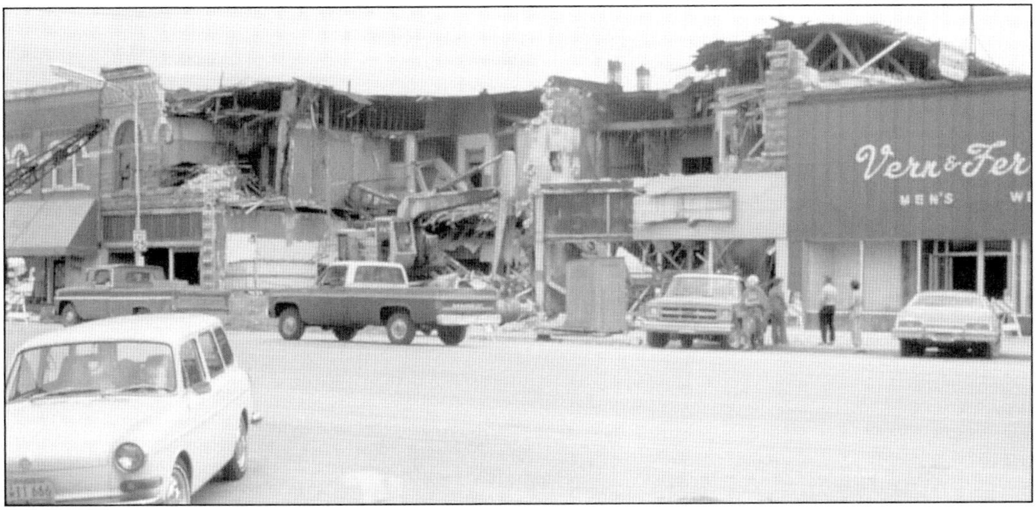

This scene shows the aftermath of Teton Dam flood. Clean up was painstakingly done to retrieve family heirlooms while others had nothing to retrieve. The spirit of volunteerism was evident as people from other towns and states descended on Rexburg to help with the shoveling of mud from homes. The view of downtown Rexburg shows the power and the wrath of Mother Nature on the monuments left by Rexburg's early pioneers. (Courtesy of the *Rexburg Standard Journal.*)

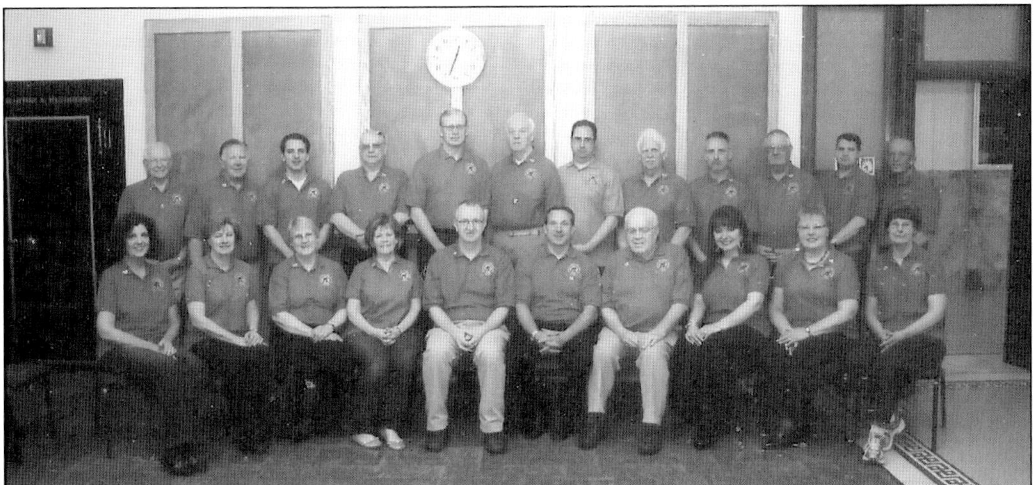

On February 18, 2013, Rexburg celebrated the 100th anniversary of the creation of Madison County. This event was the largest and longest celebration in the 130 years of the history of Rexburg, Idaho. The county commissioners—Jon Weber, Todd Smith, and Kimber Ricks—spearheaded the centennial committee with Vicki Grover and Shauna Ringel as cochairs. In this picture are the members of the centennial committee; from left to right are (first row) Sally Smith, Diane Fuller, Shauna Ringel, Vicki Grover, Todd Smith, Jon Weber, Kimber Ricks, Christine Campbell, Mardi Parkinson, and Loretta Smith; (second row) Dewey Furnace, Bart Webster, Jace Kellogg, Jerry Glenn, Sid Muir, Bryce Rydalch, Matt Eichner, Lowell Parkinson, Kent Arnold, Bob Schneider, Lane Steel, and Randy Huskinson. The yearlong celebration started with the ribbon-cutting ceremony and photography display in the courthouse, followed by a centennial dance, parade, circle wagons, a potato dig, a history fair, a branding irons showcase, the designing of a commemorative throw and token, a citizen centennial climb, a concert at fairgrounds, and the creation of a centennial park. (Courtesy of Allan Morton.)

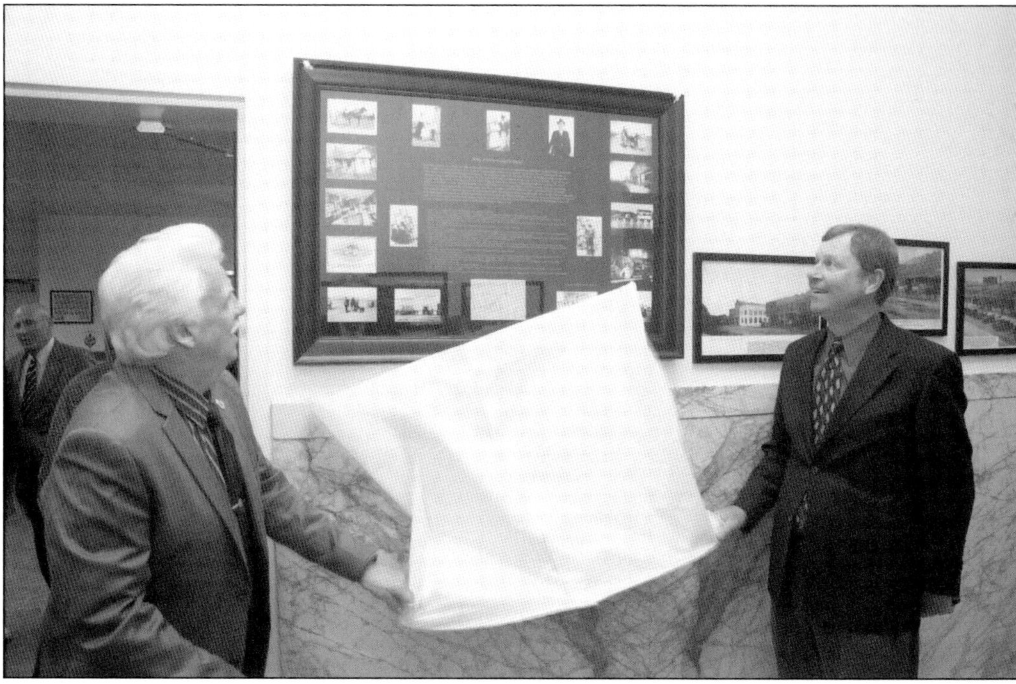

Lowell Parkinson (left) and Dr. Brent Peterson unveil a pictorial mural of the 1911 first Rexburg Fair recognizing the Henry Bigler family, who were responsible for creating an ideal atmosphere for the fairgrounds. Parkinson designed eight murals with historical pictures, 70 photographs of Main Street, and 25 historical maps, and also designed a centennial throw and coin. (Courtesy of Allan Morton.)

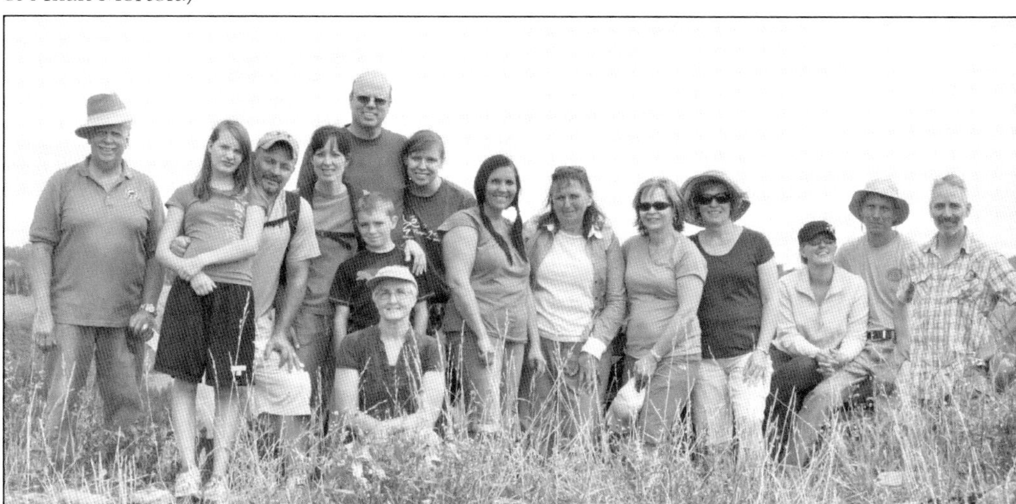

On September 6, 2013, the Citizen Centennial Climb took place with 19 people participating. The group ascended the 8,108-foot Red Butte Mountain. From left to right are (sitting in front) Terri Hepworth; (standing) Lowell Parkinson, Kayla Parkinson Eric Parkinson, Monica Parkinson with Carsen Parkinson (in front), Doug Conway, Amy Conway, Shellie Woolstenhulme, Carolyn Bratt, Barbara Summers, Lori Robertson, Shannon Hansen, David Moon, and Kent Arnold. Not pictured are Allan Morton, Mardi Parkinson, and Joseph Law.

The USS *Rexburg* was a rescue ship built by the Pullman Standard Car Manufacturing Company in Chicago, Illinois. These ships served three missions: damage control and firefighting, casualty treatment and evacuation, and patrol and guard ship. The USS *Rexburg* had a short but remarkable war record during World War II. The bell to this ship is on display at the Rexburg Flood Museum. (Courtesy of Upper Snake River Valley Historical Society.)

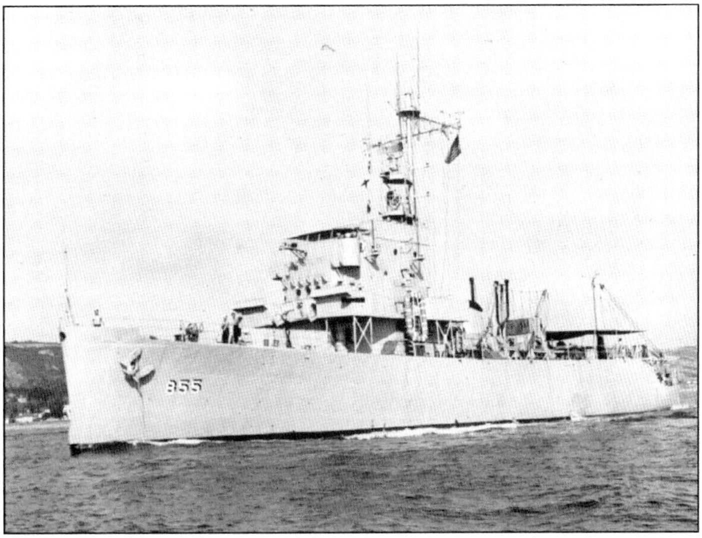

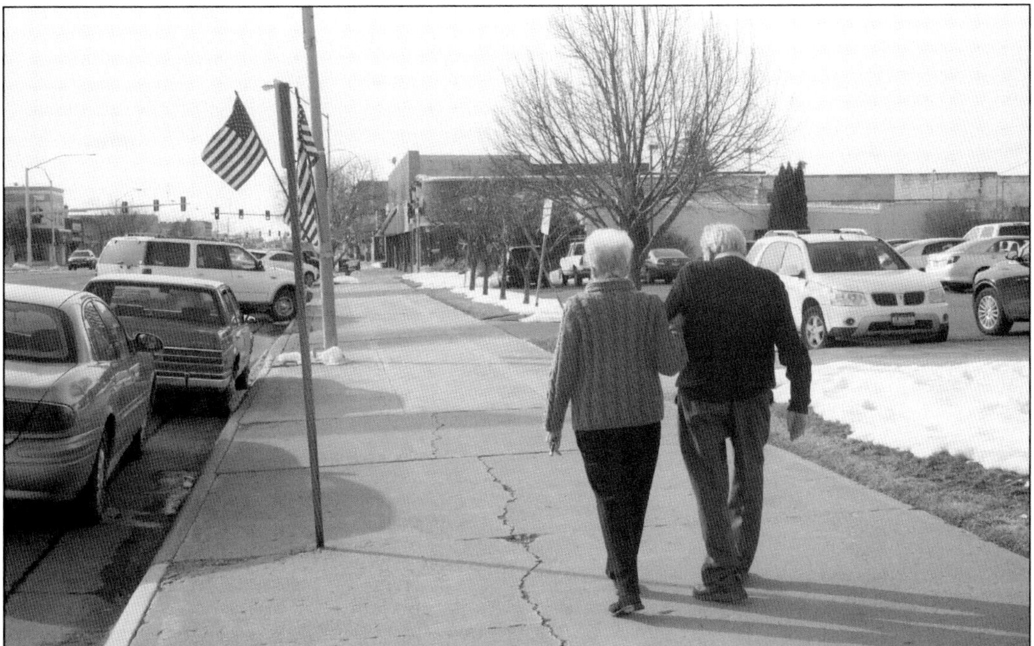

On February 18, 2013, Terrell and Margaret Porter Arnold leave the Madison County Courthouse after attending the opening ceremonies of the Madison County centennial event. As they stroll arm and arm together down Main Street, so goes the greatest generation and the history they had lived and witnessed. (Courtesy of Allan Morton.)

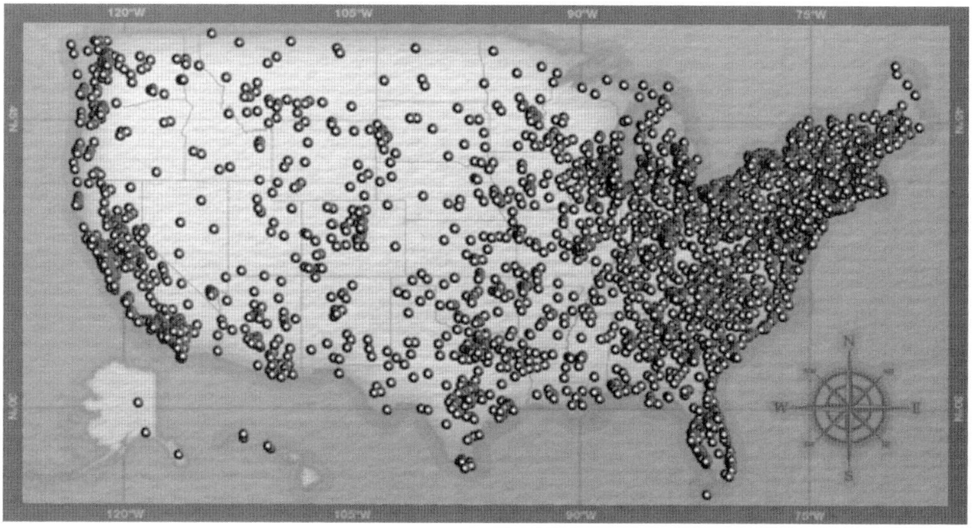